Three Generations of
Irish Middle Class Experience
1907, 1932, 1963

Ordinary Lives

The private worlds of three generations
of Ireland professional classes

Tony Farmar

A. & A. Farmar

© Tony Farmar 1991, 1995

All rights reserved. No part of this book may be
reprinted or reproduced or utilised by electronic,
mechanical or other means, now known or hereafter
invented, including photocopy and recording,
or any information storage of retrieval system,
without permission in writing
from the publishers.

British Library Catalogue in Publication Data
A CIP Record for this books is available from the British Library

Cover design by Alice Campbell
Produced by Betaprint

ISBN 1 899047 10 7

A. & A. Farmar
Beech House
78 Ranelagh Village
Dublin 6
Ireland

*For my friend
David Butler
(1940–1989)*

Contents

Acknowledgments		
Introduction		1
Part 1 1907		5
Chapter One	A World of Hierarchies	7
Two	Getting and Spending in 1907	19
Three	Daily Lives in 1907	34
Four	The Great Edwardian Collection	47
Five	Becoming Irish	59
Part 2 1932		71
Six	An Exciting Year	73
Seven	Getting and Spending in 1932	87
Eight	Symbolism and Daily Life	99
Nine	Digging the Political Trenches	110
Ten	The Kneeling City	124
Eleven	The Sweep	137
Part 3 1963		147
Twelve	Melting	149
Thirteen	Getting and Spending in 1963	165
Fourteen	Daily Lives in 1963	178
Fifteen	The Moral Irish	190
Sixteen	The Nice Man Cometh	202
Notes		213
Index		225

Acknowledgments

Many people heard a great deal about this book while it was being written. Foremost among these of course was my wife Anna who among other shaping contributions bravely allowed me to read and quote from her student diaries. Frank Litton and Geoffrey MacKechnie will be glad to find other years out of the millennia cropping up during seminars. Peter Costello was particularly helpful with references and illustration sources. The original idea was Peter Thew's.

Garret FitzGerald with his letter about Kennedy's death, Nick Reddy of the Department of Finance, Sue Naughton of Naughton Books, Michael O'Brien, Tom Garvin, Eddie O'Donnell SJ, and Tim Cleary of the Civil Defence School, all provided useful sources.

Illustrations come from the following sources: Fr Browne Collection (112), E. Chandler (21), Civil Defence School (162), Clery's (29), Peter Costello (52, 72, 112), L. Doyle *The Spirit of Ireland* (1935) (78), Dublin Civic Museum (44), *Dublin Opinion* (74, 101, 105, 121, 141, 158, 185), G. A. Duncan (16, 41, 44, 162, 166, 181, 188, 196, 209), *Irish Independent* (88, 94, 118, 125), *Irish Jesuit Yearbook* 1932 (84), Neville Johnson (150, 185), *Lady of The House* (10, 29), Lensmen (84, 156, 173, 188, 206), *Lepracaun* (36, 51, 61), National Museum (61), *Punch* (8), *A Hundred Years of Service* (St Vincent's Hospital, 1934) (21, 94), Brian Seed (196, 209), M. Sheridan *Monica's Kitchen* (181), *Sinn Féin Yearbook* 1908 (51), *Record of the International Exhibition* (1909) (52, 56 and 57), *Pictorial Record, Eucharistic Conference 1932* (130, 135), Royal Society of Irish Antiquaries (16), Turf Club (36).

Introduction

HISTORY has traditionally been concerned with wars, with political manoeuvrings, or with social and economic revolutions. For most of us, however, politics and matters of high state are spectator sports. Only the young and the committed worry more about political change than about the daily pressures of life: the mortgage, the overdraft, the job, the children's education.

Unfortunately, unlike political crises, these pressures are not neatly documented in official files. As a result they tend to disappear beneath the horizon, overlaid by 'important' events such as changes of government. We can date to the minute when the first Late, Late Show went on the air, but how can we date its various influences thereafter on Irish attitudes? The coming of the fridge to Irish households in the 1960s freed Irishwomen from the necessity of daily shopping—what were the implications of that? We know when the miniskirt first appeared on Parisian couture platforms, but how can we date its effects on sexual attitudes in south Dublin?

The history of ordinary lives is about how childhood; family and working life; retirement; the pleasures of books, food and friends; attitudes to ourselves and others, mould and are moulded by our identities. In any individual life the family is the critical influence. Behind the family, however, lie four more general determinants of personal identity. These are gender, class, religion and nationality.

These terms need to be defined more precisely. By gender I do not mean only male or female: the spinster and the bachelor have long had a different position to the married. Class refers to the way individuals and their families get and preserve their means of living. Religion in this society means the religion into which one was born. Nationality is less about 'four green fields' issues than the jointly recognised icons that every group preserves. Thus Brian Inglis identified the 'symbols of the old order' that represented Ireland for the Anglo-Irish in 1910 as: '*Punch*, Gilbert and Sullivan, Trinity Week, the Shelbourne Hotel, the Irish Mail at Euston, Fitzwilliam Lawn Tennis Club, Punchestown, the Prince of Wales, Horse Show Week and Mazawatee Tea'.[1]

Normally, I believe the relative strength of the factors is in the order given. Gender is the deepest barrier; class is a more important indicator than religion—a Catholic lawyer has more in common with a Protestant lawyer than with a Catholic labourer—and so on. Only for exceptional people, or by exceptional dislocating forces such as a revolution or a religious mission, could the normal order be changed, and then just briefly. On a great march in Dublin in 1907 to protest against the French Government's treatment of the Catholic Church, journalists noted with surprise how, among the 30,000 in the procession, 'well-known professional men could be recognised in the same rank with others, who, though neatly attired, were evidently of the labouring classes'.[2] The heat of religious feeling aroused was sufficient to overcome for the day the normal class barriers, but not the sex barrier: the procession was for men only.

The past, wrote L. P. Hartley, is a foreign country; they do things differently there. This book tries to get the flavour of that difference by taking snapshot pictures of three individual years of this century. During the period spanned by the three years—1907, 1932 and 1963—a great change took place in Irish society. A revolution occurred which unseated the British and the Anglo-Irish from the commanding heights of the social and political economy and established in their place the Catholic urban middle class.

The success of this relatively small group of the population was not a result willed by anyone in particular. Indeed the ringing phrases of the Democratic Programme of the First Dáil went in the opposite direction—'We declare that the Nation's sovereignty extends not only to all men and women of the Nation, but to all its material possessions, the Nation's soil and all its resources, all the wealth and wealth-producing processes within the Nation.'

Many citizens took the view that a class system did not exist in the new Irish state: there was only 'twopence-halfpenny looking down on twopence'. No doubt compared to the systematic elaboration of the British class system, the Irish version is meagre and unworked-out; but it has never been non-existent. There was also no powerful political pressure sponsoring the Catholic middle classes as such. Fianna Fáil, since 1932 the dominant political party in the state, has as its declared objective: 'to make the resources and wealth of Ireland subservient to the needs and wealth of all of the people of Ireland . . . [and] to carry out the Democratic Programme of the First Dáil'.[3]

Notoriously, nothing like this has happened. The most recent estimates published in the 1980s suggest that nearly half of gross national income goes to the top-earning twenty per cent of the population; that five per cent of the population own nearly two-thirds of the wealth;

Introduction

that two-thirds of government ministers since the foundation of the state came from the professional classes; that the middle classes have a grossly unfair share of many benefits, especially access to education and health care; that perhaps one-third of the population does not have 'an adequate share of the produce of the Nation's labour'.[4]

Ordinary Lives does not attempt to investigate the mechanics of how this came about. Its purpose is to explore how the urban middle classes went about daily concerns such as work and pay; shops and spending; clothes, food and life-style; comfort and entertainment; religion and sex. The poor in agricultural Ireland and in urban Ireland have been studied at length—the relatively well-off have not, despite (or perhaps because of) their grip on the levers of power and wealth. These answers to the question—what was it like to be a Catholic urban middle-class person in 1907, 1932 and 1963?—may go some way to addressing the problem.

To keep the research within bounds I have concentrated largely on Dublin, where of course the bulk of the target population lives, and where their influence is strongly felt. Three groups who might have been discussed are, as a result, mentioned only glancingly. These are middle-class Catholics in the North, those in other urban centres in Ireland, and strong farmers.

The Catholic professional and middle classes in the North have suffered from a prolonged reversal of the normal order: economic and social relations were organised according to religious affiliation rather than class. To describe the impact of this requires special knowledge. As it happens the North was not high on the political agenda in any of the three chosen years. It was not a critical issue in 1907, or in the 1932 election, and the resignation of Brookeborough in 1963 and the accession of Captain O'Neill was but faintly applauded. Not until the American civil rights movement of the mid-1960s provided a model for non-violent, non-IRA activism in the North did the middle classes in the South become widely engaged, however briefly. For the other two groups I have had generally to let Dublin speak for the rest. This is not entirely unwarranted, for a large proportion of those who ended up in professional and civil service positions in Dublin came from the country and from Cork in particular.

Note: The Cost of Living 1900–1990
The equivalent values of money between one period and another are always difficult to compare. On the other hand it is helpful in such a book to have a rough and ready 'exchange rate' in one's head. For that

purpose I have used the following multipliers to obtain 1990 values. They are based on an arithmetical combination of the official cost of living indices.

To get 1990 values multiply sums of money as follows:

Year	Index	Multiplier to Use*
1907	55	50
1932	34	33
1963	11	10

*These figures are much easier to multiply in your head, and are well within the boundary of error of the index figure.

Part 1
1907

Chapter One

A World of Hierarchies

THE world of 1907 is divided from us by more political, military, social and technological activity than had ever before split a century. A long series of revolutions, world wars, economic developments, and technological and ideological changes have destroyed a world that seemed to most middle-class Europeans to be largely and comfortably fixed.

In 1907 the world seemed naturally ordered into hierarchies. Just as Darwin had demonstrated the survival and dominance of the fitter in the natural world, so in the human world men dominated women (had they not after all larger brains and stronger arms?), and strong countries dominated weak ones. Races, sexes, social classes and species were all ranked in the world as a result of basic, probably God-given, fitness. There was hardly any point in resisting this natural order of things. This view was of course convenient: just over eighty per cent of the world's population lived in some form of colonial or semi-colonial regime. Any proposal for change, such as Home Rule for Ireland, was a challenge to the natural order. Since 23 per cent of the world's population was under British control, didn't this prove that the British were natural rulers?

Ireland, as Britain's oldest overseas colony, fitted uneasily into the political categories of the day. In some ways it was so deeply integrated into the domestic British political scene as to seem inseparable (in language, in markets, in the tax system, in political representation and so on); in other ways the Irish remained obstinately separate. Not least of these was in time. Dublin time was twenty-five minutes after London: every day the city stopped as men checked that their watches showed 11.35 as the time ball on top of the Ballast Office dropped at 12.00 noon Greenwich Mean Time.[1] By 1907 the excitements of the Land War and Parnellism were twenty years in the past; now the United Irish League (the reunited Parnellite and anti-Parnellite wings of the old Irish Parliamentary Party) dominated the hustings both for the Imperial Parliament in Westminster and in local elections. So complete was their political hold that some (particularly southern unionists) complained of their oppressive dominance of local affairs. However John

A DIVIL OF A GAME.

John Redmond having as much trouble balancing the Irish Parliamentary Party as others had with the fashionable new game, Diabolo (*Punch*)

Redmond, the leader of the party, was not especially secure in his tenure; his followers' allegiance was known to be volatile, and to require considerable reinforcing by local priests, by nationalist journalism as exemplified by the *Freeman's Journal*, and by judicious patronage.

A similar piercing scrutiny held for every member of parliament. The *Freeman* regularly published lists of attendance records at Westminster, and questions to the Chief Secretary in Parliament had the particularity, aimed at local consumption, familiar from the reports of the Dáil. In March, for instance, the Chief Secretary was asked about a pier in Gooseroun in Kerry, about a teacher's salary in Ballybunion, and a robbery from a postman in County Cork; in April Mr Jeremiah McVeagh asked the Chief Secretary if his attention had been drawn to the condition of the schoolhouse in Barnmeen, Co. Down (it had); in Augustine Birrell was asked if he was aware that the schoolhouse at Ahascragh, near Ballinasloe, which was used as a Church of Ireland parochial hall, had been vandalised. He was, and he said he couldn't understand it since the Rector was, as far as he knew, one of the most popular men in the community.

By 1907 the land aspect of the Question had been largely solved, by the simple means of the government financing tenant purchase of the land. Since the Land Act of 1903 some 90,000 holdings had been bought out, and the landlord class was fast disappearing. In 1907 there were less than 15,000 landlords left, sharing an income of some £8 m. in rent, or under £600 each. This represents about £30,000 in 1990 terms.

With the defusing of the land situation, some of the fervour departed from politics. There remained, however, in the jargon of the day, the Home Rule Question, the University Question, the Town Tenants Question and the Labourers Question to perplex the politicians at Westminster. Perhaps the most sensitive of these to the Catholic middle-class supporters of the Irish Party was the University Question, in particular the establishment of a university acceptable to the Catholic hierarchy. Advanced education of the future leaders of the country was seen as essential to national progress.[2]

The titular head of the British regime in Ireland was the Lord Lieutenant. With the recent change of government from Tories to Liberals, the dashing Lord Dudley had been replaced by Lord Aberdeen in this post. The Aberdeens, known to Dublin wits as Jumping Jack and Blowsy Bella, were, as one of their officials put it 'an earnest, kindly, well-intentioned couple'.[3] Nobody could deny that they did a tremendous amount of good work; they used their influence among the poor, for the battle against the 'white plague', tuberculosis, which was then killing 12,000

The Lady of The House, published for the up-market grocery chain, Findlater's, claimed a circulation of 20,000 copies.

people a year, to aid local industry and so on. Unfortunately they lacked the vice-regal style.

The Dudleys, on the other hand, had this quality in abundance. One morning, for instance, Lord Dudley noticed he needed a haircut, so he sent to London for Truefitt, his hairdresser, whose man arrived by the night mail. Unfortunately Lord Dudley had an important yacht race at Kingstown the next day, and couldn't spare the time for a haircut, so the barber had to wait. Next day Lord Dudley motored to Meath, and on his return was summoned immediately to London. On arriving in London he noticed to his surprise that his hair still wanted cutting, so he summoned Truefitt himself by telephone, and the job was done. The following day he returned to Dublin, and he was reminded that Truefitt's man still waited to cut his hair. 'Too late, too late,' said Dudley, 'send him back to London. Why can't these people come when they are wanted!'[4]

The Aberdeens' lack of style was translated into their entertaining, which became deliberately democratic. This did not please the establishment. As Page Dickinson, a Dublin man about town, put it in his autobiography: 'Social amenities were thrown to the winds, and the rag-tag and bobtail of Dublin went to Court. Without being a snob, it was no pleasure and rather embarrassing to meet the lady at dinner who had measured you for your shirts the week before.'[5]

Of course people still went to the Castle. The *Freeman*'s report of a levee in February veered between the sarcastic and the sycophantic. 'The usual small crowd of leisured folk assembled along Cork Hill and round the tow path of the Upper Castle Yard and took the customary interest in and made the customary remarks, occasionally more candid than complimentary, about the occupants of "growlers" and "outsiders" and carriages. The visitors, the officers of the garrison being especially to the fore, began to make their appearance before midday. The Viceroy having taken up a position in front of the throne . . . the visitors filed in from the Picture gallery, making their obeisance in passing.' The paper rounds off its report with two whole columns of the names of those who were presented and who presented them, including nearly fifty ladies and three times as many military and police officers.

Below the Lord Lieutenant were the real political and administrative powers, headed by the Chief Secretary, Augustine Birrell, who had a seat in the cabinet, and senior civil servant, Sir Anthony MacDonnell, who had made his name as an administrator in India. Below them Boards and Offices dealing with national and intermediate education, local government, public works, congested districts, prisons, trade, lunatic asylums—enough boards to make Ireland's coffin, as the nationalists frequently said.

Many of the Castle officials were English and conscious of the anomalies of their position. As Birrell himself said in a speech in the House of Commons in March, 'I do not think that any Chief Secretary with the slightest tincture of popular feeling in his bones could enter the gloomy portals of Dublin Castle without a sinking of the heart . . . No pulse of real life runs through the place. The main river of Irish life as it rushes past its walls passes by almost unheeded. There it stands "remote, unfriended, melancholy" regarding this great stream of National life and feelings with a curious expression of cynicism and amusement, coupled also I admit, with a passionate tutorial desire to teach the wild Irish people how to behave themselves (laughter).'[6]

The gradual dismantling of landlord power by the Land Acts, and a simultaneous waning of confidence on the administrative side meant that the Protestant community increasingly took its tone from the military. The system of massing troops in large barracks adopted after the Crimean War, and the disproportionate tendency of the Anglo-Irish to go into the Army or Navy had spread a loyalist and military influence throughout the class. Country society in Ireland no more than Jane Austen's Hampshire was able to resist the exciting influence of so many smart young men readily on tap for dances, theatricals, picnics or tennis. 'It was only a convinced anti-Britisher who could hold off his daughters from associating with these fascinating creatures, so . . . well turned out and so ready to enjoy themselves.'[8] Even in Dublin the military were conspicuous at social events.

Class distinctions were, as the militant Irish-Ireland journalist D. P. Moran put it, 'ridiculously minute and acute in Ireland'.[9] Only at the very top of society did the two religious and racial groups mingle easily. Nora Robertson, who was related to the Parsons of Birr Castle, described the line-up from the Protestant point of view.

> Row A: Peers who were Lord or Deputy Lieutenants (of counties), High Sheriffs or Knights of St Patrick [there were only 25 of these latter] . . .
> Row B: Other peers with smaller seats, ditto baronets, solvent country gentry and young sons of Row A . . . Row A used them for marrying their younger children.
> Row C: Less solvent country gentry, who could only allow their sons about £100 a year . . . they were recognised and respected by A and B and belonged to the Kildare Street Club.
> Row D: Loyal professional people, gentlemen professional farmers,

trade, large retail or small wholesale . . . such rarely cohabited with Rows A and B, but formed useful cannon-fodder at Protestant Bazaars and could, if they were really liked, achieve Kildare Street . . . There were perhaps a dozen (also very loyal) Roman Catholic families who qualified for the first two Rows; many more, equally loyal but less distinguished, moved freely with the last two.[10]

Even in nationalist circles, class was an important token of personal identity. D. P. Moran continued his article quoted above by deploring the failure of the Gaelic League 'in attracting the active co-operation of the professional and middle classes; it has thousands of sympathisers among these classes, but too few attend the branches. These classes have to be de-Anglicised, but they stubbornly refuse to be de-classed.'[11] Nationalist fervour was not yet strong enough to break the class barrier. Moran's point was taken extremely seriously by Gaelic League organisers, and for some years afterwards they insisted on officers of the League wearing evening dress at the more important functions.[12]

In *Dublin Made Me*, C. S. Andrews described the class line-up from his viewpoint:

> At the top of the Catholic heap—in terms of worldly goods and social status—were the medical specialists, fashionable dentists, barristers, solicitors, wholesale tea and wine merchants, owners of large drapery stores and a very few owners or directors of large business firms. These were the Catholic upper middle class; they were the Castle Catholics . . .
>
> Below the Castle Catholics were the Catholic middle middle class. They were the general practitioners, less successful solicitors, grocers, publicans, butchers, tobacconists who did not live over the shop (when they moved from over their shops they ascended in the social scale), as well as corn merchants, civil servants, journalists, coal merchants and bank managers. In politics these people were Nationalist, and from them came the municipal politicians . . .
>
> Lower down the scale were the shopkeepers and publicans who lived over the shop, as well as clerks, shop assistants, lower grade civil servants, and skilled tradesmen . . . at the bottom of the heap were the have-nots of the city, consisting of labourers, dockers, coal heavers, messenger boys and domestic servants.[13]

The minuteness of the grading was deeply felt at all levels. Beatrice Elvery's father was rich and presentable, but he ran a very well-known shop, specialising in indiarubber and guttapercha goods, and lawn tennis and cricket equipment. She recalled being told by a little friend, the daughter of a no doubt much less successful professional man, after Sunday school: 'We're not allowed to play with you, because your father has a shop.'[14]

The census of 1901 had revealed that the population of Dublin City was 290,000 of which 82 per cent were Catholic; about two-thirds had been born in the city. An additional 91,000 people lived in the suburbs of Blackrock, Rathmines and Rathgar, Pembroke and Kingstown, to which the middle classes had retreated during the nineteenth century. Only 61 per cent of these were Catholic. (The population of Cork at this time was 76,000.) Though their numbers were waning, the Protestants still held a disproportionate grip on the top professional and business jobs. Protestants represented more than half the doctors, engineers, bankers, lawyers, pharmacists and JPs, and only just under half the accountants.[15]

It has been estimated recently that in income per head Ireland (excluding the North) was in 1907 the tenth richest country in Europe, and ranked perhaps fifteenth in the world. It was richer per head than Italy, Japan and Norway, and only a little behind France and Austria. It was not by then, as it was so often painted, 'the most distressful country'—Irish average income was in fact about average for Europe at the time.[16] Emigrants' remittances, which had been estimated at £700,000 a year between 1852 and 1872, were now running at some £2 m. a year.[17] Such estimates are of course extremely subject to error and ignore the distribution of income which was very uneven. The best official salaries were about £2,000 a year, while a labourer working for Dublin Corporation would get £55 a year plus a suit of working clothes. The range therefore between the highest and lowest official incomes was over 30 to 1; in 1990 the equivalent range was more like 8 to 1.

In Dublin the scandal of the tenements was only just breaking through into widespread public awareness. A quarter of the city's population lived in 22,000 single rooms, of which 13,000 were occupied by three or more persons. In October the *Freeman's Journal* reported the case of Thomas Doran, of no fixed abode, who broke two panes of glass worth £20 in McBirney's and two worth over £40 in Todd, Burns. In its editorial comment the paper took a stern line. 'The man, if his account was true, was starving. He could not raise a copper for food. But in a few minutes he could do at least sixty pounds' worth of damage, for which the citizens must pay. Assuming he is imprisoned for the offence there is no security he will not repeat it when he comes out. Meanwhile it is probable he will be housed, clothed and fed at the expense of the taxpayers. One thing is abundantly proved: for such offenders, prison is no deterrent. It is indeed wages, not punishment...' During the case the magistrate of the police court, Mr Drury suggested that flogging would deter such offenders, but Doran said 'if you gave me a thousand lashes of the "cat" it would not stop me. I have been sleeping in hallways. I could get no food. I am destitute and I must do something.'

There was very little serious crime in Dublin. There was of course the famous Monto, the brothel quarter to the east of O'Connell Street. One estimate suggests that there may have been as many as 4,000 prostitutes in Dublin, most of them no doubt part-time.[19] The area was also notorious for late-night drinking parlours and other shady activities. Certainly it was dangerous for the unwary: in April a young Corkman was enticed into a house in the area and severely beaten by two men.

What other crime there was was strongly connected with social circumstances. In the country there was illegal poteen making and faction fighting. In April a faction fight between the Delargys and the M'Auleys in Cushendall, Co. Antrim, resulted in several injuries, and the death of a man who was struck on the head with a ten-pound coal-hammer.

The willingness of the authorities to intervene in some matters and not others was quite different to the present pattern. In some ways they seem to be excessively intrusive (in August Edward Sherlock of Tallaght was fined one guinea for using obscene language in his mother's house); and in others absurdly casual. In October a wall collapsed in Park Street, off Hanover Street W., crushing a schoolboy; on Wednesday it was reported to the police that a man had been missing since Saturday—the fire brigade was called for, and the pile of rubble from which the boy's body had been removed was sifted. Another body (the man's) was found. The Coroner asked why the rubble had not been removed, and was told that since it wasn't causing any obstruction, they just left it there. In October a woman was sentenced to six months' imprisonment for attempting suicide by throwing herself in front of a car in Stephen's Green. This was her second attempt.

Despite the enormous problems of the country and the city, despite widespread poverty, especially in the tenements, Dubliners knew that their city was remarkable. Everything that London provided, except a parliament, was to be found there: art, theatre, culture, wit. Even a parliament was, possibly, not far off: at the opening of the parliamentary session in Westminster the King's speech described the government's intention to 'introduce ... means for associating the Irish people with Irish affairs'.

A quarter of a mile apart: a typical tenement (note the chamber pot in the corner), and the Gresham Hotel, a popular centre of middle-class social and cultural activities

At the lower level it was not possible to participate in the great revolution of the age: personal transport. Until very recently, personal transport had been confined to the very rich. There was however a wide variety of public transport: on his visit to Cork the journalist, William Bulfin, noted automobiles, tramcars, jaunting cars, landaus, inside cars, hansom cabs and covered cars jostling each other in the streets.[18] With the recent perfection of the bicycle (the 'Safety' as it was called, to distinguish it from the 'Ordinary' or penny-farthing), complete with pneumatic tyres, the exhilarating freedom of the open road became widely available, at least to the middle classes. 'For those who want to keep business appointments', ran a regular ad in the *Freeman*, 'a bicycle is necessary—5 guineas to 15 guineas.'

For the better off there was the still greater excitement of the motor car. In January 1907 the first Irish Motor Show was held in the RDS, with over 400 different vehicles on display, ranging from a six-horsepower Rover at £130, to a twelve to fourteen-horsepower Singer for £295. Also on display was the only Irish-made car, an eight-horsepower vehicle from Chambers & Co. of Belfast for £182.

For most people the only interest they had in the motor car, as D. P. Moran put it, was in getting out of its way. This was not always easily done. Road discipline was not good, and the combination of inexperienced motorists and maladroit cyclists frequently resulted in accidents. In August, for instance, Major A. W. Clarke was accused of running down a cyclist, a Miss Nora Phelan, in Ranelagh. She was, she claimed, cycling from Clonskeagh to Ranelagh when Major Clarke dashed out in his motor car round the corner of Milltown Road and Eglinton; he was on the wrong side of the road and failed to sound his horn; she turned towards the footpath, but the car caught her back wheel, smashed the bicycle and knocked her down. Major Clarke counter-claimed that he had sounded his horn, and that Miss Phelan was swaying about the road; she was some fifteen yards away and he could not get out of her way, so he stopped while she ran into him! In the end the Major settled for six guineas.

Part of the problem was that cars were capable of quite unfamiliar speeds. For 'scorching through Grafton Street, College Green and Westmoreland Street at fully fifteen miles an hour' in June, a chauffeur was fined £25, which was probably not far short of half his annual salary.

Not that horse-drawn traffic was much safer. Horses were always running away, to the great danger of everyone. On 6 December three such accidents were reported on the one day. In one a horse, attached to a van, was stopped in Grafton Street while the owner was delivering goods. It took fright at a motor car and ran away. Plucky postman, J. O'Connor, rushed into the street and succeeded in capturing the animal as it was nearing the end of the street. (This was a genuinely brave thing to do—a few weeks before, a man had been killed nearby, stopping a runaway horse, and two men had recently lost their lives in Fitzwilliam Square in similar attempts.)

On the same day a horse, attached to a float carrying four calves, bolted and charged through the North Circular Road 'which was rather thronged at the time, it being market day . . .' Luckily Constable 176D rushed up and seized the horse before any damage could be done.

The Anglo-Irish snob could feel comfortable that, as the egregious Page Dickinson put it, 'there was little commercial element in the best of social life. No pushful newspaperman had captured the public taste; few profiteering industrial magnates had attained social success through the power of their purses. Dublin was more free from the meaner elements in its social life than was London of that time.'[20]

Nationalists could reasonably feel that their country was on an upward spiral: an American journalist quoted the veteran campaigner John Dillon as saying that 'Ireland has made more progress in the last ten years than during the previous two hundred years... the whole face of the country is changing, and the spirit of the people with it.'[21] The enormous success of the Gaelic League, which by 1907 had nearly 900 active branches, underpinned a growing self-confidence in being Irish. Naturally there was much to do: industrial regeneration was high on the patriotic agenda, along with the clearance of the tenements, the conquest of tuberculosis and the improvement of agricultural products.

It was clear enough that the British had lost the battle for the hearts and minds of the Irish; many people felt it was simply a question of when and how much Home Rule would be won. On St Patrick's Day the *Freeman's Journal* picked up the mood: 'Now', wrote the leader writer, 'from the ends of the earth comes a chorus of confidence, a voice that brings not merely cheerfulness but strength... this celebration of the National Festival has been marked by a brightness and hope too often lacking in the past.'

Chapter Two

Getting and Spending in 1907

BY 1907 Ireland's urban middle classes were comfortably benefiting from the economic boom of Edwardian England. The poor on the other hand had lost out when the emphasis of Dublin's economy had shifted in the second half of the nineteenth century from manufacture and industry to the less labour-intensive import/export business. In recent years the proportion of unskilled to skilled workers in the workforce had greatly risen. Rates of pay and security of employment were worsened as a result. Despite the fact that the population had risen from 325,000 to 404,000 since 1861, by 1911 there were actually ten per cent fewer people employed in manufacturing industry in the city.

To enjoy the delights of Dublin you did not need to be particularly well off. In his memoirs describing life in pre-war Ireland, Page Dickinson noted that 'people could do themselves well in Dublin at that time, and hunt or yacht or go in for any similar sport on incomes that would scarcely have covered living expenses in London. A poor man's paradise, surely.'[1] This last sentence could have been more sensitively expressed. Dublin's have-nots, as has been well documented, lived in some of the worst slums in Europe.

In his *Reminiscences* Sir Charles Cameron, Dublin's Medical Officer of Health, described the results of various surveys of Dublin's poor that were carried out at this time. The wages of unskilled labourers were generally less than £1 a week, and often as low as 15s. (Sir Charles himself was paid £1,200 a year by Dublin Corporation). With this level of earnings a working man, even though sober and with a small family, found it was virtually impossible to provide adequately for his family. As a result the family diet was usually poor and insufficient. (£1 a week is equivalent to £2,850 a year in 1990 terms.) Rent was another major item: 3s. a week for a single room might have to be found.

The constant items of a working-class diet were bread, usually without butter, and well stewed tea with sugar. Cocoa was occasionally used, coffee never; beef and mutton were hardly ever found on the table, nor was pork, except in the form of crubeens (trotters); bacon and cabbage was common, usually American bacon at 5d. or 6d. a pound. Very few vegetables other than potatoes and cabbage were eaten. Fruit was a rare treat for the children. The milk was either condensed (at 1*d*. to 3*d*. a tin) or supposedly whole, but in fact frequently adulterated, watered and diseased.³ Cheese was never eaten, a prejudice the Dubliners held on to for generations.

By contrast Dickinson and his friends frequently enjoyed what he describes as 'a simple and very cheap dinner' at a little pub in Leinster Alley before going to further entertainments at the newly founded Arts Club. A typical menu ran as follows:

A steak or chop	6*d*.
Potatoes and bread	no charge
A glass of draught stout	1*d*.
Cheese, bread and butter	2*d*.
Glass of port	2*d*.

Total, elevenpence, plus a twopenny tip for the waiter—say £2.80 in 1990 terms, with the glass of stout at the equivalent of 20p.³

The division of Dublin into the haves in the suburbs and the have-nots in the city was well advanced. The census of 1911 showed a marked difference in the social structure in the two areas. Nearly one in five of the suburban population was independent or professional, while only one in twenty of the city's population fell into that class. As many as forty-three per cent of the suburban population pursued clerical, managerial or professional lives: less than a quarter of the city's population fell into those categories. No wonder then that the new food and grocery chains, Findlaters, Leveret and Frye and Bewleys all set up branches in these lucrative middle-class areas. At the other end of the scale eighty-eight per cent of the conurbation's unskilled workers lived between the canals.⁴

The range of incomes in all areas was very wide. By modern standards the men at the top earned extremely large sums, and those at the bottom relatively small ones. The senior civil servant, the Under-Secretary, Sir Anthony MacDonnell, got £2,000 (equivalent to £110,000 in 1990—the Secretary of the Department of Finance in 1989 had a basic salary of £55,000); the Inspector-General of police got £1,800, the Crown Solicitor £2,200, the Recorder of Dublin £2,400. Judges earned more than this: the Lord Chancellor had £6,000 (recently reduced from £8,000), and other judges £3,500. Lesser functionaries earned considerably less: the Treasury Remembrancer received £1,200, as did the Registrar-General, and Sir Arthur Vicars, who was to lose his job during the year over the theft of the Irish Crown Jewels, had £500. One hundred and twenty-seven officials in the Board of Works

Surgeon Tobin: 'An Irishman's first duty is to keep clean.'

Surgeon Johnny McArdle

The Fusilier's Arch in Stephen's Green was unveiled on 19 August 1907 by Lord Aberdeen; immediately after the speeches a rainstorm scattered the crowd.

earned an average of £285 a year; a national schoolteacher as little as £100 a year (£5,000 in 1990 terms).⁵

University teachers were luckier: the Provost of Trinity earned £1,751 in 1905, and the Senior Fellows had between £1,300 and £1,600 each. The famous Mahaffy earned £1,495. 2s. in that year. Junior Fellows averaged £800, while the top college officers, the Assistant to the Registrar and the Accountant, had £450 each.⁶ The (Jesuit) Fellows of University College Dublin earned £400 a year.

In the professions the range was equally wide. The Mastership of the Rotunda was said to be worth 'some thousands a year',⁷ and certainly Surgeon McArdle of St Vincent's had no trouble building himself a substantial house and elaborate garden in the Wicklow mountains, where he lived for two months of the year, taking few or no cases.⁸ Dispensary doctors, the GPs of the day, lived on a different scale, as George Birmingham's Dr O'Grady discovered. 'He enjoyed, as a dispensary doctor, £120 a year. He received from Lord Manton an additional £30 for looking after the health of the gardeners, grooms, indoor servants and others employed about Clonmore Castle. He would have been paid extra guineas for attending Lord Manton himself if the old gentleman had ever been ill. He could count with tolerable certainty on two pounds a year for ushering into the world young O'Loughlins. Nobody else in the district ever paid him anything.'⁹

The few top barristers could earn as much as £5,000, though the average of those in practice was nearer £800–£1,000;¹⁰ the senior partner of Craig Gardner, the leading accountancy firm, had £2,700; the five executive directors of Boland's averaged £1,400. An alimony case in June 1907 revealed that a well-off Derry merchant, with three boot and shoe shops, had £700 a year. In another alimony case (4 December) a jeweller in Nassau Street was judged to have an income of £300 a year. (There was some argument about this: his wife said he had at least £600, while he claimed he had only £100 a year. Her counsel was felt to have made a point when he queried the possibility of dining regularly at Jammets, Dublin's top restaurant, on £100 a year.)

Down the social and economic scale, though still in the 'middle classes', the wages in the retail department of Eason's for a few years before 1907 show the range possible. The head of this relatively unprofitable department, an old and respected employee, had £4. 10s. a week, but only one other employee in the department had as much as £2 a week; there were three at £1. 18s. and nine below that, with figures ranging from £1. 10s. to trainees at 7s.¹¹ In the larger stores it was common for staff to be provided with accommodation: contemporary censuses record that over one hundred employees of Clery's slept on the premises at this time. A small ad in the *Freeman* in January announced: 'Young Lady engaged in City wants situation immediately as Assistant to general Drapery, can also help as Milliner, able to serve through; good reference: salary £12 (indoor) six years experience.'

The top employees in Eason's earned £9 a week at this time. In Eason's at least, therefore, a young starter on a few shillings a week could look forward to a steady and secure job, with his income steadily progressing to £100 a year, then £200 and perhaps even to the giddy heights of £400 or £500 if he was really successful. On this there was no problem in keeping a modest yacht in Dublin Bay—indeed an Eason's executive was one of the founder members of the Dublin Bay Sailing Club. Not only were there enormous differences between the earnings of one group and another, but even in a man's own lifetime he could without excessive optimism expect to run from comparative poverty to riches as he grew older.

Then as now the successful business venture was a possible route to rapid riches. Ernest Bewley was one example. In 1890 Bewley's was a modest coffee and tea-selling business: the cousins' businesses, in shipbuilding, in import/export and in wines and groceries, were much better known. In 1894 the first Bewley's café was opened, to be followed in 1896 by another in Westmoreland Street. By the 1900s Ernest Bewley was rich enough to leave his house in Rathmines for the much more substantial Danum, in Zion Road, Rathgar, which he built for himself on the grounds of the old Rathgar Saw Mills. He also bought new premises in Fleet Street, intending to diversify into bicycle repair, an idea which came to nothing. By 1907 he had developed the Fleet Street property into a series of offices above an extended café, had started his famous jersey herd, and had just been elected an Alderman of the City of Dublin. (When Bewley died in 1932, his will was proved at £99,333—the equivalent of 800 years' earnings at the then average industrial wage.[12])

Another, more traditional route to riches was demonstrated with the death in December of 'Banker' Patterson, an illiterate miser. The *Freeman's Journal* reported that he commenced business as a loan shark after finding a sum of money on his way to Belfast. He loaned single shillings at a penny a week interest. To save money he sat in the dark, wore no trousers in the summer, and possessed only a cup, a plate and a knife. He left all his money, £80,000, to charity.

The problem, then as now, was how to get started. The first significant factor was religion. Many firms and other organisations deliberately or effectively discriminated against Catholics. Nationalists frequently complained that the best civil service and other government appointments went to Protestants. In the Local Government Board, for instance, there were 34 Protestants and only 13 Catholics; in the Board of Works the 79 Protestants earned an average of £326, while the 48 Catholics averaged only £197.

For many of the brighter Irish recruits the wider possibilities of the Empire must have been tempting: could they too not become, like Sir Robert Hart, head of the entire Chinese Customs service, or like Sir Anthony MacDonnell, administrator of millions of Indians in Bengal?

Because businesses generally lacked elaborate staff organisation, recruitment was a very personal matter. Modern executive functions such as finance, marketing, quality assurance and personnel were completely unknown; in general the employment of such experts, even in accounting, was a late development—not until 1945 were there as many chartered accountants working in industry as in professional practice. As a result, except in places such as the railways, banks and enormous firms such as Guinness's, opportunities were few. *Thom's Directory* listed only thirty-eight public companies registered in Dublin, excluding banks and insurance companies, and while there were companies such as Guinness's and Gallaher's registered elsewhere, the corporate sector was not large. As a result personal introductions were vital. Naturally recruits tended to follow the religious adherence of the owner and his friends.

For a variety of reasons sons tended to do the kind of work their fathers had done. Few fell or rose much out of their original sphere. One sample suggests that eighty-five per cent of the sons of professional or independent fathers worked as professionals, employers or managers; three-quarters of the sons of employers and managers earned their living as white-collar workers. Only three per cent of the sons of unskilled labourers penetrated into clerical work.[13]

Some of this immobility was caused by the fees, premiums and capital investments that employers demanded of their recruits. Professional firms such as solicitors and accountants might ask for £150 or more as a premium, and then pay little or no wages during the period of training. Similar arrangements applied to trainee barristers, with the added penalty of a hazardous earning pattern in the early years. Banks and large firms such as Guinness's frequently demanded a surety payment of £100 (equivalent to £5,500 in 1990 money) as well as a personal introduction and the passing of a stiff examination. Competition for eligible jobs was severe. In November Kingstown announced that it had sixty-nine applicants for the post of librarian of the municipal library. It was eventually offered to a woman librarian at 30s. a week with residence, coal and light.

Once the money was earned, the question of what it was to be spent on could be addressed. Full-blown middle-class family respectability was difficult to maintain on much below £250 a year. The Andrews family, with only two children, and living in the parental home, found life a hard struggle on £150 a year.[14]

Several books published around this time addressed the question of *Marriage on £200 a Year*—to take the title of one published in 1903. Because of the way the distribution of incomes was arranged, young middle-class men, whatever their prospects, could hardly earn enough to keep a wife and family until their thirties. The problem was, at the author Mary Halliday put it, that 'because a woman has decided to marry on a small income, she is no whit changed as far as her tastes and likings are concerned; that it will be her aim and ambition to live as far as possible in the old manner, to drop none of the refinements to which she has become accustomed, and to bring up her children as she herself has been brought up'. In these circumstances the maintenance of respectability at all levels was extremely important. Appearance was much cherished. Mrs Andrews, for instance, who ran a dairy and provision shop in Terenure, 'never went out in the street with ungloved hands (she would regard it as not respectable to be seen without gloves)'.[15]

The first item to acquire was some form of accommodation. At this time, and for years afterwards, only the very rich bought their houses: nearly everyone else rented. The question was: where? A clue to the most desirable areas can be gleaned from the results of the annual collection of Peter's Pence, the annual collection for the Pope. The *Freeman* devoted two whole pages in early August to an elaborate record of the donation of every parish in the diocese. By this listing we can detect the richer Catholic parishes. Top of the list was Haddington Road in the Pembroke area, which donated £59. ('The Roads' as they were called—that is Clyde, Elgin, Morehampton and Pembroke—were occupied by the most successful of Dublin society. Haddington Road church was to become the only Catholic church in Dublin to erect a memorial to its parishioners who fell in the Great War.)[16] Next came the fashionable church of St Andrew, Westland Row, which catered for the doctors and professional families of Merrion and Fitzwilliam Squares; they gave £54. The Pro-cathedral, with its huge but not wealthy catchment area, gave £50. Kingstown gave £38 and Monkstown only £16, reflecting the fact that, uniquely in Dublin, it still had a minority Catholic population. By contrast, the predominantly working-class area of Ringsend gave £6. The two churches in the centre of the grander and older (and more Protestant) districts of Rathmines and Rathgar, the Three Patrons and Rathmines itself, gave only £30 and £32 respectively, while Cullenswood and Milltown (Beechwood Avenue) gave £42.

This area of Ranelagh was at this time expanding rapidly with smaller houses to appeal to the newly-wed and less well-off middle classes. In one advertisement, Macarthur's, the prominent auctioneer, offered 78–80 Lr Beechwood Avenue, described as 'two good modern houses, 5 bedrooms, bath (hot and cold) separate wc, to be let at £42 each pa'. At the same time two three-room cottages off the North Circular Road in Drumcondra were available for £5 or £6 per week, and in the 'nice quiet neighbourhood' of Sandymount houses were available for £24 a year.

The next item to buy was food. For the working-class family this might account for as much as two-thirds of the average income.[17] For the average middle-class family food represented considerably less of the budget. In the *Economic Cookery Book*,[18] first published in Dublin in 1905, Mary Redington suggests that the following expenditures would be typical at certain levels of income.

Expenditure by income range

Expenditure	Income in 150–220 %	£ per year 250–300 %
Food	50	45
clothing	18	17
lodging	12	12
fuel	5	4.5
education	5.5	8
tax, rates	3	4
health	2	4
recreation	3.5	5

In *How to Keep House*, Mrs Peel provides a guideline to the quantities of certain staples that might be required for a normal family spending, which she calculates would cost between 8s. 6d. (for 'plain but sufficient living') to 10s. (for 'nice living') per head per week:

Meat – ¾ lb (uncooked) per head per day
Table butter – ½ lb per head per week
Bacon – 1 lb per head per week for breakfast rashers
Sugar – 1 lb per head per week
Tea – ¼ lb per head per week
Milk – ⅓ pint per adult per day
Jam – 1 lb per head per week
Eggs, bread, fruit etc. are extra according to the household's taste.[19]

There had been a significant change in the supply of food over the previous thirty or forty years. Instead of loose goods such as tea, sugar and flour selected and purchased by skilled grocers, manufacturers were beginning to provide pre-packed and branded goods. The old skills of the grocery trade, however, were still in strong use: selecting and washing fruit according to season (oranges only between November and April and so on); blending tea to suit exactly the local water; chipping salt and sugar from large blocks into saleable quantities; ripening cheese, selecting and buying butter by the barrel and patting it into saleable blocks; smoking hams; attending to special customers—a chair for madam, and a biscuit for her dog—down to folding twists of brown paper into cups to carry loose goods such as flour, rice, semolina. No wonder there was a seven-year apprenticeship to the trade.

By 1907 products unknown before were rapidly gaining popularity: branded packaged tea, such as Mazawattee (the up-market favourite), and Lipton's; biscuits, from Jacobs and from English firms such as Peak Freen and McVitie; jams, from Williams and Woods in Great Britain Street; pickles and sauces, Lever's heavily advertised Sunlight Soap, margarine, Cadbury's Cocoa, Bovril, Cherry Blossom boot polish, ginger ale from Cantrell and Cochrane. The new packaged products always made a great play of their purity and wholesomeness, for adulteration was known as the besetting temptation of the old-style grocery trade.

Chains of grocery stores supplied the needs of the middle classes: Findlater's, with fourteen stores, distributed through the suburbs in such places as Rathmines, Foxrock, Bray and Howth. Leverett and Frye, based in Grafton Street, but with branches in Sandymount, Rathgar, Rathmines, Bray and Dundrum; and Bewley's—run by distant cousins of the café family, and much better known in 1907—had its head branch in Henry Street and branches in Howth and Blackrock.

> Milk was a special case. It was supplied to the customer by one of the two hundred or more private dairies scattered throughout the city, often with their own cattle sheds and herds. In the winter there were as many as 6,000 cows housed in byres and yards in the middle of the city, some of which, as Dr Flinn, Medical Inspector of the Local Government Board, reported, were in an intolerable condition. 'Some time since I visited a number of dairy-yards at milking time. The cow byres were then in a very filthy state, full of recent manure . . . the hands of those milking were not in a cleanly condition. . . In a few places pigs were kept on the dairy premises, a condition fraught with danger where there is a supply of milk being daily distributed to the public   . . . In many cases the surface is very irregular and soft, and consequently in damp or wet weather pools of stagnant water are in evidence . . .' The country dairies, said the *Freeman*'s leader writer, were even worse than those in Dublin. No wonder then that the milk supply was a prime target of the anti-tuberculosis campaign.
>
> The supply of meat was not much more enticing: three-quarters of Dublin's meat was slaughtered in private slaughterhouses of which there were still more than fifty around the city. Dubliners were well used to straggling herds of cattle winding their way through to the abbattoirs in Moore Street, Townsend Street, Westland Row, Thomas, Francis and Dorset Streets and elsewhere. Because of the condition of some of these yards, they were a serious health hazard. Ramshackle huts and shanties permanently stained with offal, blood and entrails vividly suggested the less than humane methods of slaughter frequently used.[20]

Findlater's even had their own woman's magazine, *The Lady of the House*, which claimed a readership of 20,000, distributed to the firm's customers.

For those who didn't go to the chains, there were individual grocers who often still brought traditional skills to bear, such as Murphy's in Mary's Abbey, at the end of Capel Street, a large draughty shop where Austin Clarke's mother bought the best Danish bacon, butter, eggs in winter, and in summer the best Irish bacon, butter, eggs. Behind the shop was a smoke-house, with glowing ashwood and, almost hidden in the gloom above, hung the Limerick hams; or Barry's sweetshop, where Mr Barry boiled all the sweets himself, rarely emerging from the hidden sugariness, the thickenings, skimmings and ladlings.[21] C. S. Andrews' mother had a similar provision shop in Terenure, with 'two counters facing one another, from one of which was dispensed eggs, butter, bread, cheese, tea and sugar, and from the other sweets. Behind the shop was a parlour which we used as a living and dining room.'[22]

For all sorts of products other than food, Dubliners were beginning to be able to experience the pleasure that comes from exchanging money for things. Elizabeth Bowen and her governess used to shop in

DAINTY THINGS FOR DAINTY DAMES.

A very pretty evening gown is made of primrose net, the body and skirt ornamented with frills, edged with the narrowest black velvet. A belt of black velvet, shaped, but not gathered, is worn.

Lace and ribbon dresses are very pretty if a little expensive. Tall people can wear wider ribbon and insertion than small ones. If the rows of lace and ribbon are arranged horizontally, they tend to give an effect of shortness to the figure. Small women, therefore, will find perpendicular rows more becoming.

An extremely effective evening gown is made of rows of black velvet ribbon and white valenciennes insertion. A flounce of white lace, edged with three rows of black velvet completes the skirt, and a frill of the same kind is arranged round the top of the bodice.

The same idea can be carried out in coloured velvet. Pale violet and deep cream lace is an artistic combination, and red or orange looks well with black lace. In these cases a lining of the same colour as the velvet should be used.

Pearl grey tulle looks well when made up in a cloud of tiny frills. The colour is particularly becoming to people with a high colour. It requires a touch of colour, dull pinks and reds being the most suitable.

The tightly corsetted S-shape figure, with tiny waist and exaggerated bosom, was still very much in fashion.

See our MODEL AEROPLANES.
From 2/- to 2 Guineas.

PEPPER FULL of FUN and LAUGHTER

No. 222 TY.
Card Games (as Illustrated), 1/-.
Large Assortment of various New Games.

No. 228 TY.
The Latest Novelty.
Walking Dolls from 4/6.
Undressed do. from 2/6.

No. 221 TY. "Billy" Figure.
Rival to Teddy Bear, 3/6.

No. 224 TY. Plush Balls.
Light and Harmless. No Dye to come off.
6d., 1/-, 1/9, 2/6 each.

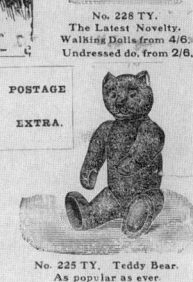

POSTAGE EXTRA.

No. 225 TY. Teddy Bear.
As popular as ever.
1/-, 2/-, 3/-, 4/-, 6c.
"VERY SPECIAL LINE."

No. 226 TY.
Maple Furniture for Little Girls.
Washstand ... 1/6, 3/6, 7/6 (as illus.)
Bureaus ... 1/6, 3/6, 7/6.

No. 223 TY. Character Dolls, dressed to represent Dutch Boy or Girl, Sailor Boy or Girl, Territorial Boy or Girl. 2/6 each.

No. 227 TY.
Jointed Dressed Doll,
14 ins. high, 1/- each,
In a Variety of Dresses.

Toys for Christmas from Clery's catalogue for 1909

Upper Baggot Street, where 'two rows of well-to-do shops faced each other over the wide street . . . [there was] a chemist, with the usual giant bottles of violet and green, a branch of Findlater's, a baker's, a post-office (encaved at the back of a fancy stationers) and a draper's . . . everything was, in its way, classy: where white cotton coats were worn. these were chalky clean, and sweet dry sawdust covered victuallers' floors'.[23] The Junior Army and Navy in D'Olier Street was another favourite haunt, as was the high-class grocers, Andrews', in Dame Street. This shop had a unique arrangement for collecting change from the cash office. In common with many shops of the time, the assistants didn't handle money, but sent the cash received and the invoice ticket to a central cash office. In Andrews' the money and the ticket were screwed into a wooden ball which was then hauled to the ceiling and tipped into a runway; the ball then rolled extremely slowly to the cash office, announcing its arrival with a crash. The return journey was equally time consuming.

Christmas was, then as now, a big time for shopkeepers. On Christmas Eve 1907, The *Freeman*'s reporter noticed that

> Dame Street was dull and dirty. Most of the shops were closed and the only gleam of brightness came from the passing brilliantly illuminated tramcars. But when one turned into George's Street there was a complete change of scene. All the shops were doing a furious business, crowds filled the side walks; happy children grabbing their mothers' skirts halted in front of the windows, where confectionery or toys were displayed . . . in Thomas St and James St there are still stalls on which were displayed turkeys and geese that are to be got cheap . . . the shops suggest a conspiracy on the part of poets, pastry cooks and butchers to over-feed us . . . every window front appealed irresistibly to the passer-by, from the time-honoured sawdust doll and dancing nigger, the model motors, the silks and satins, the turkeys and the geese, down to the fragrant mixtures of Apothecaries Hall. O'Connell St and the other business streets in the area presented constant streams of people crossing by Nelson's pillar between Henry St and Earl St . . . shops which catered for the Christmas card traffic continued thronged throughout the greater part of the day. The provision shops, too, of O'Connell St, Henry St, Mary St, Capel St remained open after most of the other establishments had put up their shutters, and they continued to be well patronised even up to midnight, many of the poorer classes

with slender purses waiting till an advanced hour in the hope of getting the bargains . . .

Clothing, especially fashion clothing, was always an exciting buy, full of tricky choices. For men a suit was *de rigueur*: with a waistcoat, complete with boots and a watch chain, and underneath a long-tailed shirt (with detachable collar), a tie, and long underwear. The prices varied widely depending on cloth and cut. In April the Henry Street Warehouse, a department store, had flannel suits at 10/6, 15s. and 21s.; striped tweed suits at 15s. and 21s.; and Irish tweed suits at 22/6, 27/6 and 35s. For more sporting occasions jacket and trousers might be adopted; Irish-Irelanders, following Douglas Hyde's lead, frequently sported kneebreeches.

For women, clothing started with long knickers, still usually made by themselves or by devoted elderly relatives;[24] a chemise and a corset, which ran from the breasts to the thighs, shaped the body into the conventional S-shape, with a narrow waist and protruding chest and bottom. Over this another petticoat and a dress, or a skirt and blouse. For day wear the throat was closed; in the the evenings the arms and some (a little) of the chest might be revealed.

The long-term trend of twentieth-century fashion, attributed particularly to the influence of Chanel, has been increasingly to adopt sporting clothes to more formal occasions. Bulfin noted an early version in Cork, at a Regatta. One tall girl, he noticed, wore 'a motor cap, cycling shirt, golf blouse, and walking shoes' while her companion wore 'a yachting cap, tennis shoes, and a man's light waterproof coat worn over a dainty muslin costume'.[25]

The department store M'Birney's great sale in January gives some idea of the prices paid for these garments (5s. then was worth just under £14 in 1990): French flannel blouses were 3s. 11d., in all wool delaine 6s. 11d.; ladies evening gowns in Japanese silk, or in satin—'very smart styles' 55s., a reasonable discount off the usual price of £3 10s. (Yet it was still some three weeks' wages for an ordinary labourer.) Silk moirette underskirts were 6s. 11d., while ladies' ribbed cashmere hose were 8½d. per pair. Box calf boots, with stout winter soles were 9s. 6d. Ladies, suede and kid evening gloves 4s. 6d.

For both sexes hats were much more important. No respectable man would venture into the street without a hat, and for women the hat allowed play for creativity and display of panache. In May the well-known milliner, Holmes, announced its summer season's offerings:

Picturesque, charming and original, for river, race meetings, fêtes, restaurant and matinée wear.
Lovely Tuscan model, with a crown of Eighteenth Century Quillings of Valenciennes, Clusters of Roses, Wisterias or Lilac 25s. 6d.
Lovely Mauve Tegal Straw Model, New Droop Shape, bouquets of forget-me-nots, heliotrope, and Roses, also in Mignonette Green 29s. 6d.

Personal tailoring was so prevalent that for some it was a luxury to buy shop goods; Austin Clarke remembered Mrs Carney, 'our family tailoress' who used to make his boyhood suits, and how he envied his school contemporaries their 'splendid shop suits', and how he lived in constant apprehension 'lest the boys from the high-class suburbs should detect a woman's hand in the cut of my breeches'.[26] Another innovation was dry cleaning, announced as 'the new French process, *nettoyage a sec*' by Prescott's laundry.

A family that had comfortably covered the basics could start to look round. Education was generally the next priority. As income went up, so did expenditure on education, which meant in exam results. For the Intermediate exams of 1907, the top boys' schools were five Christian Brothers' Schools, then Clongowes, Blackrock, Inst., Belfast, Rockwell, O'Connell School; for girls the Loreto convents took the place of the Christian Brothers' schools, with five out of the top twelve placings; then St Louis (three convents), Victoria High School, Londonderry, Victoria College, Belfast, Dominican Convent, Eccles Street. The exam orientation of the intermediate system was deplored by educationists: the Chief Secretary (in words echoed later by Pearse) described it as a system of 'cram, cram, cram . . . which murders the growing intelligence of the people . . . turning the little boys and girls of Ireland into money-making machines'. The *Freeman* would have none of this: 'the only reason he and his advisers are against the system', it wrote, 'is that Irish Ireland is using it for self-advancement'.[27]

Transport was normally the next consideration. The bicycle was extremely popular, and at £5 for a reasonable model, just about affordable. It was only for the reasonably athletic though, for the roads were generally rough, and spills were frequent. For richer excursionists the choice was between a carriage or a motor car. In the long run, a motor car worked out cheaper. A four-seater car costing £300 with 53,000 miles' capability at 4,000 miles per year would cost £167 a year to run, while a brougham and two horses, with harness etc. also costing £300, would cost £244 a year and be capable of only some 3,000 miles a year. The car was also more rugged: 'In the majority of places the carriage horses are not taken out at night. The motor can be used at all hours and in all weathers. It makes distant places accessible that with a horse are impossible.'[28] But the motor car was not only a status symbol. It was also a powerful instrument of government. Sir Henry Robinson, head of the Local Government Board, pointed out that with a motor car a Chief Secretary wishing to find out at first hand about conditions in Dingle or Ballycroy could arrive and visit more places in twenty-four hours than he could have seen in five days with horse-drawn transport.[29] He was no longer dependent on the reports of local magistrates and police for information.

Chapter Three

Daily Lives in 1907

IN 1907 people married, had children, fought with in-laws and neighbours just as we do; they enjoyed themselves at the races, or went to the theatre; they tut-tutted over the details of the latest daring robbery and fussed about clothes; students got tight and larked about, to the alarm of the respectable; earnest citizens worried about the poor, and complained about the incompetence and self-seeking of politicians; Catholic prelates worried about the decline of religious worship.

Yet there is an indefinable difference. On a random news day (17 July 1907), for instance, the *Freeman's Journal* reported 'the smart capture of a pickpocket at a tram stop in Marine Road, Kingstown'; that a barmaid in Tyrone was suing her customers for libel; a shopkeeper was fined for selling margarine as butter, and another for watering milk; a proposal to set up a women's parliament (without legislative power) was reported from a London paper; seventy-three different clergymen were listed as attending the Month's Mind of the parish priest of Moy, Co. Galway; a Scottish excursionist was decapitated by a railway train near Croke Park; and Hobbs, playing at the Oval for Gentlemen v. Players, was LBW for 5.

Some things were of course radically different. The most fundamental perhaps was the position of women. The rise to economic and social prominence since the Famine of a celibate clergy and the strong farmer had made Ireland an increasingly male dominated society; women had been hemmed more and more into a narrow sphere. By 1907 British suffragettes had been agitating for many years for the vote and for greater participation in public affairs by women. In isolated areas this call had also been heard in Ireland; but for most people (male and female), the position of women was clearly in the home.

In June the *Freeman's Journal* gave its plain man's view: 'The "smart" woman and sometimes the advanced woman sneers at the old-fashioned notion that a woman's life should be lived for her husband and her children. The man who is worth his salt realises that his first duty is by the toil of his brains or his hands to make and keep a home for his wife and family. The woman can have no higher duty than to make that home happy . . .'

These views reflected traditional Catholic ideas which were discussed in detail in the popular treatise, *The Mirror of True Womanhood*, by Rev. Bernard O'Reilly, subtitled 'A Book of Instruction for Women in the World'. For Fr O'Reilly and his readers, 'no woman animated by the spirit of her baptism . . . ever fancied that she had or could have any other sphere of duty than that home which is her domain, her garden, her paradise, her world'. Women were warned against vanity, and the appetite for display and enjoyment. The wife was urged never to seek to please 'any eye but that of her husband, or to value any praise on dress, personal appearance, accomplishment of any kind, but what falls from his dear lips; or to wish for any amusement that is not shared by him; or to wish to have any theatre for the display of any gift, natural or otherwise, save in the bosom of one's family'.[1]

Father O'Reilly also warns against the family trap of 'giving the boys, as they grow up, so large a place in the home that the daughters either seem in the way, or are obliged to devote themselves to the pleasure and caprice of their brothers'.[2] (This injunction at least fell on deaf ears. In 1966 a sociologist reported that in both working-class and middle-class homes in Dublin, the boys still did absolutely no housework whatever, and the girls frequently cleaned their brothers' shoes and performed similar tasks for them.[3])

Feminism was not strong in Ireland. Men generally took the view that woman's suffrage was probably against the natural law—since marriage made man and wife one flesh, why did they need two votes? Even if it was not, there were more important things to be worrying about, such as the National Question. In the universities, the middle-class students took little interest in their sisters' position. In the University College Dublin debating society, the Literary and Historical, there was a long-running battle to prevent women students attending the debates. The President of the College, Fr Delany, SJ, was as unenthusiastic about the idea as most of the students. As he pointed out, it would involve the ladies in the great dangers of being out late at night, and having to cross the city on their return home; furthermore, he worried about the male students, whose morality might be jeopardised by conversations with the ladies, not to mention the possibility of the undesirable or unhappy marriages that might be brought about. The society agreed, until December 1910, when a vote to allow their entry was passed by nineteen votes to seventeen.[4]

There was also the business of the low marriage rate. At 4.8 per 1,000 this was 40 per cent below that of England and Wales, and 35 per cent below that of Scotland. Some blamed feminism, others blamed

'Boss' Croker, who made his money from protection rackets and property scams in New York, was a popular winner of the 1907 Epsom Derby with his horse, Orby.

The Lepracaun, an Irish version of *Punch*, unsympathetically notes the loss of Cook's perks under the Prevention of Corruption Act.

The Expulsion from the Modern Paradise.

(Christmas Boxes given by Tradesmen to the Servants of their Clients are regarded as illegal under the Prevention of Corruption Act.)

men. The *Freeman* took the middle line: 'It is said that men have grown selfish. They shirk the trials, the expenses, the dangers of matrimony. They prefer the selfish ease of bachelor life. But men are not wholly to blame. If men are no longer attracted it is because women are no longer attractive. It is the domestic virtues that make a home desirable. For womanly women there will always be marrying men . . .' (June 1907).

The home was for the middle-class housewife not quite the lonely place it can now be in the modern estates: the smallness of the city enabled clerical workers to come home for lunch every day, and every middle-class home had at least one servant. There were in fact 28,000 servants in the city area, or just over one servant for every four members of the middle classes.

At the simplest level the household would run to only one servant, usually living in. With complete board and lodging, this was not expensive: in March a lady in Kingstown, with three in the family, offered a wage of £8 (per year), and that was typical. In November Mary Foley sued her employer for loss of wages under the newly passed Workmen's Compensation Act. She had badly burned her hand with a defective gas iron, and was off work for a month. Her wages were 3s. a week (£7. 16s. a year) and her board 7s. (she obviously lived out), so she was claiming 10s. a week. She was awarded £4.

As well as board and lodging, there was the possibility of the servants' living standard being boosted by perks, though these depended on the mistress. Garments that the household no longer wanted were frequently given. With luck there might also be a chance of a few backhanders. The rag-and-bone man would pay for items such as bones, dripping, empty bottles and jars, and tradesmen frequently gave the cook Christmas presents, and occasionally a commission on purchases. (The recently passed Prevention of Corruption Act made both of these perks illegal, to the consternation of many a pantry.) More legitimately, visitors would give tips: for those staying a few nights, tips of as much as a week's wages were normal.

While the servant saved her tips, there was much hard work to be done.

The larger and richer the household, the more elaborate the division of function. There was a fine gradation of skills. Cooks, for instance, were either Plain Cooks, who worked on their own, and also did housework; Cooks-General, who usually had an assistant; or Professed Cooks who had at least a scullerymaid and a parlourmaid under her, and possibly a 'tweeny'. This last was the lowest form of servant life and was frequently worked into the ground by her fellow servants.

> **The servant's daily routine in a small household with only one servant:**
> 6.30   Open house: see to kitchen
> 6.50   Sweep and dust diningroom; lay breakfast
> 7.20   Brush boots
> 7.30   Brush stairs
> 7.40   Clean front door and hall
> 8.00   Make breakfast
> 8.15   Serve breakfast
> 8.45   Take pail upstairs, empty slops (from the utensils in the bedrooms); strip and make beds, tidy bedrooms
> 9.30   Wash breakfast things
> 10.00 Allocated work for that day—e.g. washing, clean kitchen, ironing etc.
> 12.00 Prepare vegetables for dinner—the mistress will actually cook the meal
> 12.30 Change into more formal wear
> 1.00   Serve dinner
> 1.45   Wash dinner things
> 2.30   Afternoon walk (with children)
> 4.45   Prepare and serve nursery tea
> 6.30   Bath children
> 7.00   Wash tea things
> 7.30 – 9.00 own time, except on Monday and Thursday
> 9.15   Serve supper
> 9.45   Bedtime.[5]

In a well-off town household, the servants might consist of a professed cook, a parlourmaid, a housemaid and a tweeny. More specialist functions such as a lady's maid, and a nurse or governess could be added to the household as required. So far all the servants are female: grander arrangements started with a boy (for messages, boots, etc.) and progressed through a single-handed manservant, a footman, a valet and a butler. The bachelor household of Sir Arthur Vicars and his friend Francis Shackleton, the Dublin Herald, with a joint income of some £750 a year, consisted of a cook, a manservant, a boy and a coachman.

By the nature of things, the servants lived very close to the family, and particularly to their mistress; privacy in these circumstances was impossible, as the evidence in divorce cases regularly revealed. The fashionable female costume of the day was designed to be donned with the skilled help of a personal maidservant; it was quite a puzzle for anyone intending a rendezvous to wear garments that could be easily pulled on and off without arousing her maid's suspicions.

Daily Lives in 1907

In March 1907 Henry Byrne of Castlenock sought a divorce from his wife Edith on the grounds of misconduct with a certain Richard M'Dowell, described variously as a commercial traveller and as secretary of a trading company. Annie Cavanagh, Edith's paid companion for sixteen years, was put into the witness box, and declared that she had lived with Mrs Byrne for years at Prince of Wales's Terrace, Blackrock. At the end of Horse Show week she had accompanied her mistress to the Metropole Hotel in O'Connell Street, and there they met M'Dowell, presumably by arrangement. The three of them dined there, and afterwards went to the Empire where M'Dowell had arranged a box. They then went home.

M'Dowell, she said, afterwards frequently visited them at home. Annie said she had frequently been asked to have the blue room prepared, as a gentleman was coming to stop. Her mistress often had breakfast in bed and M'Dowell would be there in the room. On one occasion they travelled down to Cork, where they were sworn to by the porter of the Metropole, Cork. He remembered the lady's luggage and two little black dogs. They stayed in the hotel as Mr and Mrs M'Dowell. A divorce was granted and the details reported in the *Freeman's Journal*.

(A few days after this case, that highly respectable body, the Irish Commercial Travellers' Association met, and among other things they instructed the Association's Secretary to point out to the press that Richard M'Dowell was not and had never been a commercial traveller.)

Drink was an essential part of Dublin entertaining life: from the solitary black bottle with the harp on it put on the Clarkes' table when grandfather came to Sunday lunch, to more wholehearted affairs, such as the Lord Mayor luncheon on Easter Sunday 1907. After Solemn High Mass at the Pro-cathedral, the Lord Mayor and his Lady Mayoress greeted His Grace the Archbishop and over a hundred other guests. The menu was plentiful but not imaginative:

Soups: clear mock turtle, thick macaroni;
Fish: salmon, sauce tartare, cucumber;
Entrées: braised cutlets, green peas, tomato salad;
Joints: boiled chicken and ham, cauliflower, roast sirloin of beef, French salad;
Sweets: fruit jellies, apricot creams;
Savoury: anchovies on toast;
Coffee;
Fruit: pineapples, grapes, apples, oranges;

Wines: Amontillado, Nierstein. Champagne: Ayala 1893. Sandeman's old crusted port. Claret—St Julien, Medoc. Liqueurs.

Champagne was 'almost invariably given for a formal party', as Mrs Peel put it; port, sweet sherry and claret were served with the dessert. For a small luncheon, claret or hock might be served instead of champagne.

With the wine came wit; or at least that was the theory. The favourite form of humour was the epigram and the *bon mot*, the witty saying which was apparently spontaneous, but in fact could be prepared, ready for release at suitable moments. Oscar Wilde was the greatest exponent of this highly artificial art, but Dublin was well supplied with lesser versions. The Trinity academic, Mahaffy, was one of the best known, not least for his snobbery. Dubliners took a malicious delight in the report that he had referred to a certain distinguished personage as 'quite his favourite Emperor'.

Sayings of the mildest humorous content were retailed and preserved in such a way as to make one wonder about the rest of the conversation. Puns were especially popular. During the long and admittedly boring hearings of the Railway Commission, a complaint arose about the charges for carriage of chickens.

Judge: 'They think you want to pluck them (laughter).'
Counsel: 'My lord that is a fowl suggestion (renewed laughter).'
Judge: 'I think the subject is exhausted.'
Counsel: 'There is still a merrythought or two (renewed laughter).'

Not everyone appreciated the reign of the wits. One Trinity colleague noted that Mahaffy always insisted that conversation at dinner be general—his golden rule of conversation was 'to know nothing accurately'—in practice, 'This meant that he talked and we listened.'[6] In a lecture to the RDS in February 1907, Canon Carmichael reported a similar exasperation. 'Society in Dublin was', he reported, 'on the whole, hospitable, genial and pleasant; it was perhaps most agreeable in coteries, for in them there was free speech. In mixed society the acute acerbities of religion and politics rendered two of the most interesting topics of conversation quite taboo . . . Men's dinners were not much better—they heard the same old stories over and over again. Whatever the neglect of tree planting in the streets, there was no lack of chestnuts at the dinner table.'[7] For those in retreat from the wits, there was music; for those not musical, more eccentric entertainments. The adult crazes of 1907 were diabolo, in which a cone is tossed between

The long Edwardian afternoon: racing on the Liffey at Chapelizod, and strolling down Sackville Street

two sticks, and the blind pig party. At this blindfolded guests drew the outline of a pig in a book, to the great amusement of the fellow guests. M'Birney's sold a pig book in various bindings from 2s. to half a guinea, complete with quotes from classical and modern authors relating to the pig.

Despite the country's continuing reputation for drunkenness, in fact there had been a remarkable transformation in the previous thirty years. In Dublin arrests for drunkenness had considerably reduced (from 5,200 per 100,000 population in 1870 to less than 1,000 per 100,000);[8] there were still problems, however, especially with those for whom, as Sir Charles Cameron tolerantly put it, the pub was the equivalent of the club. A regular stream of tragedies and crimes connected to drink were reported in the papers. In January, Jane Bowen, her husband and her neighbour, Margaret O'Grady, spent a companionable Sunday drinking in their house in Rathmines. The drink ran out, so Jane went to get some more. On her sudden return she found her husband and neighbour 'together, in suspicious circumstances', as the court was told. She lost her temper and hurled a lamp at Ms O'Grady, who rushed out in a sheet of flame. She afterwards died. The jury found the accused guilty of manslaughter but under great provocation.

For serious drinkers, the beginning of 1907 brought a change to the law. A new licensing Act enforced weekend closing at 10 p.m. and extended the 'bona fide' distance from three to five miles. (Bona fide travellers were by law entitled to a drink at any time; thus to get a drink out of hours you had to prove that you had travelled at least the decreed distance.) The new law enabled small traders such as drapers and grocers in the city, which normally stayed open until 11.30 or later at night to catch the post-pub business, to close earlier on Saturdays. Reporters noted that streets normally crowded at that hour were deserted. Temperance restaurants and shellfish establishments also did better business as a result of early closing.

The extension of the bona fide limit affected pubs in outlying districts considerably: a pub in Rathfarnham, which had made quite a business of catering for the bona fides under the three-mile rule saw only three such customers on the first Sunday in January; in Booterstown and Blackrock passengers on the trams, used to alighting there, had to travel on, and were seen waving through the windows at their former haunts before moving on to Kingstown; while outlying townships such as Howth, which was clearly outside the new limit saw a great increase in trade, especially since, unlike Blackrock, Dollymount and other places, Howth was outside the jurisdiction of the Dublin Metropolitan Police.[9]

Non-drink related crime was relatively slight, though 1907 saw one of the century's great unsolved mysteries, the robbery of the set of jewels known as the Irish Crown Jewels from the centre of Dublin Castle itself. The crime was first reported on Monday 8 July. On the previous Saturday the safe had been found open, and the jewels, valued at £50,000, gone. The detectives of G Division and the Castle official declared themselves mystified. 'On all hands there is a feeling of blank amazement at the absolute audacity and consummate ingenuity with which the theft must have been executed', reported the *Freeman*. At first suspicion fell on professional burglars from Britain, many of whom had come over to exploit the opportunities offered by the Irish International Exhibition in Herbert Park. Several teams of pickpockets and con-men from London had already been apprehended by the DMP.

There was also an exciting awareness that technological advances had occurred in the burglary business as in other more legitimate trades. 'No craft', enthused the *Freeman*, 'in these days of wonderful enterprise has so modernised its tools as the burglars, and what with master keys, "jimmies", "feather-heads" and "solvers", the most ingenious piece of mechanism with a suitable time spent on it falls prey to their designs.'

After a few days suspicion was beginning to fall on insiders in the Castle establishment, such as the keeper of the jewels, Sir Arthur Vicars. Sir Arthur's responsibilities as Ulster King of Arms were to advise on matters of protocol and to control access to the ranks of the Irish nobility; to help in the work he had a secretary and a staff of young men, including the good-looking Francis Shackleton. During the course of investigation it transpired that Shackleton was connected with a certain ring of homosexuals in London, and was also an acquaintance of the King's brother-in-law, the Duke of Argyll.[10]

Sir Arthur himself had a considerable quantity of his own family jewels in the safe which were also stolen, which tended to exculpate him. From the beginning there were odd things about the investigation: no reward was offered for information until quite late, and in September rumours were flying around Dublin that the authorities knew where the jewels were, and that the inaction of the police, which had prompted much comment, was caused by the fact that three days after the discovery of the loss, the Home Office had instructed Scotland Yard that it was unnecessary to make any effort to find them.[11]

Two of Dublin's favourite 'characters': (*left*) the Professor; (*right*) Endymion, complete with cavalry sword under his coat. *Below*. Blackrock, about midday

This was later connected with a sensational report from Germany about scandalous goings-on at the German court. During a libel case reported from Berlin, Count Kuno von Moltke, the French Chargé d'Affaires at Berlin, Prince Eulenberg, the Secretary of State for Foreign Affairs, and various others in a group of friends around the Emperor were described as taking part in abnormal orgies at Potsdam.[12] Writers about the mysterious and continued disappearance of the Irish jewels have speculated that Edward VII, who was undoubtedly extremely angry at the loss of them, knew of the homosexuality of the group around Shackleton, and preferred the police not to explore too deeply, lest a similar scandal brush near the British court.

The *frissons* provided by these insights into misdoings in high places were reserved for the comparatively few newspaper readers. The country's best-selling daily, the *Irish Independent*, sold a mere 30,000 copies a day. By 1934 this had risen to 123,000 a day. Mass readership of daily newspapers was a thing of the 1910s and 1920s. For others the entertainment of the street and the music hall had to suffice. And there was plenty of it. C. S. Andrews remembers street organ grinders complete with monkeys, ice-cream carts proclaiming their wares with little brass horns; policemen taking a drunk or a snatch-thief to the station; military display, whether for ceremonial or recruiting purposes; cattle being prodded through town to the slaughterhouses; occasionally a fight—perhaps, as Andrews once saw in Gardiner Street, between two young women, drunk, clothes torn to the waist, streaming with blood from scratches.

Well-known characters roamed the streets, such as the Professor, or Endymion, a pensioner from a brewery accident who always carried a cavalry sword and an umbrella, or 'Sackcloth and Ashes' who would hire a jaunting car and then walk through Dublin following it, praying loudly. The familiar photographs of the day cannot report either the noise or the smells of the streets. In parts of Dublin, such as College Green, the noise was incessant: over the granite sets clopped horses, clattering iron-wheeled carts, and trams grinding round corners without differentials. Added to these interests were the smells. The basic smells were of dust, hay, straw and horse droppings, and the Liffey. There was also, depending on the wind, the malt and barley from Guinness's, the rich baking of biscuits from Jacobs in Bishop Street, the suds from Barrington's of Great Britain Street (now Parnell), where, as Austin Clarke wrote, 'It was always washing day, always Monday.' Individual shops had their own smells: the sugary tang from the sweetmaker, the cool milky dairy shop, the spicy and curranty grocer, the keen reek of drugs and the dusty dry smell of the loofah from the chemist ('smell almost cure you, like a dentist's doorbell', thought Leopold Bloom) or the hucksters' shops which sold bread and paraffin oil and kindling sticks and hot boiled peas, or the less pleasant smells from the shop at the corner of Marlboro Street where tripe, crubeens and puddings were made.[13]

Chapter Four

The Great Edwardian Collection

BETWEEN May and November a splendid entertainment, a mixture of museum and funfair, bandstand and fashion parade, was open daily in Dublin's southside. Both before and during its six-month run, the last great international exhibition before the World War was a constant source of gossip, of news, of drama and of simple jollity. Over two and three-quarter million visitors streamed through the turnstiles of the Irish International Exhibition whose halls and entertainments were spread over fifty-two acres of Herbert Park. They came to see the stands of over a thousand exhibitors of commercial and industrial products, to listen to a long series of concerts by military and civilian bands, to see the native Somalians in their village (complete with spears and shields), to admire the paintings in the Palace of Fine Arts, to watch the performers, or to try out the water-chute that whooshed with much splashing and shrieking through the lake. ('Much too dangerous', said Mrs Andrews to the seven-year-old Todd, who longed to try it.)[1]

The idea of an international Exhibition was quintessentially Victorian. It combined instruction with display, commercial advantage with the pursuit of excellence; in its original and purest form, it attempted a comprehensive survey of human products carefully arranged, like exhibits in a museum. The most celebrated of its kind, the British Great Exhibition of 1851, split the fourteen thousand exhibitors into five major divisions, and then into thirty classes, ranging from Class I: Mining, Quarrying etc. to Class XXX: Art. Each class had an international jury which awarded prize medals, proud replicas of which so often graced Victorian packaging.[2]

The success of the Great Exhibition led to the establishment of others: the first major one in Ireland was in 1853, sponsored by the engineer and railway magnate, William Dargan. There had in fact been smaller exhibitions in Ireland before this, organised by the Royal Dublin Society, notably in the 1830s and 1840s; consciousness of these was part of the background to the establishment of the great Crystal Palace venture. The 1853 exhibition attracted just under a million visitors, including Queen Victoria and Prince Albert. It was housed in a purpose-built hall covering the lawns of Leinster House, but also extending into the area now covered by the National Gallery and the Natural History Museum.

The next Irish International Exhibition was in 1865, in the buildings now occupied by the National Concert Hall; it attracted just over 700,00 visitors. By the 1860s the exhibition movement was well into its stride, with the United States and France holding them every decade; it was for the 1889 Exposition that the Eiffel Tower was erected.

These exhibitions had four functions: they stimulated trade, by allowing manufacturers to display their wares in a world where retail outlets were few and advertising was inadequate (trade fairs still perform this function); they educated the public, in taste and in the organisation of ideas; they attracted foreign tourists; they encouraged artists and others to deploy their talents in the creation of beautiful and practical objects. That at least was the original motivation; by 1900, when the most luxurious of the great nineteenth-century exhibitions, the Paris Exposition of 1900, took place, the element of tourist show was predominant. The promoters of the Irish International Exhibition of 1907 were working a seam that was past its best.

The project started with the International Exhibition held in Cork in 1902–3. It attracted many visitors, and William Dennehy, the editor of William Martin Murphy's newspaper, the *Irish Daily Independent*, wrote a series of articles praising the venture and suggesting that something similar should be done in Dublin.[3] He also suggested that there be set up a national Institute of Commerce and Industries. This idea, which was apparently a cross between the IMI, Coras Tráchtála and the Irish Goods Council, never got off the ground. The exhibition idea did, however, and by 1904 a committee had been set up and a guarantee fund was being gathered from interested parties. It was originally planned to hold the Exhibition in 1906.

The question of the site had been settled. At first the Phoenix Park was proposed, and was an obvious starting-point, but it was strongly felt that the southside would be more financially attractive. Accordingly the forty-acre site of rough wooded ground between Donnybrook and Ballsbridge was investigated. This land had already been promised by Lord Pembroke to Pembroke District Council for a park, and they were quite happy, in exchange for a fee, to waive their claim for a year or two.

The site was well supplied with handsome trees, but was frequently flooded in winter, so considerable work had to be put into draining and landscaping it before the exhibition buildings could be erected. During the course of clearance the workmen came across a mysterious and macabre find: a body, buried without a coffin in the seated position, about two feet from the surface. No police action was taken. Once cleared, the park was filled with great halls and a lake, like a city created by a mad dictator, with all public and no private buildings.

By May all was ready, and the exhibitors were largely in place. There were over one thousand of these, of which 538 were Irish, 278 French, 187 English; other exhibitors came from various countries including Hungary, Italy, Holland, Germany, Japan, Armenia and the Argentine. Unlike previous exhibitions, it had been decided not to allocate space according to a definite scheme: as a result the visitor was exposed to a wild mixture of products natural and manufactured, serious and trivial. The exhibition movement, which had begun with the products of the nations carefully segregated into thirty categories had, for whatever reasons, lost faith in the ability to order the world.

The *Freeman's Journal* described the effect. 'The stalls are arranged in the buildings without any reference to their contents . . . commencing at the Central Hall the visitor meets the following stands, taking them in order: printing, furniture, evening gowns, post cards, woollens. In the North Wing off this hall, walking along one avenue, are jewellery, carpets, pianos, furniture (again), upholstery, church decoration, sewing machines. In the South Wing, taking them in order, comes: matches, photographs, glass bottles, laboratory stores, ropes, electricity, account books.'[4] At least, as the official record noted, monotony was avoided.

The *Freeman*, along with most of nationalist Ireland, was by this time an increasingly hostile witness, a stance taken from the beginning by the Gaelic League. In January 1907 the League issued a statement urging all Gaelic Leaguers to have nothing to do with the project and to give it no support. There was even talk of boycotting exhibitors. The League feared that local manufacturers would be swamped by foreign companies, who would use their presence in Ireland to explore and penetrate the Irish market. The Irish Industrial Association battled continuously in the courts against British manufacturers attempting to ingratiate themselves in the Irish market by the use of Irish-sounding trade names. In flour alone, British brands were called 'Slainthe', 'Faugh-a-Ballagh', 'Emerald' and 'St Patrick'; still others put harps, shamrock and similar symbols on their bags. The story was repeated with other products. In June several Irish societies in London including the GAA, the Gaelic League, Cumann na nGaedheal, and the Dungannon Club issued a joint manifesto denouncing the Exhibition, and the Irish Party maintained a constant posture of denouncing the Exhibition. In the event only 308 out of 2,371 Irish firms listed in the *Irish Manufacturer's Directory* were represented.

The organisers certainly had a knack of alienating opinion. No doubt the choice of a British building contractor was influenced by the £26,000 Humphreys put into the guarantee fund, but the handling of the catering tender was bungled. J. Lyons of London eventually got the job, but only after dark accusations that they had been given an inside track in the bidding. Quite soon after the opening, when it was discovered that the appallingly bad weather and perhaps nationalist doubts had reduced the expected stream of visitors, 200 Irish workers were sacked from the catering staff. Lyons had brought over 400 English people of their own, who of course were kept on. Though this was understandable from Lyons's point of view, and the blow was softened by a hand-out of £7 each to the disappointed workers, this was a stick readily to hand with which to beat the organisers.

The choice of some of the paintings in the displays of Fine Arts could also have been more tactful. Not only were there vivid representations of the martyrdom of sixteenth-century Protestants at the hands of Catholic priests, but also there were, as one complainant put it, 'a couple of glaringly naked pictures . . . to the naturally refined tastes of the ignorant world, which have not been vulgarised by education, such things are repulsive and disgusting'. In a society where even the words of the Hail Mary (particularly 'blessed be the fruit of thy womb') could cause a rictus of embarrassment, as it did night after night in Austin Clarke's family,[5] such things were deeply offensive.

The organisers persisted to the very end with a myopically Protestant view of the world. Among the hymns chosen for the closing ceremony was a Protestant favourite, the Old Hundredth, which was a red rag to the ultra-Catholic bull. Fr Ambrose Coleman, OP, editor of *The Irish Rosary*, described the tune as that to which Cromwell and his men massacred thousands of poor Irish Catholics. 'It is therefore', he went on, 'the most barefaced impudence and hypocrisy on the part of the Ascendancy clique at the Exhibition to invite Catholics to voluntarily join in prayers, whose ancestors suffered heavy fines and rigorous imprisonment for refusing to have anything to do with them.' (The same hymn had been sung at ceremonies for Dargan's Exhibition of 1853, but the Church had not felt strong enough then to protest.)

The official opening of the Exhibition was on Saturday 4 May. Great crowds attended the route to watch the procession of the Lord Lieutenant, Lord Aberdeen, and his Countess to the Donnybrook entrance and thence to the official opening ceremony. It was a bright day, but very windy and abnormally cold. In fact the weather throughout the six months of the Exhibition's life was to be markedly bad. As

Uninhibited anti-semitism: (*left*) an advertisement from Leabhar na hÉireann, the Irish Yearbook 1908, issued by the National Council of Sinn Féin; (*below*) Shanks, the manager of the Irish Exhibition, depicted as the Modern Moses, excluding honest Irish manufacturers in favour of the Jews

NO JEWS Connected with our Business. Only IRISH Tailors employed.

THE IRISH TWEED HOUSE.

Cash Tailoring Co.,

ONLY ADDRESS: **4 CAPEL ST., DUBLIN.**

Branch—50 Upper George's Street, Kingstown.

DO YOU KNOW

"CONWAY'S," 35 EXCHEQUER STREET, DUBLIN?

(Leading thoroughfare between Grafton and George's Street.)

Everything in the Tobacco line there, and of the Best. Irish Manufactured Goods always introduced. One Quality—the Best.

NOTE ADDRESS: **35 EXCHEQUER STREET.**

DUN EMER GUILD, LTD., DUNDRUM, CO. DUBLIN.

Secretary: EVELYN GLEESON.

Weaving—Evelyn Gleeson. Book-binding—Norah Fitzpatrick. Enamelling—Emily MacCarthy.

Silver Medal, Milan International Exhibition. Bronze Medal, Munster-Connacht Exhibition. First Prizes three years in succession, Royal Dublin Society.

CARPETS AND RUGS TO ORDER. Any Design, Size, or Colour required. Price from 25s. per Square Yard. The Materials employed are all the best Irish Wool, and the work is done by a Co-operative Society of Young Girls, under the direction of Miss Evelyn Gleeson. The Designs are original, unless when adapted to order in harmony with any special scheme of ornament.

HAND-BOUND BOOKS. ENAMELS.

LATEST BOOKS.

	s.	d.
The Idea of a Nation. By "CHANEL"	0	6
Irish Made Easy. By SEAN O CUIV	0	6
Nationalisation of Irish Railways. By WILLIAM FIELD	0	3
Lally of the Brigade. By L. MAC MANUS	2	0
Patsey the Omadaun. By M. McD. BODKIN	2	0
History of Ireland in the 19th Century. By D. COSGRAVE	1	0
Moments with Heaven. The New Manual of Prayer. Third Edition. Prices 1s. 6d. to	4	6

JAMES DUFFY & CO., Ltd., 38 Westmoreland Street, Dublin.

THE MODERN MOSES.

Left. William Martin Murphy, one of the most successful Irish businessmen ever. Organiser of the Exhibition, owner of the Dublin Tram company, Clery's and the *Irish Independent* group, not to mention extensive overseas interests. *Below*. Edward VII and Queen Alexandra went blandly and amicably round the exhibits, expressing general but vague enthusiasm.

a result regular attendances were well down on expectations. On the first day 25,650 turned up to find the famous water chute still being tested and the Canadian pavilion still undergoing finishing touches.

For those who braved the weather there was always plenty to see, quite apart from the formal displays of products. On a typical day the grounds would open at ten o'clock, and the various entertainments, such as the water chute, the helter-skelter, the Indian theatre, the switchback railway, and the displays of the Rivers of Ireland, ants and bees, the Somali village, the crystal maze and the shooting range would open at 10.30. From 12.30 to 10.30 at night military and civilian bands, organ recitals and other musical entertainments filled the air. In the afternoon and evening there was often a 'cinematograph performance', and later at night fireworks. As well as these regular entertainments, there was a constant stream of special attractions such as Japanese jugglers, tight-rope walkers, novelty bands and trick cycling displays to keep up the public interest.

> The Somali village was by far the most successful side-show, grossing nearly £10,000 in 6*d*. entrance charges. In this various native Somalis went about their daily lives in as near a replica of home as the damp of Dublin would allow. Early on a correspondent of the *Freeman* described the scene: 'The Somali Village was more active than on the opening day, but the coloured gentleman who walks along outside, uttering hideous noises, making faces, and brandishing his spear might usefully be allowed to moderate his zeal somewhat. Ladies and children are apt to be startled suddenly coming upon him thus enraged . . . .' Later on another correspondent described the villagers as uttering grunts and whoops of joy at the visit of King Edward, which was explained as the nearest they could get to cheers.

(There was a strong element of the zoo about the village. For those brought up in a post-Holocaust world, the casual racism of one's ancestors is breathtaking. Jews were of course the most frequent butt. During one Dublin assault case the magistrate declared: 'These gentlemen are protected by the law here, if they are not in the countries they come from, and they must conform to those laws. I am sorry that the way the summons was taken out does not allow me to send him to jail.' The plaintiff, who announced that 'she wouldn't allow one of these Jewmen into her house', was commended for her behaviour in telling the plaintiff to clear off.[6])

The visit of King Edward VII and his Queen Alexandra took place on one of the few fine days in this dismal summer. The royal couple, accompanied by Princess Victoria, stayed on the royal yacht in

Kingstown harbour. On the morning of 10 July they landed and took carriages to the Exhibition grounds, pausing only to receive a loyal address from the burghers of Kingstown. This was the first of thirteen sycophantic addresses from various organisations that the King had the pleasure of receiving that day. On the way to the Exhibition the royal couple were greeted by the Irish people with what the *Freeman's Journal* (in a burst of nationalism) described as a 'respectful and hostlike attitude to their foreign visitors'; it was reported that large and enthusiastic crowds were marked only in such areas as Ailesbury Road, Donnybrook and near Trinity.

On arrival the royal couple went blandly and amicably around the exhibits, expressing general though vague enthusiasm. A small incident marred the occasion for Lord Aberdeen, who as Lord Lieutenant was the host. It was decided that William Martin Murphy, as the leading organiser of the Exhibition should receive a knighthood. Unfortunately no one mentioned this to Lord Aberdeen, so there was no ceremonial sword; furthermore no one had mentioned it to Murphy either, and he declined the honour. There followed a pause, which, as Lord Aberdeen describes the scene in his autobiography, was 'exceedingly awkward . . . during the subsequent brief interval before the luncheon some obser-

---

The Exhibition presented an opportunity for larking that was more than the students of Trinity could resist. On the very last night, in November, a large body of students assembled at eight o'clock by the bandstand. They had an apparently unlimited number of fire crackers and other fireworks which they let off with great abandon. Led by a young man in Turkish fez, and another who waved the Union Jack, a group rushed over to the Somali village where they caught a man, hoisted him high, and vociferously demanded that the unfortunate Somalian make them a speech on the fashionable subject of technical education. (This is no doubt the source of the Dublin folklore that relates how certain Trinity students actually kidnapped a Somali baby for a few days during the Exhibition.) After they had rampaged about for a while throwing fireworks, the police charged them and they scattered.

About two hundred of them quickly regrouped and took control of the central bandstand. At this the police vigorously intervened. They scaled the platform, and after a fierce tussle the intruders were hurled off. The students then began to tear bits off the pillars and throw them at the police; the students were again routed, so they surged off to the outside bandstand, where they seized a bandsman, put him on a chair and hurled him over the stand. They then began to smash the chairs and throw squibs at the crowd. Eventually they were ejected bodily out of the grounds just before midnight.[8] It was not for nothing that the nationalist MP, Tom Kettle, joked that the reason Dublin needed such a large police force relative to other cities was nothing to do with the lawlessness of the Irish, but was to keep the loyalist Trinity students in order.

vations of a very emphatic sort were addressed to myself'.[7] Coming on top of the recent theft from the heart of the Castle of the Irish Crown Jewels, this incident cannot have left the King with much confidence in the efficiency of the vice-regal establishment in Ireland.

By the last weeks of the Exhibition's course it was clear that the takings were simply not enough to cover the costs. In the event the accounts showed that the total expenditure had been £340,000, and the receipts, including the organisers' shares from all the concessions was £240,000—a loss of £100,000. There was talk of extending the life of the Exhibition, even of making it permanent. (Part of the failure was blamed on the weather, which had been exceptionally wet and cold all summer. Not only was the Exhibition hit, the Horse Show was also rained out, as a *Freeman's Journal* reporter graphically described. 'Rain, rain, rainclouds like dirty blankets, not a vestige of life in the air, underfloor inches of slush, beauty checked, restrained, marred, almost destroyed; not a horse in good humour, horsemen scowling and growling, not a bit of colour or picturesqueness about; nothing but a wearisome, monotonous, merciless downpour.'[9])

J. P. Nannetti, the nationalist Lord Mayor, took the opportunity to renew the attack on the Exhibition as a whole. The traders of Dublin, he declared, generally believed they had lost by the Exhibition. 'Hotels, restaurants and theatres had all lost money through the Exhibition being here', he claimed, somewhat wildly. 'Instead of spending money in the city visitors went to the Exhibition and traders in the city never saw them.' A director of two city centre hotels, the Metropole in O'Connell Street and the Grosvenor in Westland Row, disagreed; in the event his receipts were more than doubled. Many restaurant keepers undoubtedly had had a bad start to the year, but as the Hotel and Tourist Association confirmed at a meeting a few days later, the Exhibition generally had been a boon. One Association member spoke of trebling his business and sending away thirty or forty people every night. After all, he said, a million people had visited the city. In the official *Record* of the Exhibition, published two years later, William Martin Murphy noted that the chairmen of public companies were all having to apologise for the relatively dull performance of their companies in 1908 compared to 1907.[10]

In the event the pressure was not enough to keep the Exhibition afloat; Pembroke councillors wanted the excursionists removed from their leafy and secluded streets, and eventually Lord Pembroke decreed that the lease should not be extended. The land was cleared and returned to the people as Herbert Park.

An afternoon on the terraces at the Irish International Exhibition in Herbert Park, 1907

The creation of the park was the most tangible result of the Irish International Exhibition of 1907. For various reasons, its aims in stimulating Irish industrial enterprise were particularly ineffective. For Irish life as a whole, however, the most powerful single result of the Exhibition was the stimulation and direction it gave to the anti-tuberculosis campaign, which like the Home Industries Section, was chaired by Lady Aberdeen. In 1907 deaths from all forms of tuberculosis numbered 11,679; this represented 15 per cent of all deaths in that year. It was a fearful, mysterious disease, which struck particularly at the young, the female and the urban dweller. Rates seemed, if anything, to be getting worse, fluctuating between 2.7 and 2.9 per 1,000; thirty years before, the rates had been 2.3 and 2.5 per 1,000.

From the beginning the campaign was recognised to be one of social education. The women's National Health Association of Ireland was set up to promote the values of fresh air, clean homes, nourishing food and clean drink, especially milk. Habits such as spitting, breathing through the mouth, kissing bibles and kneeling in church on soiled handkerchiefs were all deplored.There was much to do. Simple cleanliness could not be relied on in the best homes: Straffan House, with at least nine guest bedrooms, had only one bathroom (most people had tubs brought to their bedrooms). Beneath every bed lurked a chamber pot, and the heavily furnished rooms would have been difficult to clean even with modern equipment. In the city, opening a window to air the room simply let smoky smuts in.

In *Ulysses*, the characters shave, urinate, fornicate, eat in bed, and perfume themselves, but they rarely wash: Stephen Dedalus apparently hadn't had a bath for nine months. No wonder then that at the opening session of the medical year at St Vincent's Hospital, Surgeon Tobin urged two rules on every individual patriotic Irishman: 'firstly cleanliness of body . . . secondly self-restraint in regulating his appetites'. Bloom himself is the exception: he buys with pleasure a bar of Barrington's lemon soap (price 4*d*.) and enjoys a bath in the Turkish Baths in Leinster Street. This was no doubt an accurate reflection of his background. Jewish women, who for ritual reasons bathed at least once a month, had a reputation for exceptional cleanliness.[11]

Travelling caravans were established by the WHNA to bring the message of fresh air to the country; model dairies, selling pasteurised milk, were set up; lectures, leaflets, booklets and other instruction methods were exploited. In her autobiography Lady Aberdeen details the continuing success of this campaign: by '1913 the rate had fallen to

2.15 per 1,000, meaning 9,387 deaths; and thus in 1913 there were 44 fewer deaths every week from tuberculosis than in 1907 . . . in 1924 the rate of deaths from all forms of tuberculosis had fallen to 1.45 per 1,000, meaning 4,582 deaths'.[12] By 1932 the rate had dropped to 1.32 per 1,000. Even if this had been the only effect of the slightly absurd Lady Aberdeen and the Irish International Exhibition of 1907, they were well worth it.

Chapter Five

Becoming Irish

THOUGH the country was quieter politically than it had been for generations, it seemed to some that there was a malaise in the Irish air. To one observer the Irish could be seen as a 'weakened and exhausted race', battered by centuries of famine, emigration, alcoholism and colonial exploitation. Those remaining, on this gloomy reading, seemed scarcely to have the will to thrive. The birth and marriage rates were actually the lowest in Europe; nine per cent of the population lived off the poor rates; emigration seemed an unstaunchable haemorrhage; the number of lunatics per head of population had quadrupled since 1851; the 'white plague' (consumption) was killing 12,000 of the youngest and most hopeful of the country's citizens a year; 30,000 licensed public houses (one for every 146 people) extracted their toll.[1]

Compounding all these problems, it seemed that with the increasing penetration by English habits, English media and English mass-market fashions, Ireland was in danger of becoming an English shire, a province of England as had Scotland and Wales, and before them Cornwall. Extensive circulation of British weekly and daily mass-market publications made obvious what was often called the 'slow process of denationalisation', as English goods and frankly vulgar mass-market English publications flooded into the new markets.

Many who were later to become ardent Republicans, such as C. S. (Todd) Andrews, imbibed their first ideas of the world from English comics such as *Chips, Comic Cuts, The Magnet, The Gem* (Billy Bunter's home territory), and the *Union Jack*. Andrews' life-long nickname was actually derived from a character in *The Magnet*. Adult publications such as *Titbits, Photo Bits, Pearson's Weekly, Lloyd's Weekly News* (all of which were read by Leopold Bloom and his milieu), were deplored by churchmen and puritanic Gaelic Leaguers alike.

In the theatre, the Dublin audience was equally lacking in discrimination and 'national-mindedness'. In the same week that the Abbey showed *The Playboy of the Western World*, less serious citizens enjoyed Casey's Circus at the Empire ('Screamingly funny acts! Roars of laughter with the Latest English and American sensation! Man versus Motor—a wonderful cycling and motor racing exhibition'); or the last week of Sinbad, the pantomime, at the Gaiety, and Mother Goose at the Theatre Royal; at the Tivoli, Chas. Fisher and Co. played their musical farce, *The Music Master*; finally, there was Living Pictures at the Rotunda. These were short one-reel films in a wildly mixed programme. A typical selection would include: *The Short-sighted Sportsman's Mortification, Canadian Salmon Fisheries, A Model Husband, New Tour in Switzerland, The Sultan of Morocco and his Army, Flowers for Mother's Birthday, Professional Skiing from Norway*, and so on.

Later in the year the Empire (always the raciest of the theatres) had 'artistic' poses 'representative of undraped statuary' by LaMilo, and in May an exhibition by Miss Juno May, the female wrestler. Wrestling was extremely popular with both sexes: in July the *Freeman* noted the presence of a 'galaxy of ladies' at a contest between the great Russian George Hackenschmidt and the Belgian Constant le Marin in the Theatre Royal. Later that month the 'knights of the grip and tumble arena' were part of a variety programme that began with the 'accomplished comedienne', Kitty Wagner, and included Collins and Rice, who called themselves the Breezy Comedy Duo.

Traditionally nationalists had reacted to these feelings of economic or cultural oppression by demanding Home Rule; once things were managed by Irishmen for Irishmen, matters would rapidly right themselves. On the other hand, it has been the experience of nationalist movements that abstract ideas of political and economic freedom are by themselves insufficiently exciting to inspire fighters. To stimulate a more aggressive enthusiasm required the heat fuelled by a legendary past, a flag, a national anthem, a traditional enemy, a language and a literature, and the hatred aroused by a sense that these rights are denied by the occupying power. The Gaelic League set about self-consciously inventing, or at least rediscovering, a powerful myth to fulfil this requirement and to re-establish the Celtic race in its rightful place among the nations of the world.

The Irish/Ireland movement was aware of the essentially synthetic nature of the task: 'we are nation-makers' wrote a correspondent to the Sinn Féin paper, *United Irishman*.[2] Enormous effort was put into monuments to the heroic past: in 1907 the nationalist movement erected statues to the Manchester Martyrs (in Tipperary), to the Irish 'wild geese' who fought at Fontenoy (in Belgium) and to Parnell (in O'Connell Street). At the very beginning of the year a massive 'indignation meeting' gathered in Dublin to prevent the despoliation of Conquer Hill, which was described as 'the venerated and historic mound under which have lain for 900 years the relics of the Irish heroes who fell in the Battle of Clontarf'.[3]

THE RIVAL HURDY-GURDYS.

MISS ERIN.—"Go away, please, gentlemen; this noise is awful. If you expect me to pay you for discord, you're quite mistaken. When you've practised a little harmony you can call round again."

Above. Not everyone appreciated the wrangling between the nationalist parties. *Below*. 'The lion whelps of Gaeldom': the GAA was a favourite recruiting ground for nationalist activists. Future president Sean T. O'Kelly holds the ball.

A good deal of windy rhetoric always accompanied these meetings. At the unveiling of the monument to the Manchester Martyrs, one of the speakers claimed that 'the longest war in history was only a fraction of that between Ireland and her enemies . . . the Manchester Martyrs died defending the flag that had floated for 1,000 years in the face of the enemy'.

This rhetoric was characteristic of the time. One cynical commentator years before had noted that if words could do all, Ireland would be the richest and strongest country in the world. The journalist, William Bulfin, was a typical enthusiast: his account of a cycle tour round Ireland was published in 1907—the 'pleasantest book in the year's list' enthused Sinn Féin's *Irish Year Book*. As he cycled through Ireland Bulfin reflected on ancient glories, waxing lyrically over Tara ('old when Christ was born, for it had held the throne of Ireland from days far back beyond the morning of our history . . . one of the world's chief capitals, and a great centre of political, legislative and literary activity')[4], and seeing in every mountain and field some echo of the greatness of the Gael. Viewing the country through his eyes, the reader was urged to feel in himself 'the unconquerable spirit of the lion whelps of Gaeldom'. Only in Belfast did Bulfin's enthusiasm for things Irish fail. He disliked the place intensely. It was not, he thought, an Irish city. It seemed foreign; the street life lacked Irish geniality, it was cold, austere, rigid, grim—in the very primness and newness and spaciousness of the city there was something basically unIrish.

Throughout his rambles, Bulfin met enthusiasts for Irish-Ireland, grave clear-sighted scholars, laughing young athletes, bright-eyed girls, all imbued with Sinn Féin ideas very like his own. He asks a Cork schoolboy (who had 'a wealth of Munster fun in his big blue eyes, and the Munster music in his soft and mellow speech') who was the patron saint of Cork. 'St Finbar is the patron saint of the Irish part of Cork', said the boy dutifully, 'but the king of England is the patron saint of the shoneens.'[5] All over the country the Gaelic League was building on local enthusiasm: in some cases already with militaristic overtones. Thus in Nenagh Percy French's collaborator, Houston Collisson, was jostled by a group who objected to his songs. They were 'a body of youths, some of whom were dressed in suits of the knickerbocker kind, and some poor fellows in ragged garments. They were trying to march in step, two and three deep. Their manner was objectionably aggressive, a something undefinably rude and coarse about it all . . . their leader addressed me in "school" Gaelic . . . my seeming indifference was met with hissing, hooting and cries of "Sassenach".'[6]

For many the re-creation of Irish pride started with the language. It was felt that there was a unique fit between the Irish people, the country and the climate, the mind-set and the language. The language had evolved over countless generations as the one perfect key to unlock the Irish creative and religious spirit. Without this key a vital part of the Irish spirit must remain in the dark, and the race remain suppressed. There were other motivations. For some the appeal of the language lay in its origins in a purer time: 'in these days of coarse materialism, Gaelic is for the Gaels an intellectual stimulant and a moral anti-septic', wrote one commentator.[7] Others, following Davis, saw the language as a surer barrier and a more important frontier for a nation than a mountain or a river. Douglas Hyde put it at a Gaelic League meeting in May 1907: the League was engaged in 'the last struggle of the Irish race to preserve not its language, but its identity as a nation'. Despite wistful glances, however, towards the revival successes of other European languages, such as Czech, Flemish, Polish, few saw Irish totally replacing English. English was a commercial necessity, said Hyde, but Irish was a national one.

The political aspects of the language movement were obvious. Those opposed to Home Rule therefore vigorously ridiculed the movement. Page Dickinson echoed the feelings of the ordinary Anglo-Irish when he described the revival of Irish as being about as useful as teaching people in Devon the Saxon tongue of pre-Norman times. Hyde's disciples, he claimed, were grocers' assistants and solicitors' clerks in Dublin and the provinces, whose motivation was not so much pro-Irish as anti-British.[8] From Trinity, Mahaffy described the non-religious writings in Irish as either silly or indecent, adding that the delicacies of Irish were as untranslatable as its indelicacies. Those mainly concerned with the industrial regeneration of the country were inclined to feel that perhaps German or French might be more useful.

By far the most exciting outing for Irish-Ireland in 1907 was the protest against the staging of Synge's *The Playboy of the Western World* at the Abbey in the early part of the year. As is the way of these things, few of the participants came out of the affair with credit.

The Abbey was in the habit of announcing its new offerings in advance, and in late January a small paragraph appeared in the papers, which with hindsight appears as a pathetically doomed attempt to ward off trouble. 'Mr Synge's new three-act comedy *The Playboy of the Western World* will be played for the first time on any stage tonight at the Abbey Theatre. It is a peasant play pure and simple, and the scene is laid in the vicinity of Belmullet. No one is better qualified than Mr

Synge to portray truthfully the Irish peasant living away in western Ireland. He has lived with them for months at a stretch, in the Aran Islands and Mayo. He has noted their speech, their humours, their vices, and virtues. He is one of the best Irish speakers in the country, and is thus brought into the closest contact with the people. The *Playboy* is founded on an incident that actually occurred.'

Synge had, it was clear from the start, chosen sensitive ground. The quality of Irish peasant life was an especial boast of the Gaelic League: it was well known in those circles that the parts of the country where Irish was spoken were, 'morally, on a higher level than those of other parts of the country'. Hyde himself maintained that native Irish speakers were cleaner, more virtuous, better mannered than others, and churchmen declared that their faith was stronger and their religious feeling more profound.[9]

The incident on which the play was founded was equally inflammatory to upholders of the new tradition. In 1894 James Lynchehaun of Achill Island had brutally assaulted and probably raped a woman called Agnes MacDonnell for whom he had acted as agent. Having escaped from the police he was hidden by his friends and relatives for several weeks before eventually getting to America. British attempts to have him extradited made him something of a famous Irish rebel figure there.[10]

The *Playboy*'s first night was Saturday 24 January. On the following Monday the *Freeman* contained a review and an indignant letter about the play, though there was no mention of riots or large-scale disturbances. The reviewer started by saying that 'a strong protest must be entered against this unmitigated, protracted libel upon Irish peasant men and worse still on Irish peasant girlhood'. However, according to the reviewer's report, the audience was quiet though restless until the third act, when Peg ties Christy and prods him with burning turf. At this point 'angry groans, growls, hisses and noise broke out, while the pinioning of Mahon went on. It was not possible—thank goodness—to follow the dialogue for a while. The groans, hisses and counter-cheers of the audience drowned the words . . .' In his final summing-up, the *Freeman*'s reviewer came out strongly against the play. 'The mere outline of the plot does not convey the offensiveness of the piece. No adequate idea can be given of the barbarous jargon, the elaborate and incessant cursings of these repulsive creatures. Everything is b_ _ _ _y this or b_ _ _ _y that, and into this picturesque dialogue names that should only be used with respect and reverence are frequently introduced. Enough! the hideous caricature would be slanderous of a Kaffir kraal.' With this racist remark, so characteristic of the times, the reviewer closed his piece.

Just below this attack the paper printed a letter from 'A Western Girl' which introduced the 'shift' theme into the debate. The writer knew the West as well as Mr Synge did, she claimed, and 'in no part of the South or West would a parricide be welcomed'; what's more, she added, 'not only would such a man be shunned, but his brothers, sisters and blood relations would be more or less boycotted for generations', thus somewhat weakening her case for the innate Christian sensitivity of the region. Her main concern was reserved, however, for 'a word, indicating an essential item of female attire, which the lady [i.e. Miss Sara Allgood, who played the Widow Quinn] would probably never utter in ordinary circumstances, even to herself'.

These articles alerted some attention, for the reaction on the Monday night was considerably more volatile, and well prepared to be shocked. The audience, however, was small: it was described as 'a very thin house', which received the curtain-opener, *The Riders to the Sea*, most favourably. The *Freeman's* reporter described what ensued: 'For a few minutes after *The Playboy* had started the rather smart dialogue was applauded. As soon as Mahon was taken to the arms of the peasants, and it became clear that Margaret was to be left alone with him, the uproar reached massive proportions. Stamping, booing, vociferations, in Gaelic, and striking of seats with sticks were universal in the gallery and in the pit.

'Amidst this babel of sounds the refrain of *God save Ireland* was predominant . . . cries of "Sinn Féin for ever" were also heard. Someone shouted "Such a thing could not occur in Ireland." A gentleman whose proclivities were not exactly on the popular side rose and shouted, "What about Mullinahone and witchburning?" This query was responded to with very emphatic execrations.'[11] Eventually the police were called and the noise calmed down a bit. At the end of the act the police left (perhaps thinking the play was over), and the nationalists began singing again songs such as 'The West's Awake', 'A Nation Once Again' and other patriotic compositions.

By Tuesday night farce began to follow tragedy. Everyone knew that a thoroughly enjoyable confrontation was in the air. Thirteen-year-old Walter Starkie went that night, and 'found a great crowd assembled in the streets adjoining the theatre. Inside the atmosphere was electric . . . as if everyone was expecting a political revolution to break out.'[12] Starkie noted that in addition to the usual middle-class theatre-goers, there were numbers of workers, and various Dublin intellectuals who had come to see and be seen.

At 7.30 the police arrived at the Abbey, as well as a mysterious group of young men, not apparently Trinity students. One of them stripped off his overcoat and offered to fight anyone in the audience who disagreed with him—an offer received with great hilarity. He then announced (to no one's surprise) that he was 'a little bit drunk' before moving to the piano and playing a waltz, very badly. The stewards eventually hustled him away from the piano. At 8.15 Yeats entered and the curtain went up. *Riders to the Sea*, the curtain-opener, was again received with general applause. Then Yeats stood up and suggested that there should be a public debate on the issues raised by *The Playboy*. At this stage a number of Trinity students appeared in the stalls, with the avowed intention of suppressing interruptions.

A few minutes into the play, uproar began, a good deal of it contributed by the drunken gentleman who once again offered to fight all and sundry—he was eventually persuaded to leave. The noise continued throughout the play; as the *Freeman*'s reporter put it 'not half a dozen consecutive sentences had been heard by the audience . . . groans and hisses greeted the sentence "You are a man who killed your father: then a thousand welcomes to you." This revolting sentence led to further disorder . . . [as did reference to] an article of female attire.'

Yeats and his supporters ran up and down the aisles, acting as spotters for the police, pointing out people who were making noise, with a view to having them ejected. They succeeded in getting a number of the most vociferous ejected in this way. Among those arrested was Padraic Colum's father, later indicted in the magistrate's court. Yeats gave evidence in court against him, claiming there was an organised attempt to prevent the play being heard, which was in effect true. A 40s. fine was imposed (perhaps half a week's salary for a clerk).

The fun continued on Wednesday. By this time the lines of confrontation were clearly drawn, and everyone came expecting a row, especially the police, who this time were lined up the side of the pit. The *Freeman*'s reporter was there again, and described the scene. 'As usual the first ten minutes passed off quietly, in fact there was a fair share of applause . . . however when the self-described parricide was greeted with open arms by the peasants things changed. Shouts of "get out" were hurled from all directions, whilst catcalls, strident bugle notes, and fierce denunciations added to the terrific din. But, on the other hand, there were shouts of "order" and "fair play".'

During the second act 'a low-sized Englishman in the stalls, who was an upholder of the play, got into an altercation with a young gentleman in the pit . . . at length the former challenged the latter to fight him . . . the combatants made their way into the vestibule and there exchanged several blows'. A considerable number of the patrons accompanied the pair into the foyer to see the fight.

In the third, act, with old Mahon chasing after Christy, one of the cast, Philly Cullen, says, 'I'm thinking we'll have right sport before night will fall.' At this point the combatants in the pit momentarily forgot the deep seriousness of the issues. 'This was so very apropos to the exciting situation', wrote the *Freeman*, 'that all parties in the theatre joined in an outburst of hearty laughter.' However things quickly reverted, and the police were kept busy ejecting interrupters. At the end of the play the audience hung on, and a number of gentlemen stood on the seats and began to make speeches to knots of their supporters.

By Thursday night some of the more objectionable passages had been cut out of the play, and additional bits of dialogue put in. By now the Dublin combatants had had their say, and the excitement had worn off. The *Freeman*'s reporter noted that 'quietness prevailed in the house last night . . . every word that was spoken on the stage could be heard'. A few hisses and yells and shouts of disapproval were heard, but the heavy police presence, and a detachment of plain-clothes police in the pit deterred any very violent demonstrations. It was noticeable, said the reporter, that many ladies were present at this showing.

D. P. Moran's journal, *The Leader*, the original of much Irish-Ireland thinking, was predictably against the play. 'Had the production been submitted to the less artistic appreciation of the commercial audience it would have been hooted off the stage in half an hour . . . throughout the play there runs an undercurrent of animalism and irreligion really as rare in the much-decried Theatre of Commerce as it is undesirable in the National Theatre of Ireland. One looks in vain for a glimmer of Christianity in the acts of utterances of the characters. Superadded must be the frequent repetition of words for the use of which any corner-boy would be arrested, and touches of coarse buffoonery which would not be tolerated in a pantomime.'[13]

For the moment the excitement about *The Playboy*, which was to recur when the play was taken abroad, ended with a great debate on the subject at the Abbey on 5 February. Yeats opened the batting, and there were contributions from Sheehy Skeffington (who said he was both for and against the play), Cruise O'Brien, leader writer of the *Freeman*, Jack Yeats, Joyce's friend, C. P. Curran and others, most of whom took up more or less predictable positions.

An extraordinary contribution from Mr D. Sheehan, a medical student and later a GP in Kerry, took the debate to an arena that appealed to neither side, but certainly let a few deeply hidden cats out of the bag. He was, reported the *Freeman*, strongly in favour of the play, which he said represented in Christy the widely distributed type of sexual melancholic. This comment was greeted with hisses and disorder. Sheehan went on to say that he had come that night to object to the pulpit Irishman just as they objected to the stage Irishman (renewed noise) . . . they ought, he said, to defend the women of Ireland from being unnatural pathological—(the rest of the sentence was lost in the noise).

Mr Synge, Sheehan continued, had drawn attention to a particular type of marriage law, which, while not confined to Ireland (disorder), was very common here (disorder). It was with a fine young woman like Pegeen Mike (hisses) and a tuberculer Koch's diseased man like Shaun Keogh (some laughter, groans, hisses and noise). When the artist appears in Ireland who was not afraid of life (laughter) and his nature (boos), the women of Ireland would receive him (cries of shame and great disorder).

At this stage in the speech, reported the *Freeman*, many ladies 'whose countenances plainly indicated intense feelings of astonishment and pain', rose and left the place. Many men also retired. The rest of Mr Sheehan's speech was drowned in noise. The new tradition was in thorough agreement with the old as to the necessity for reticence on sexual matters. Sheehan's note of blunt speaking was hardly to be heard in public debate again for sixty years. After some more speeches the meeting broke up with cheers and hisses and the singing of 'A Nation Once Again'.[14]

These activities were exciting, but still of minority interest. Even students and young intellectuals did not automatically become Irish-Irelanders. De Valera, for instance, was twenty-four in 1907 and spent his time teaching in Carysfort and playing rugby; he did not join the Gaelic League until 1908; nor did he, so it is said, consider seriously the idea of an Irish Republic until 1911.[15] For Joe Brennan, later to become Secretary of the Department of Finance and first Governor of the Central Bank, the *Playboy* row was less interesting than the Jesuit Rector of UCD's attempt to censor a student paper. In the University College Dublin debating society, the L & H, those students with political views tended to support the parliamentary party; Irish was never spoken.[16] At a less intellectual level, only three of the thirty-two playing fields in the Phoenix Park were required for Gaelic games, the rest being used for soccer.[17]

The new tradition that was so earnestly being created had still to become the dominant orthodoxy. For most people in 1907 the connection with the British Empire, with at the same time increased political, cultural and economic independence, was as much as they demanded. In pursuit of this the United Irish League was steadily pursuing the parliamentary road to Home Rule and was widely regarded as the reasonable political option. Sinn Féin was seen as clearly extremist: *The Leader* (2 March) reported as typical the reluctance of one man to join the Gaelic League, which was in theory non-political, because if he did so he would be expected to adopt Sinn Féin policies.

Part 2
1932

Chapter Six

An Exciting Year

THE political and social fixtures of the Edwardian era had collapsed by 1932; throughout the world, the war years and the 1920s had been hectic and unsettling. In many countries monarchies had tumbled, and in Russia an aggressive and avowedly atheistic communism had prevailed. Hoover was President of the United States, Chiang Kai-shek of China; Hitler was still an opposition leader. Salazar took power in Portugal in 1932, but Franco was still just a soldier. In October the newspapers reported the first successful flight from Ireland to Berlin—it took eight hours, as opposed to three days by the overland route. The *Irish Independent* commented that we were 'accustomed to think of Central Europe as a place almost as far away from us as America; in some respects indeed much further'.[1]

Societies were experimenting with divorce, with prohibition, with birth control, and had experienced social upheavals in general strikes and coups. Ireland was not immune: in the late 1920s the Cosgrave Government was worried by signs of militant communism in the IRA, and many (especially *An Phoblacht*, the IRA newspaper) saw de Valera as an Irish Kerensky, the bourgeois preliminary to Lenin's communist revolution which had taken place in Russia only fifteen years before.[2] The assumption of government early in 1932 by Fianna Fáil was a moment full of menace. In late February the *Irish Press* noted rumours that a Cumann na nGaedheal clique were plotting a coup, and these rumours were sufficiently believable to encourage several deputies to enter the Dáil armed.[3] In August 1933 a proposed mass march of Blueshirts in Dublin awoke vivid images of a similar march by Mussolini's blackshirts before he took power, and it was banned.

It seemed that the forces released during four years of war might never be channelled into a new stability. Right at the end of the 1920s the economy of the USA, the richest country in the world, had collapsed like a punctured balloon. With it the world economy itself had gone into serious recession, spiralling down over the following years to a fraction of its former activity levels. World unemployment levels stood at over twenty per cent; coal production dropped thirty per cent between 1929 and 1932.

"Yeah. Same everywhere. Nothin' but unrest!"

Dublin was easy to live in: a traffic-free Stephen's Green, and *Dublin Opinion*'s view of the impact of world crises

An Exciting Year

For many serious people the terrifying, but also exhilarating, realisation came that capitalism (and perhaps democracy itself) had apparently been shown not to work. The pompous and aggressive empires of the pre-war era had largely gone into the dustbin of history with feudalism, and it seemed likely that their replacement, liberal democracy, was going the same way. There was now a chance to create a new world that would not make the same mistakes. Many people agreed with H. G. Wells, who looked forward to a world state, run by an upgraded League of Nations.[4] These earnest souls struggled with Esperanto or Volapuk or one of the many other 'universal languages' that had such a vogue. In Germany and Russia two different utopias seethed in the minds of Herr Hitler and General Secretary Stalin.

Various mixes of fascism, communism, corporatism and other theories were in the air. The good and the bad in these ideas were not always adequately distinguished. (For years Canon Hayes, the founder in 1931 of Muintir na Tíre, kept a photograph of Mussolini above his desk.) The more conservative members of the Catholic Church favoured a return from the hated liberalism to the feudal theocracy of the thirteenth century.[5] From the Communist Peadar O'Donnell to the Jesuit, Fr Cahill, theorists shared a belief that the basic liberal democratic model was for one reason or another no longer appropriate. The world was felt by many to be a cusp, and it could with the slightest pressure roll one way or another.

'The year 1931 has departed, unwept and unhonoured', wrote the leader-writer of the *Irish Independent* on 1 January 1932. 'It was a time of almost universal distress and anxiety . . . in Germany alone it is said that almost 20,000,000 citizens are living on relief . . . But unemployment has not been the only spectre . . . budget deficits, increased taxation, and political crises have been the lot of the wealthiest nations. In Great Britain and Austria political landslides have brought new Ministers into power. In Spain the last of the Bourbon dynasties has given way to a Republic. In India the year has ended with rumblings of a storm that may soon become a terrifying hurricane.'

For Ireland (that is, the Irish Free State of the twenty-six counties) the *Independent* was perhaps a little smug: 'Ireland has come through the ordeal of the world waves of depression and distress with fewer bruises and a greater residue of vigour than most countries . . . foreign observers speak with envy and admiration of conditions in this country and of its sound Administration.'

This last remark must be taken with a grain of salt. Unemployment was high, emigration continued (though at a reduced rate), and both rural and urban poverty were marked. It was also an election year, in which Fianna Fáil were going to make another attempt to unseat William Cosgrave's Cumann na nGaedheal Party. The *Independent*, along with most of the business establishment and the strong farmers, supported Cosgrave warmly.

Like its readers, the *Irish Independent* was pious, nationalistic (though not Republican), right-wing in its instincts and conservative in its opinions and its style. With audited sales of 130,000 copies a day it was the mouthpiece of Catholic middle-class Ireland, the successor to the *Freeman's Journal*, and the voice of the new establishment. The *Irish Times* was still resolutely ascendancy, and the *Irish Press*, which was launched in 1931, was vehemently and vigorously a party paper. The *Independent*'s values were largely Dublin based, with a nod in the direction of England. The social column always led off, if possible, with some titbit about the British royal family: on 1 January for instance, readers were told that the Queen, with a number of friends, had driven to the sea at Hunstanton from Sandringham; the party walked on the front and then on the beach and stayed by the sea for some time. The Irish interest was catered for a few days later by the intelligence that the Marquess of Waterford had given up the Mastership of the Waterford Hunt, 'a decision', said the *Independent*, 'that would be regretted by every hunting man and woman in the country'.

Some of the *Independent*'s smugness reflected the fact that for the middle-class, urban Irish, it was a comfortable world. Ten years before, a political revolution had resulted in their gaining increased control of events. The shadow of the gunman still hovered in the Free State, particularly behind Fianna Fáil, but for the moment the dapperly formal Cosgrave, their own man, was President. There was an interesting year ahead, full of exciting happenings. As the *Independent*'s New Year's day leader continued: 'We face the year with confidence. It will be a year of memorable events. The general election, the Tailtean Games, our participation in the Olympiad, will contribute to make it a year out of the ordinary. But all these things will be overshadowed by the Eucharistic Congress, coinciding as this great event does with the 15th Centenary of the coming of St Patrick.'

In his guide to Ireland, published in 1935, the humorous writer, Lynn Doyle, listed the chief preoccupations of the Irish people as, in order of priority: 'the struggle for existence, religion, politics, betting and gambling, drink, sport, the cinema, the theatre, literature, the other arts'—a list that would have been happily subscribed to by most Irish men for most of the century. For Dubliners, Doyle noted, the struggle for existence was not as keen as in most other towns in the British Isles. In fact Dublin was, in 1932, the most prosperous town in Ireland, north and south. At least for the middle class, it was, as the expression went, 'easy to live in'. The beauty of the surrounding country flowed up to the suburban streets, and 'the people [were] as carefree as if Ireland had never known a sorrow'.[6] Living was relatively cheap, and successful people didn't choose to work too hard (businessmen regularly met at Bewley's twice a day); senior civil servants were entitled to six full week's holiday.

There was also the fun of being once more a capital: the new ambassadors (from the US, France and Germany) were the great catch at parties, and the burgeoning civil service promised jobs at home for the sons and (at least until they got married) the daughters.

The best of times, wrote Doyle, was Horse Show Week.

> There is nothing on earth like those Horse Show Week dances, a phantasmagoria of lights, laughter, mischief, and reckless gaiety; a babel of voices (you can dance to them if you like, for you won't be able to hear the band) a pageant of dress from the newest of Paris to the Silurian, and a pageant of people from Connemara to Jerusalem; lean hunting girls who could speak to Galway without using a telephone, and their bronzed men-folk; an Irish peeress or two, with the Irish predominating triumphantly over the peeress; sleek well-groomed doctors and barristers from Fitzwilliam Street and Merrion Square; long-haired intellectuals who think deep thoughts and don't drink shallowly; a Minister or so, trying to look European . . .[7]

The city was still small—Greater Dublin held only half a million people, less than Dr Johnson's London. Many of these still lived in great poverty and squalor in what were believed to be the worst slums in Europe. During 1932 the *Irish Journal of Medical Science* published the results of Nurse M. O'Leary's four years of district visiting to children in the poorer areas. One in eight suffered from malnutrition, over half from dental caries, one in five from eye trouble.

Inside the limits of a pre-Keynesian budget balanced in the traditional way, the government was slowly trying to do something about rehousing and clearing the slums. Great estates at Fairview and Marino had been built, though there was, as Fianna Fáil bitterly pointed out during the 1932 election, much to be done. And if the poor stepped out of line, punishment could be severe: in October Annie Duggan

Above. Horse Show scenes: smoking in public, particularly for a lady, was considered somewhat raffish. *Below.* A Feis in County Galway: the man in the front of the platform is evidently delivering his party piece.

(aged 45, of no fixed abode) was sentenced to one month's imprisonment with hard labour for being drunk and using obscene language at a Garda station.

There was a different law for the rich: a County Clare District Justice complained bitterly about drunkenness at the Shannon Lawn Tennis Club dance. 'The trouble', he said, 'is that there has never been a prosecution against persons for drunkenness on such occasions, although at any of the dances I have attended I have seen drunkenness, even at so-called reputable dances in the county. It might be [that the Guards thought] that the people drunk were too respectable to be prosecuted, but they were not, and what's more (he went on) he didn't care whether it was a he or a she getting drunk . . .'

The extreme squalor of Joyce's Dublin was slowly being cleaned up. The brothels of the Monto area had been cleared out by the guards and the Legion of Mary in the 1920s; as a result of the anti-tuberculosis campaign, personal hygiene was gradually improving—spitting in the streets was virtually a thing of the past, and people washed more, pushing the city's consumption of water up by thirty per cent in twenty-five years. It was therefore a pity, as the critic of the *Irish Builder* pointed out, that for reasons of economy, bathrooms were not included in the design of the houses of a new estate in Carlow.[8]

> Food hygiene left much to be done. The city's milk was still supplied by city dairies such as Rafters of New Street, where over 150 cows were housed in strong-smelling barns in the shadow of St Patrick's. Despite its importance, milk was in fact a highly dangerous substance: an article in the Irish women's magazine, *Model Housekeeping*, warned mothers of 'the chance of your child getting tubercular meningitis, or tuberculosis in some other form', and described filthy pails, manure and other dirt falling from cows' legs and flanks into the milk. A report published in 1924 found a quarter of Dublin's cows had tuberculosis, and the *Irish Medical Journal* in 1932 reported that the worst milk was often that which had been pasteurised, since many dairies pasteurised only bad or aged milk—what after all was the point of pasteurising good?

Women had achieved the vote, and shorter skirts and shorter hair; even at the height of fashion they were now able to dress themselves without the help of a maid, which had not been possible twenty-five years earlier, but they had gained little more control of their lives. Indeed in Ireland divorce was banned; more and more women habitually lost their jobs on marriage (this was introduced in the teaching profession in 1932), and even information about contraception was censored. During the year the parish priest's 'trade journal', the *Irish Ecclesiastical Record*, solemnly quoted with satisfaction the opinion of an eminent UK specialist in mental diseases, who announced that 'birth control leads to increased lunacy in women'.[9] In the recent encyclical, *Castii Connubii* (1930), Pope Pius XI had written: 'if the woman descends from her truly regal throne to which she has been placed within the walls of the home . . . she will become as among the pagans, the mere instrument of man'.

In a book published in 1932 Edward Cahill, the Jesuit Professor of Social Science at Milltown Park, gave a summary of the Church's position. Woman's natural qualities 'fit her especially for the activities and the life of the home'. Indeed for her to work outside the home, especially with men, would risk violating the requirements of Christian modesty. For the Church (whose views in this matter were more or less enshrined into the 1937 Constitution), the family was the key unit of society, with the man as leader, natural head, provider and protector, and the woman 'by her life within the home' giving the state a support without which the common good cannot be achieved.[10] A favourite joke told of the bridegroom who stood up at the wedding meal and said: 'Mary and I have become one—and I'm the one!'

Cahill even raised the question of the universal franchise; he personally favoured the idea of giving the vote to the family rather than the individual, with the vote being expressed, of course, by the male head of the family, and having a value based on the size of the family itself. In this suggestion the good Father showed himself more a theoretical than a practical sociologist: according to the 1926 census, less than half of the adult population (of 20 or over) were married, so the majority of both men and women lived either by themselves or in extended family groups. This point also escaped Sean MacEntee, who as Minister of Finance a few years later lyrically described the 'sound organisation of immemorial memory, deeply rooted in the traditions of our race, based on the patriarchal principle that honour, respect and obedience were due to the heads of the household . . . Today [he complained] the man and his wife carrying the whole burden of their families has no more voice in the direction of our public affairs than the flapper or whipper-snapper of 21.'[11]

The new state had not changed the fact that society was carefully divided into layers, both in the country and in the city. In financial terms the gulf between the rich and poor was still wide, though the erosions of inflation and social change meant that the gap was not as wide as it had been twenty-five years previously. The top civil servants now earned £1,500 (plus cost of living and children's allowances), whereas a casual labourer in the city, such as a jobbing gardener, was glad to work for 6s. or 7s. a day, or £100 a year—a labourer in the country might get less than 15s. a week. The range of incomes in the city was therefore up to 20 to 1, compared to the 30 to 1 ratio before the war.[12]

In the country things were relatively simple: Dervla Murphy's parents went from Dublin to Waterford to run the County Library in 1930, and found that 'on one side of the deep rural divide were the gentry and aristocracy, mainly Anglo-Irish and Protestant, and on the other were the farmers and tradesmen, mainly native Irish and Catholic. No true middle class had yet evolved . . . and professional men were usually either the sons of impoverished gentry or of prosperous farmers.'[13] Many of the gentry lived in a Somerville and Ross world, complete with servants and hunting: in January, for instance, the *Independent* reported the result of a stag hunt in Portrane, Co. Dublin. After a long run, the stag headed straight for Portrane House; it leaped through an open kitchen window, hotly pursued by the hounds, to the consternation of the maids. 'The stag was safely taken, but not until considerable damage had been done to the delph.'[14]

In Dublin, where Dervla Murphy's parents had been born and brought up, structures were considerably more complicated. Sets interlocked and intermingled (giving the illusion of classlessness) but were quite exclusive in their family affairs. Still with considerable prestige, though to a diminishing extent setting the tone, were the survivors of the Anglo-Irish ascendancy, becoming fewer and more isolated year by year. The Protestant business class still dominated the financial institutions, many of the largest businesses, and the clubs. Catholic professionals formed a distinct and well-off set, the sleek doctors and barristers that Doyle spoke of. Other sets included owners of smaller businesses, senior officials, intellectuals, bank employees; and finally ordinary clerks, middling civil servants and employees of businesses.

By 1932 about seven per cent of the Free State's population was Protestant, and half of the Protestants lived in Leinster. Every business, club or organisation was clearly defined in people's minds as either Catholic or Protestant (a feature of Irish life that persisted until the 1960s). Dervla Murphy recalled shopping at Miller's of Dungarvan, an old-fashioned Select Family Grocer, and being surprised to notice that a neighbour never entered the shop. 'Mrs Mansfield', she was told, 'doesn't believe in supporting Protestant shops.'[15] Protestants were expected to support Protestant firms, which in turn recruited their staff from Protestant schools.

The social division between the two religious groups could be deep. The day a Catholic consciously met his or her first Protestant was a memorable one. Olivia Robertson, whose father had come from England to be Dublin's City Architect, records a scene a few years after 1932 in the playgroup she ran.

> One day a crowd of children appeared before me, dragging with them a rather mentally deficient girl. The children's spokesman, a fair little girl called May, spoke up. She was furious with their prisoner.
> 'Miss Robertson, Delia's after saying somethin' awful about you!'
> 'Oh dear.' I looked round the circle of angry faces, 'What did she say?'
> 'She says you told her you were a Protestant!'
> There was a horrified pause. Then May, her face pink and anguished, spoke for them:
> 'Oh Miss Robertson, say you're not a Protestant, say you're not a Protestant!'
> If only the children had been hostile it would have been easier. But they were incredulous, shocked. To complicate matters, my Anglican training had taught me that I was an Anglo-Catholic. Still I knew what they meant. I had to rescue Delia.
> 'Yes,' I said. 'I am a Protestant. Lots of people are Protestants,' I said. 'The King is a Protestant.'
> This was not enough. I thought again. 'The film stars are Protestants.'
> It was all right.[16]

The most common (and exasperating) Church of Ireland attitude to the new state was to be patronising. Many Protestants, as Brian Inglis testified, 'as soon as they found that the new Irish Government could be trusted not to expropriate their land, debase the currency, or make general legislative mayhem, settled down to ignore its existence'.[17] However for some, such as the formidable Dr Gregg, Church of Ireland Archbishop of Dublin, the severance from Great Britain was a disaster: for him the British were the trustees of Christianity in a pagan world, and as his daughter put it 'in 1922 he felt that he had been banished from the Garden of Eden'.[18] Others retreated into arrogance. Evelyn Waugh, taking his tone from the friends he met in Ireland, relates how the Countess of Rosse 'was taken to a turf cabin where a crone sat in pig dung smoking a pipe and complaining of the roof. "My dear", said the Countess, "don't change a thing. It's simply you!"'[19]

In the end, some accommodation had to be made to demography. Brian Inglis describes the nice calculations by which the Protestant committee of the Island Golf Club regulated its affairs. Other things being equal, families in trade, Roman Catholics and Jews were excluded. 'On R.C.'s, as we called them, the rule was flexible. It had to be because there were many people of what we called "good" families in Ireland who "dug with the wrong foot"; (the Jamesons for instance, and Sir Arthur Chance's family). There were also a few members of good Protestant families who had made mixed marriages. Parental opposition was often fierce before the match, but it rarely survived the birth of children . . . so, infiltration was in progress all the time . . . but a Catholic without social status stood little chance of becoming a member. A man who was "in trade" stood even less.'[20] Class was finally a more important determinant of acceptability than religion.

On the Catholic side there was, in theory at least, no class system. This was one of the canons of the Republican Movement before the Treaty, and was, in the teeth of the evidence, happily rehearsed to English visitors until the 1970s. 'We assumed', wrote C. S. Andrews, 'that except for the usual tendency of tuppence-halfpenny to look down on tuppence the Irish nation in the mass was a classless society. There was no social immobility based on birth or inherited wealth.'[21] This was in practice no more than pious aspiration, as no doubt the less well-off members of his Republican group could have told him.

Andrews himself was typical of the men who were to run the new state. His parents ran two small but prosperous businesses—an auctioneer's and a dairy. He himself went to university (then as now largely a middle-class privilege). Among his fellow students were the later chief executives of Aer Lingus and the Industrial Credit Corporation. At university he was looked down on as a wild Republican by the sons and daughters (especially the daughters) of the professional classes. When he married he was presented with a house by his father. His brother joined the civil service, and he contemplated becoming a professional accountant. The apprenticeship fee of £200 (at this time the average civil service salary was £179 a year) was a disincentive, so he joined the newly-formed Tourist Board as an administrator at £4 a week. These things were not even possibilities for the likes of Patrick Kavanagh, born five years after Andrews in a small farm in Monaghan, or indeed the huge bulk of the population.

In the late 1920s the urban republicans who had fought against the Treaty were, as Andrews describes with some irony, 'puritanical in outlook and behaviour. We didn't drink. We respected women . . . and

IS AN EVENING SUIT WORTH £10 10s. ?

Buyers at "The House for Men" think the money well spent.

Other Prices 8½ and 7½ Guineas.

W. J. KELLY, LTD.,
Grafton Street, Dublin.

Left. What Clongowes and Belvedere wore in the evening: an ad from the Irish Jesuit Directory of 1932. *Below*. Seán MacEntee (1889–1984) as Tánaiste in the 1960s

knew nothing about them. We disapproved of any form of ostentation. We disapproved of the wearing of formal clothes—tuxedos, evening or morning dress and, above all, silk hats. We disapproved of horse-racing and everything and everyone associated with it. We disapproved of every form of gambling. We disapproved of golf and tennis and the plus fours and white flannels that went with them . . . We ate our meals with the same detachment with which we dressed or shaved . . . we disapproved of elaborate wedding ceremonies, we disapproved of women "making up" or wearing jewellery.' This austere creed could not last in the gregarious Dublin of the 1930s. 'Within ten years', Andrews goes on, 'we had all played golf and tennis. We had worn black ties and even white ones. We had joined Bridge clubs. We had sampled alcohol and eaten out in restaurants. Some of us had developed views on wine and how to cook steak. We had even modified our views on cosmetics and women's dress. We had visited France.'[22]

It wasn't just the gregariousness that changed views. Two new and powerful media had begun to exert their influence—radio and cinema. Irish radio, station 2RN as it was known, was state-run as a subset of the Post Office, and so was not likely to prove very revolutionary. It broadcast mostly music, solo singers and instrumentalists, some opera, and talks, for which experts were paid a guinea (about £35 in 1990 values) for a quarter of an hour. Occasionally they attempted an outside broadcast, as at Christmas 1931, when, as one publication put it, '2RN proved its value to Christianity and the country as a national radio station controlled by Irishmen replete with Catholic spirit when they broadcast from Kilkenny Cathedral a magnificent rendering of Mozart's Mass in D.'[23]

Politicians were luke-warm about radio. As Senator Connolly, the Fianna Fáil Minister of Posts and Telegraphs declared, he had his doubts 'as to the desirability of having a mechanism in the home, as against a certain culture'. Only some five per cent of households had radio licences in 1932, most of these being in Leinster. With the opening of the new high-power transmitter in Athlone in 1933, the number of licensed receivers tripled, to 100,000.

The cinema was another thing altogether. Irish people quickly established their reputation as one of the heaviest cinema-going peoples in the world. The glamorous images of Hollywood contrasted vividly with the mundanity of daily life. Films that promised to 'tear the heartstrings of all filmgoers who see this gripping drama of love and sacrifice' were a considerable change from ballads on 2RN or the local seanachaí. Disturbingly, these films began to suggest a set of values that were far removed from those of the parish priest and the matchmaker. Attitudes to sex, to marriage, to material possessions, were all challenged.

Talkie Topics, a Dublin-based magazine, quoted Dorothy MacKaill, star of *The Lost Lady* as saying, 'the first requisite for a happy marriage is love . . . there are dozens of cases where people marry for convenience—they like each other, they dance well together, they make a good team at bridge, their families approve of each other, they work in the same establishment or business, and a score of similar reasons. All of these establish some basis for compatibility, but none of these is enough. Only two people who are really in love with each other will find really lasting happiness together.' No wonder, as a writer in the *Irish Independent* sniffily noted, 'a great many wellmeaning folk might be found, especially in the ranks of the older generation, who would be prepared to see the opportunities for cinema entertainment abolished or at least very much curtailed, on the grounds that this modern form of popular entertainment is one of the most fruitful sources of vulgarity and to a lesser extent crime in the world of today'.[24]

One way or another urban Ireland in the 1930s was creating a society that suited itself. It was deeply influenced by British modes and manners, and to the great confusion of British visitors freely displayed that influence, but it was not England. On the other hand the rural idyll described by the Archbishop of Tuam, who expressed the recurrent wish in a sermon that 'Ireland would return to the simple life of our fathers with home industries, small farms worked by the family, fireside stories, Irish dances, Irish games and native music, with Irish the language of the home . . .' did not appeal in practice. The Archbishop had been told that a million pounds a year left the country to pay for silk stockings. Surely, he wondered, Irish hosiery could be made capable of supplying all *reasonable* demands?[25]

Unfortunately for such dreams of self-sufficiency, Irish men and women saw no reason why they should be deprived of silk stockings or any of the pleasures of modern life, especially the cinema. They did not of course approve of 'English paganism', so the task was to create a culture, by picking and choosing things with which they could be comfortable. The much-abused censorship was one of the key ways in which society protected itself. Lytton Strachey visited Dublin in 1931, and felt something his less sensitive compatriots tended to ignore. 'The state of civilisation here is curious, something new to me. An odd betwixt and betweenism. A curious mixture of decorum and impropriety.'[26] Like many English, and Irish too, Strachey was greatly puzzled by the first of the new post-colonial societies to go its own way.

Chapter Seven

Getting and Spending in 1932

THE census of 1926 identified a population of just under three million in the Free State. It was divided into the great majority which lived in the country, in villages and in country towns, and the minority—one in six—which lived in large cities, principally Dublin and Cork. The lives, assumptions and habits of those living in cities were very different to those living in the country. In the absence of television, which had yet to be invented, and radio, which was still largely an east-coast luxury, the forces making for homogeneity were weak.

In no area was the difference between city and country life more vivid than in the basic matter of getting a job. In the country the mass of people worked on the farm, or possibly in their parents' shop or business. The question of choosing or looking for a job hardly arose. The choice was either to do what work was provided or to leave. An American sociologist who spent several months in the depths of County Clare in 1932 believed that this remoteness from the operation of the market economy went deeper. Many people working in agriculture in Ireland, he noted, worked not for wages and salaries but by virtue of their family relationship. The 'boys' working on the family farm had literally no money; if they wanted a drink on market day or to go to a hurling match, they had to get it from their father. If they went on a message they frequently left the paying to the da, who would come later. Even money earned away from the farm (on the roads etc.) was frequently paid not to them but to the father.[1] The political implications of this detachment of large numbers of voters from daily economics must have been profound.

In the city things were different. The price of the extra freedom was uncertainty, especially in an economic crisis such as that which struck the world after 1929. Work of some sort had to be sought and found. For the middle-class male child there were several options. The civil service was secure, prestigious and pensionable; unfortunately entrance was extremely competitive, with fifteen applications for every Leaving Certificate level post, and twenty-two for those at graduate level.[2] The professions were possible only to those who could afford both the very high premiums, the long unpaid training period and, in most

How "BP" PLUS scores...

the petrol is better

BP Plus begins with this great advantage—the fact that it is to BP, famous already for its power, smooth running and invariable quality, that an addition of tetra-ethyl-lead is made. Tetra-ethyl-lead is the finest anti-knock agent yet discovered and the amount added has been proved by scientific experiment to be the exactly right proportion for BP in order to give it the greatest efficiency for ordinary motoring.

★ Plus a little something some others haven't got

With the added magic ingredient—lead

cases, the necessity to be introduced by a partner in the practice. (Premiums usually amounted to £150 or more, perhaps £5,000 in 1990 terms.) The next possibilities were the banks, the railway companies and very large firms, of which Guinness's was the best organised. In terms of numbers, the big employers were the civil service, with 20,000 employed, the railways, with 12,000, and the breweries with 4,200. The other big employer in the state was the Sweep, with 4,000 employees, mostly female clerks.[3]

After that various possibilities might appeal: the army, national schoolteaching, engineering, nursing, or if family contacts allowed, a job in Eason's, Jacob's, Bewley's or any of the number of similar businesses. The larger firms were nearly as secure as the civil service. Entrance to them was usually dependent on an introduction and the provision of some kind of security (a Guinness clerk had to provide £200 in this way, before starting work at just under £4 a week). Very few applicants could offer paper qualifications: in 1930 a mere 999 boys and girls sat the Leaving, and 2,659 the Inter. One in five national school pupils, on average, were absent every day.[4] Consequently many large firms set and marked their own entrance examinations.

C. S. Andrews described the job-hunting prospects for a new graduate from UCD in the late 1920s. 'University degrees, except in the case of the professions, had little value in the job market. Due to the activities of the ESB, electrical engineers were assured of employment and the local authority service provided openings for civil engineers though often in roles well below what their training and capacity warranted. Many of the medical graduates had to emigrate in search of employment. Apart from institutions such as the State Laboratory there were few opportunities for chemists or physicists and most science graduates were forced to turn to teaching. For arts and commerce graduates, teaching in secondary and technical schools was virtually the only source of employment apart from clerical or administrative posts in the public service. . . .'[5]

For Andrews there was the added disadvantage of a Republican background. Most businessmen were unsympathetic towards the IRA, and even if they hadn't been, few firms liked the regular raids on their premises in connection with these marked men, which were apt to happen every time the illegal IRA exploded another bomb.[6] Even the civil service was not immune: a tribunal set up by the new Fianna Fáil Government at the end of the year was asked to investigate 700 claims of victimisation since 1922.[7] No wonder very large numbers of Republicans emigrated in the 1920s.

Personal contacts were considered the key. (A contemporary joke referred to J. J. Walsh, an early Minister of Posts and Telegraphs—'Do you know Irish?', an interviewee was asked. 'No', came the reply, 'but I do know Walsh.') All applicants to banks, businesses and to professional practices had to be introduced by a director or partner. Andrews applied for a job with the Irish Tourist Authority. 'The accepted wisdom of job-hunting in Ireland in those days was that it depended heavily on "influence", and I followed the conventional route.' He called, before 9.30, on his friend, Seamus Moore, who was Secretary of the Motor Traders' Association and a TD. By 5.30 Moore called on Andrews with the good news that his potential employer (an ex-IRA man from Ballyporeen) would see him the following day. After some reminiscing about the Civil War days, Andrews was offered the job.

Whatever the job, £4 a week was a relatively good starting salary (it is equivalent to just under £7,000 a year in 1990 terms). A qualified national schoolteacher could look for £140 a year (£2 13s. a week), rising to £300; a railway clerk started at £80 a year, and on promotion could hope to rise to £350 or more. A tax inspector got £221 to start with, and a dispensary doctor £300. An executive office in the civil service started at £144 a year, and a bank clerk at £100.[8] At this time the average industrial wage was £126 a year, and a live-in cook cum general servant (referred to in the small ads as a 'general') could be had for less than £30 a year. Probationer nurses got £10–12 a year in the first year, after paying substantial fees to the hospital for the privilege.

At the other end of the scale, top civil servants earned more than £1,500 a year; the six partners of Craig Gardner shared £22,000; the managing director of Clery's got £9,460 (including £6,460 commission on profits). The Revenue Commissioners reported that some 1,500 people paid surtax, which meant that they had a taxable income of at least £2,000 a year; 28 people reported a taxable income of over £20,000.[9] The best paid people in Ireland were the three promoters of the Hospitals Trust, who received an annual fee of £80,000 each for their part in organising the Sweep—the top winners of the Sweepstake itself were considered comfortable for life after winning £30,000.

By luck we have an extremely detailed analysis of how at least one section of the middle class spent their money. A government committee was set up in 1932 to investigate the grievances of civil servants, whose incomes both in real terms and in relative terms had worsened considerably in the last few years.[10] In December the *Irish Independent* noted that a skilled tradesman's wages had gone up 2.28 times since

1914, whereas a typical civil service income had risen only 1.71 times. Furthermore this erosion had been marked in the years since 1929.

Since 1912 as much as 35 per cent of civil service pay had been based on the cost of living figure. This was fine as long as prices went up, but since 1925 prices generally had fallen, and with them civil service salaries. The Civil Service Federation, on behalf of its members, complained that the cost of living index was based on working-class expenditure patterns, not those of the middle class. The Federation's case depended on establishing that there was a significant difference in expenditure and life-style between the middle and the 'wage-earning' class.

In their submission they claimed:

> (a) that the average civil servant's household budget includes items which do not appear at all or only to a negligible extent in that of a working-class household. Such items are travelling expenses, life insurance, restaurant meals, medical expenses, books, maidservants, etc.
> (b) that prices are collected for the index which do not appear at all in the expenditure of the average civil servant. An example is margarine (third grade) . . .
> (c) that the bulk of civil servants live in the city which involves them in expenses.
> (d) that civil servants are usually obliged to purchase [in different shops] from those of the working class and that price movements in such not being subject to the same intensity of competition are different from other markets . . .
> (e) that the circumstances of a civil servant's household differ greatly from that of a working class household. At least one maidservant is normally employed, and the period of dependency of the children is more extended than in a working class family.

After close examination of various sets of figures the Committee agreed with the Federation, and recommended that a separate index based on middle-class expenditure be set up.

In August 1932 the number of civil servants was just under 20,000, of which 1,700 were in the top administrative and executive grades, 1,000 in the professional and scientific, and the rest clerical and 'minor manipulative' (i.e. postmen etc.). Sixty per cent of civil servants earned less than £150. The argument was therefore largely concerned with the top three thousand or so civil servants, whose incomes ran up to £1,500 or more a year. This was virtually all available for spending. Even after the aggressive Fianna Fáil budget of 1932, income tax rates were trifling by modern standards. A married man with three children paid less than one per cent tax on earnings of £500 a year, and at £700 he paid only £44. Four out of five civil servants paid no income tax at all.

The first call on every income was for food. At the lower levels of earnings just over fifty per cent of net income was spent on food, as opposed to less than one-third at the higher levels. In actual amounts, the higher civil service servants spent £200 a year on food (in modern terms about £22 per head per week); those earning approximately the average civil service salary spent £70 a year (about £11 per head per week). In 1932, even at these relatively comfortable levels, more money meant more and better food. The table below shows the effects of increasing promotion over time (and increasing family size), thus an executive officer starting on £144 a year could reasonably hope to increase his income three or four times over his career.

Proportionate distribution of expenditure in civil service households (1932)

	Annual Income £			
	£300	£301–400	£401–500	£501+
Average income of group	£166	£341	£451	£726
Average family size	4.3	4.5	5.3	6.2
% of income spent on				
Food	41.2	36.7	35.1	29.1
Housing	16.3	15.8	18.1	15.2
Clothing	9.1	8.8	7.7	10.5
Fuel and light	6.6	5.9	4.6	3.9
Household	5.2	6.9	7.8	7.7
Education, medical	3.7	4.5	5.7	8.6
Personal expenses	9.9	13.0	11.6	15.6
Income tax	–	0.9	1.7	4.5
Sundries	8.0	7.5	7.7	4.3

But what did this mean in terms of actual food eaten? In 1943 *The Bell*, then edited by Sean O Faolain, published a graphic series of articles exploring how people spent the money they earned.[11] Despite the huge leap in the cost of living between 1932 and 1943—the retail prices index jumped some sixty per cent in the first years of the war—to say nothing of the distortions caused by the rationing and scarcities, it is unlikely that the styles of cooking and organisation of food would have altered markedly in eleven years. Certainly such menus as these remained the staples of everyday family cookery until the 1970s, when exotics such as pizza, spaghetti, lasagne and curry became acceptable.[12]

Getting and Spending in 1932

The series began with the spending of a young solicitor who was earning the equivalent of £500 a year in 1932 values. He lived in Clontarf in a relatively new house (about ten years old); he employed a maid, and a gardener who came once a week. He had three children, a car, some books, a radiogram and a set of golf clubs. He came home from the office only at the end of the day; he did not drink any wine except sherry, but he always had a spot of Irish in the decanter. He dressed carefully, as befitted his profession, was home loving, liked opera, and occasionally went to the Gaiety, but did not care much for the cinema.

In a typical week his family dinner menus were as follows:

> *Sunday*: A roast, with two vegetables, and a sweet, usually fruit and whipped cream. Coffee is served at every dinner.
> *Monday*: Cold meat with hot vegetables; a sweet, typically rice pudding or a steamed sponge pudding.
> *Tuesday*: Soup from vegetables or stock, brown stew with mixed vegetables and again a simple sweet.
> *Wednesday*: Soup, rabbit in casserole with rashers of bacon, potatoes and one other vegetable; junket and stewed fruit.
> *Thursday*: Steak and kidney pie with two vegetables; jelly and cream.
> *Friday*: Vegetable soup, fish and two vegetables, or Spanish omelette; a milk pudding or cream cheese with biscuits and jam.
> *Saturday*: White stew or hot pot; fruit, biscuits, cheese and jam.

For breakfast there was always porridge and bacon and eggs or poached eggs or the like, and the children all had eggs. The solicitor took lunch in town every day. To meet this growing requirement, Bewley's and other eating places expanded their original menus of tea or coffee and cakes during the 1930s, and developed snack-type meals.[13]

On an income of £250 a year catering was on a much reduced scale. Mr X, a civil servant aged 45, had four children and lived in a house that he was in the process of buying. He smoked, took a bottle of stout now and then, had friends in for bridge or penny poker, and once a week went with his wife to the pictures. Two of his children went to a private school, which was a bit of a financial strain for it had already necessitated Mrs X doing without her maid, but they both felt it was necessary for social reasons. 'Well, it would be pretty awkward for Mrs X having to face the people on the road, and Mr X wouldn't feel too good about it in the office either.'

Similar enormous social pressures were felt in the costs of health care. For those who were admitted into the public wards of the charity

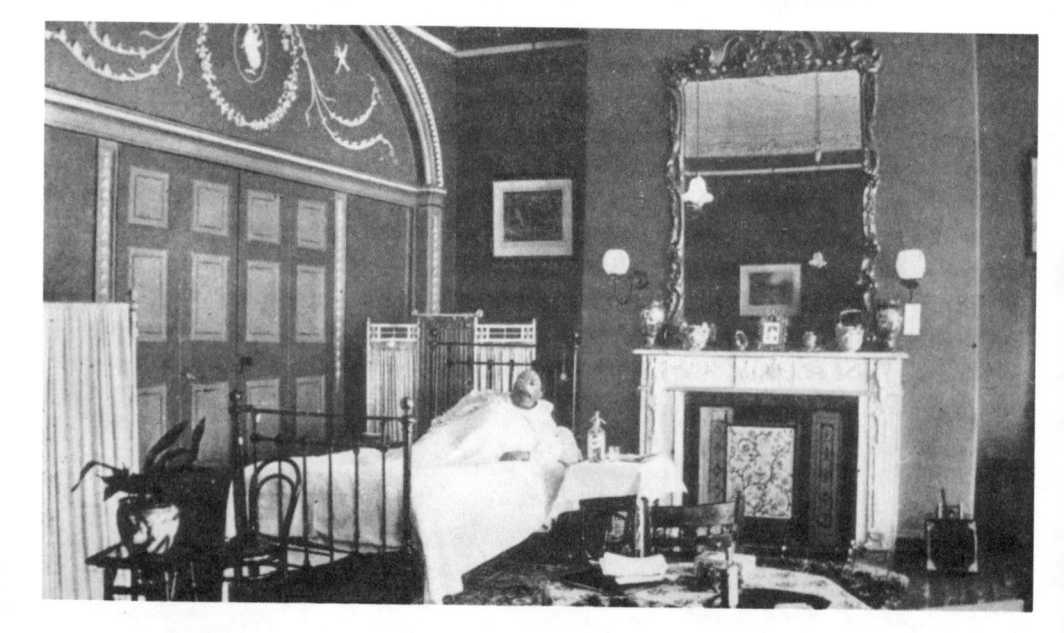

Left. What a difference that powder makes! It can even make the boss fall in love with you. *Below.* A patient enjoying the comforts of Vincent's private nursing care

hospitals, care was free; all others had to pay, and pay dearly. When the young solicitor's wife was confined with their youngest, the total costs worked out at nearly ten per cent of his income for the year. As the novelist, Annie M. P. Smithson, who was then editor of *Irish Nursing and Hospital World* noted in the July issue: 'The very rich and the very poor have no cause to complain under the present system. The hardship falls on those who are neither rich nor poor. The middle classes are too proud to go into the public wards of our hospitals, and are not wealthy enough to pay the fees required by first class nursing homes.'[14]

The Xs' menus were simpler than the young solicitor's. On weekday mornings, breakfast consisted of sausages, or porridge, or black and white pudding with fried bread; cocoa for the little ones, coffee for the grown-ups. On Sunday mornings every member of the family got an egg for breakfast. When the girls came home from school for the midday break at half-twelve there was a light lunch—usually soup with plenty of bread and a drink of milk, and whenever possible, fruit, either raw or stewed. The soup was made with stock and plenty of chopped vegetables from the garden. The children's tea was ready at half-past four. This consisted of bread, jam, cheese or potato cakes. Dinner was at half-six on weekdays and two o'clock on Sundays.

On Sundays Mrs X served a post-roast or a joint of corned beef; cold meat or shepherd's pie on Monday, and 'hamburghers' made of minced steak on Tuesday. Wednesday was meatless, and the family got a vegetable compote, or cauliflower cheese, or an omelette and a pudding of some kind. On Thursday there was Irish stew or braised steak or sausage pie. Friday's dinner menu was the same as Wednesday's. On Saturday there was nearly always fried liver and onions and, whenever the butcher was obliging, a stuffed baked heart. Supper, later in the evening, consisted of either cocoa or coffee with bread and butter and cheese.

These menus are representative of those envisaged in contemporary cookbooks, such as *The Tailteann Cookery Book* by K. Warren. This was originally published in 1929 and reprinted in 1935, was aimed at housewives and cookery students and was deliberately frugal and unadventurous. The preface notes, somewhat depressingly, that 'special care has been taken to avoid anything in the nature of lavish expenditure in purchasing the different ingredients'. *The Tailteann Cookery Book* is cookery for living, and was not written for those who lived for cooking.

Herbs are rarely mentioned, garlic never; wine or other alcohol does not appear, though occasionally a teaspoon of Worcester sauce may be recommended to add flavour; meat is heavily cooked and frequently accompanied by stuffings, fillings or additional pieces such as dumplings. Ms Warren's book contains no mention of rice, except for use in puddings, and scarcely any pasta, except macaroni; cheese is simply cheese, presumably reflecting the poor range available on the Irish market. Puddings on the other hand were prominent—rice pudding, baked bread pudding, tapioca pudding, bread and butter pudding, college pudding (another device for using up stale bread), semolina pudding—all good solid vehicles for calories and carbohydrates.

No doubt Ms Warren knew her market, and her opinion as to the conservative nature of Irish tastes is backed by anecdotes. An article in the generally quite adventurous *Model Housekeeping* by their cookery expert, Mrs Hughes Hallet, starts diffidently: 'I am sure that most of us think that the French are the only folks who can make omelets [sic] and Souffles, but with a little care and patience you will be able to make them equally well.'[15] A senior matron involved in hospital catering commented sarcastically that there was 'no use in offering cooked cheese in any form to patients in an Irish sanatorium. They will not touch it. Also not more than five per cent of them will eat tripe, oxtail or rabbits. Their gentility will not allow them to partake of what they graphically describe as "innards and vermin".'[16] The enjoyment of food was not a respectable topic of conversation: a contemporary etiquette book bluntly tells the reader that 'conversations whose only subject is eating or drinking are unworthy of a rational being, much less a Christian . . .'[17]

More sophisticated attitudes to cooking were of course to be found in individual households, and notably in restaurants such as Jammets, still the best restaurant in town, and hotels such as the Shelbourne, where the Chef, Otto Wuerst, took his job extremely seriously. In a little pamphlet published in 1930, he explained how he planned an eight-course dinner for the hotel guests (see panel).[18]

Less was being drunk. Between 1926 and 1929 the nation's drink bill was estimated to be about £16 m. or some ten per cent of the national income. Since then expenditure had shrunk to £12.7 m. in 1932, a source of some worry to the Department of Finance, since duties on drink represented over a quarter of Exchequer receipts (income tax represented less than fifteen per cent).[19]

Housing was the next drain on income. Three-quarters of civil servants still rented accommodation, but purchase was becoming more common. The grand places for the Catholic middle classes to live were still in Dublin's southside—Haddington Road Church topped the annual parish donations to the Pope again in 1932, with a donation of

> Hors d'oeuvres are a special dish to prepare the digestive organs for the food to come. Grapefruit, oysters and cocktails come under the same category.
> Secondly comes the soup. This is also a very necessary preliminary to a dinner; it promotes the flow of the gastric juices, and it prepares the stomach for work. Next comes the fish; it contributes protein, and especially phosphorus, and is rich in vitamins A and D.
> The Entrée comes next. This course has more varieties than any other; some are very rich in food values, others less.
> The following course, the Grosse Pièce, or Joint, is the mainstay of the dinner, and supplies the most nutrition, especially for tissue building. The vegetables accompanying it are not less important, since they contribute a very necessary part in our diet, principally carbohydrates and Vitamin C; they are rich in mineral matter, but have little protein and no fat.
> Next in order is the Rôti; this is mostly a bird, either domesticated or in the wild state. Salads consisting of raw vegetables are served with this; it compensates for the loss in vitamins the other foods have undergone in cooking. This is followed by the Entremet or Sweet, usually pudding, or a farinaceous substance such as rice, semolina etc. This is rich in starch, and is often accompanied with fruit.
> Then come the Savouries, of which there is a huge variety; they are dainty small morsels, highly seasoned, usually served on a canapé (or toast); they can be either farinaceous, fish, meat or vegetables. Often, especially in France, cheese is taken instead of this; it regulates the gastric glands, and brings out the taste of port, which is usually taken with it.
> Next follows the Dessert, which consists of raw fruit, nuts, dried raisins, almonds, etc. It finishes off with a small cup of coffee, mostly black, sometimes with spirits, such as Kirsch, added to it. Coffee is not a food, but a stimulant; it steadies the nerves.
> This ends the Dinner.

£113 (some £3,700 in 1990 terms—this was well up on the £2,950 equivalent donated in 1907). This time Rathmines showed evidence of Catholic infiltration of a former Protestant stronghold; their donation was only fifteen per cent less than Haddington Road. Rathgar, however, still gave considerably less than Beechwood, maintaining its exclusivity rather more stubbornly. Donnybrook was only a little behind Haddington Road, and Blackrock less than half.[20]

House prices in the most attractive parts of Dublin were not dear compared to 1990; a three-reception, six-bedroom house in Rathgar could be had for £1,400 (a mere £46,000 in 1990 money); a four-bedroom house in Drumcondra was offered at £835 (approximately £28,000). A new estate near Miltown golf course offered six-bedroom houses for £2,200, and a newly built semi-detached house in Anglesea Road, with two sitting-rooms, five bedrooms, bath (with running hot and cold water) was available for £1,650 (£54,000).[21]

After food and shelter, the family budget had to provide clothing. By 1932 the elaborate female clothes of the Edwardian era had been abandoned, though for the well dressed of both sexes it was still important to wear the right type of garment for each occasion. The rules for men were if anything more rigorous than those for women. The most formal wear was evening dress (tails and a white tie), always worn with black patent leather shoes; next came a dinner jacket for less formal occasions, a morning suit (grey tails), a business suit (in black), a lounge suit, plus-fours and a sports jacket for golf, flannels or (better) whites for tennis and so on. Each of the suits might cost anything between 30s. and 10 guineas (£350 in 1990 money). Hats were essential—men rarely ventured into the street without one, as contemporary photographs make clear. Ties, socks, shoes and accessories such as scarves, cuff-links and studs, were changed appropriately with the suit. Women's fashions on the other hand had changed so much under the influence of Paris coutouriers such as Chanel that the distinctions that formerly obtained between a dress suitable for dinner and a full evening dress, or a dress for the town or one for the country, had blurred.

To a much greater extent than now, patterns of expenditure were dictated by the kind of person one aspired to be. The middle-class civil servant members of the Federation could neither be ill in the public ward, nor be born in a hospital, nor shop in the local markets, nor appear at a party without at least a dinner jacket, without losing face. These things revealed not so much style as membership. In an age when all sorts of barriers, customs and boundaries were being broken down or changed, people clung to such things with renewed force, to a point where substance seemed to be lost behind so many symbols.

Chapter Eight

Symbolism and Daily Life

IN July 1932 a thoughtful correspondent wrote to the *Irish Independent* asking why it was that in such a conspicuously Christian country the Cross did not appear on the national flag. 'If external symbolism meant anything—as I suppose it does', 'Consistency' wrote, 'this humiliating anomaly' would be rectified at once. The appeal fell on deaf ears, but not because of a disbelief in the value of symbols; quite the contrary. In a rapidly changing world people clung desperately to the symbols of old decency. This was not one-upmanship: symbols of wealth such as cars—there were only 32,000 on the roads—were sometimes taken quite casually, as when the Secretary of the Abbey and a couple of friends found a car parked in Abbey Street, and, assuming it belonged to a friend, took it off for an afternoon jaunt. It didn't, and they were fined by the district justice.[1]

As a result of this social pressure, one of the factors in political and social life was the constant sanctifying of objectively trivial items—flags, hats, manners—into powerful symbols. From international political matters such as the Oath and the role of the Governor General, to the flying of flags, the naming of streets and of children, personal clothing, manners and times of meals, everything had an allusive significance.

In daily life one's dress had to be, said one etiquette book, 'consistent with the age and rank of the wearer'.[2] It demonstrated sex, class and status at a time when each of these things was being challenged in different ways. Even the Vatican felt the importance of clothes; in 1931 it reinforced its disciplinary rules about the necessity for priests to wear clerical garb at all times, even on holiday. By this constant display the awe in which the priesthood was held was to be reinforced; as the *Irish Ecclesiastical Record* put it, the object was to 'give the wearer the prominence and conspicuousness which naturally appertains to a member of a select and very restricted order'.[3] This idea was widely accepted. The Protestant Archbishop of Dublin, John Gregg, loved tennis parties, but was loath to lose caste by appearing in the Dublin streets in whites. 'So', his biographer recalls, 'having dressed himself up in them, he would wear over the white shirt his accustomed episcopal black garb and don the episcopal black top-hat; proceed secretly to his garage whence he would be driven—the top part of him alone being visible—in splendid state to his host's door, to whose astonished gaze he would appear in piebald state, black above and white below.'[4]

Dress should also be appropriate to the occasion; if in doubt one was urged to err on the side of formality. Occasionally the practice might be relaxed by exceptionally self-confident people. Dr Thomas Hennessy, Cumann na nGaedheal TD for South Dublin, owned a farm outside Dublin, and was in the habit of travelling to and from the farm in more or less rough clothes. One day the doctor entered a first-class compartment with the mud of the farm clinging to his boots. In the compartment sat a Dublin youth, who affected spats and a hat set at a jaunty angle, and his girl.

'This is a first-class carriage, my man,' the youth informed Dr Hennessy.

'Yes, sor,' said Dr Hennessy, entering into the fun of the thing.

'You have to have a first-class ticket if you stay here,' went on the youth.

'Yes, sor,' agreed Dr Hennessy.

After a little more dialogue on these lines, one of the station officials came along, banging the doors of the train as it was about to move out.

'Good evening Doctor,' he called out to Dr Hennessy, 'you're early this evening.'[5]

Clothes were everyone's barrier between the private body, with its mysterious life and unsettling orifices, and the outside world. The uneasy prudishness of the time made this barrier extremely important. Unfortunately for the moralists, female fashions were becoming more revealing, both in terms of the amount of leg, arm, even chest on display, and in terms of the actual female shape, no longer twisted by the corsets, hobbles and bustles of the Edwardian era. Despite attempts to create a national costume, fashion came at first or third hand from Paris, a fact deplored by more than one writer: 'the leading fashion houses in Paris and other continental cities are almost all in the hands of Jews and Freemasons of an anti-Christian type', wrote Mary Butler in a Catholic Truth Society pamphlet.[6]

The business of standing or not standing for 'God Save the King' was another symbol which provided a regular source of entertainment at the Horse Show, as loyalists attempted to make die-hards stand and remove their hats. At dances the Anglo-Irish always persuaded the band to play 'God Save the King' instead of 'The Soldier's Song'.[12] During the Ottawa conference observers watched with wry amusement

Scarecrow—New Model,
or,
Prosperity Comes to the Farm.

THE FLIGHT FROM THE TOP HAT.

" Is the Minister in ? "
" He must be. His bike's outside."

Below. Dublin Opinion characterised the republican simplicity of Fianna Fáil's style as 'The Flight from the Top Hat'. *Above*. When this cartoon was published, farm prices had plummeted to 1914 levels as a result of the Economic War.

In 1932 the spring colours were 'pale green for evening wear; among the new colours were a dark blue and a dark red; black and a colour were again becoming the uniform of the well-dressed woman, with bows and ties rather than buttons'.[7] Clothes were bought in 'madame shops' or boutiques, or in department stores. Of those surviving now, Clery's was middle of the road, and appealed especially to the country customers; Switzer's 'was the very home of Anglo-Irish clothes, sporting hats in the windows, well-cut tweed suits and linen hand-worked blouses'. Brown Thomas's ruled the other side of Grafton Street, where it catered for the new culture.[8] Shopping at these great stores was not a chore, but a new pleasure. As a Brown Thomas advertisement put it 'Thousands of women [are] finding one of their chief enjoyments in and about the great Department stores . . . women enjoyed their visits to these great emporia in just the same way as they enjoyed the theatre or the dance. . . .'[9]

One of the attractions of Cosgrave to his supporters was his dress sense. Not only was he always impeccably attired, he always, so his tailor reported, wore Irish-made cloth. With his morning suit and the silk top-hat, then the uniform of the international diplomacy, the prestige of the country was safe. Ireland could, at least in sartorial terms, take its place among the nations. The Fianna Fáil Party took a different view. Republican simplicity was their objective, in line with their appeal to the rural working class and the small farmers. They wore the formal dress of the bulk of Irish men—the dark Sunday suit. This became a political point—opponents felt that the new government was letting the country down by appearing in such informal wear as a lounge suit, much as might a modern head of state who appeared at formal occasions in jeans.

Outsiders commented on this too. When de Valera and his government met the Papal Legate at Dun Laoghaire at the beginning of the Eucharistic Congress, their refusal to wear formal morning clothes caused Cardinal Lauri a moment of doubt, as he recorded in his diary. 'When our steamer entered the harbour of Dublin, we saw the Nuncio with the diplomatic corps and an enormous crowd. We wondered if it were possible that the government were not present. Then a group of men in dark coats and soft hats, whom we had taken to be detectives, came up to us. They were the Ministers.'[10] When de Valera was planning his visit to Rome in 1933, there was a frantic exchange of telegrams between Dublin and the Irish ambassador, Charles Bewley, in Rome. Was it necessary, enquired the cables, for de Valera to wear a top-hat on his way to his audience with the Pope? The answer was yes, so de Valera took a hat and, as Bewley waspishly put it, wore it 'whenever there were no photographers about'.[11]

Not all de Valera's ministers were so scrupulous about top-hats and morning suits. At the Imperial Economic Conference in Canada in 1932, Sean T. O'Kelly, Lemass and Ryan all wore morning suits, in marked contrast to their wear for the Eucharistic Congress. The Dublin film censor and wit, James Montgomery, cracked, 'cloth caps for Christ the King and toppers for King George'.

as the ministers stood with the other delegates for 'God Save the King', but refused to drink the loyal toast.[13]

The great political struggle to remove the Oath from the constitution began with a vote in April when the combined Fianna Fáil and

Labour Parties amassed 77 votes—'one for every execution', shouted a Fianna Fáil TD in symbolist triumph. This was not the only well-publicised oath controversy in 1932. In January a rift was created in the Girl Guide movement over proposals to update the traditional oath of allegiance to the King. Strong and complicated passions were roused, and there was great backwoods resistance to any change. In the end the Head Guide, Viscountess Powerscourt, suggested a compromise which incorporated an oath of allegiance to the Oireachtas (i.e. the King, the Senate and the Dáil together). This alas was not acceptable to the die-hards, who split away from the movement.

The row naturally alerted the attention of the *Catholic Bulletin*. This publication was an ultra-Catholic version of *The Leader*, published monthly by M. H. Gill, and was written in *The Leader*'s aggressive, name-calling style, with an added sectarian twist. It claimed a circulation of 25,000 copies.[14] For them, the row simply revealed the true nature of the Girl Guides: 'these sourfaced dames are desperate to get at Catholic girls. They attempt to put a species of social souperism, of the "receptionist" type, into practice among the Catholic children of better-placed families.' The *Bulletin* continued the attack later in the year, when the Girl Guides offered to put up foreign Guide visitors to the Eucharistic Congress. These 'unsuspicious Catholic Girl Guides', wrote the editor, were being inveigled into camps so that they might be 'got at by Cromwellian Protestant women, whose very names drip the bitter hatred of all that the Eucharistic Sacrifice stands for'.[15] In another issue Dublin Corporation came under attack when they proposed to call a new road in Glasnevin (described as 'a Catholic region of Dublin hallowed by its association with the earliest and most revered of the saints of the Gael') by the 'foul and brutal bigot title of Swift's Road'.[16]

Meanwhile another symbol had been reluctantly changed. The letter boxes had all been painted green, but for many the moulded monograms—VR or ER—were still the reality. For ten years the Council of the Irish Rugby Union had refused to fly the Irish flag over Lansdowne Road ground; in February, in the middle of the general election, the Connacht Branch protested against this, describing the refusal as a gesture of contempt to the state—which no doubt it was. After political intervention from Cosgrave himself, Lansdowne Road announced, not very gracefully, that it would after all fly the flag.

After the election, the Government began a campaign of petty harassment of the Governor General, the symbol of the British connection. The first event occurred in April, when two Ministers, Sean T.

O'Kelly and Frank Aiken, in accordance with cabinet policy, walked out of a dance given by the French Legation as soon as the Governor General, James MacNeill, appeared. Dublin buzzed with rumours as to what happened, and MacNeill wrote to the President asking for an apology. Several days later de Valera replied, refusing an apology and saying that the ministers had been as embarrassed as the Governor General; would MacNeill in future please submit a list of his engagements so that this should not recur.

The following month MacNeill was effectively forbidden to invite distinguished foreign Catholics to stay with him during the Eucharistic Congress, a decision conveyed verbally to him by a civil servant. Because he was to be present at a reception for the Cardinal Legate, the Army Band was told not to be there. He was not invited to the great State reception for the Cardinal. Eventually MacNeill told the Government that unless he received an apology he would publish the letters that had passed between them, which, after some attempts to censor them, he eventually did.

In the long run, it was clear that MacNeill couldn't win, and in October he was dismissed, to be replaced by Donal Ó Buchalla, an Irish speaker. (The Cathal Brugha Cumann of the Gaelic League announced that to appoint an Irish speaker as a servant of King George was a symbolic insult to the Irish language). For symbolic reasons the new Governor General refused to live in the Vice-regal lodge in the Phoenix Park, and in the middle of the Economic War a house in Merrion was bought from state funds for him. In December the new Governor General announced that he was not going to send King George the woodcock pie for Christmas, traditionally sent by his predecessors, on the grounds that he saw no reason for continuing the custom, especially since he hadn't met King George.

The political symbolism of clothes was reflected in other aspects of daily life. At that time there were two traditions of evening eating— those who maintained the provincial tradition of high tea, and those who dined later. Terence de Vere White, who went up to Trinity in 1927, described the resulting social struggle between 'those who had brought to the city the ways of the country and refused to change them; to dine late, like wearing a top-hat, was a symptom of political unsoundness'.[17]

Dinner parties were run to an elaborate protocol, with multiple courses. Each male guest would be allocated a lady to look after. As a contemporary Irish etiquette book put it, the male guest on arrival was 'told by the host or hostess what lady he is to take to the dining room.

How is it that the wireless set is always at its worst the evening you have a few friends in specially to hear it?

VISITORS AT THE MODERN HOUSE.
HOSTESS: "I hope you'll excuse our having the tea in the garage, but it's so much more roomy."

Entertaining at home in the new Dublin

If strangers to one another he is introduced; he bows, but does not shake hands. In going down to dinner, the host offers his arm to the lady of the highest importance present, the others follow . . . each lady sits at the right hand of the gentleman who escorts her, and claims his attention.'[18] At the end of the meal the women would withdraw, leaving the men to their politics or their bawdy jokes. Lytton Strachey, on a visit to Dublin in the early 1930s, noted 'the indecency question . . . certain jokes are permissible, in fact frequent . . . but oh! there are limitations. And I must say I am always for the absolute. And the young men invariably leap to their feet when a young woman enters a room.'[19]

There were less formal entertainments, of course. For those with invitations, there were 'at homes'—Gogarty's in Ely Place, where the famous throat specialist paraded, or Sarah Purser's Second Tuesdays in Mespil House. Less formal occasions were provided by AE at his Sunday evenings, where the guests ate slab cherry cake while perched on various uncomfortable chairs and boxes, and listened while AE, a mixture of sage and Buddha, boomed away.[20] 'Wit' in the old style was taken extremely seriously. At one of these parties (which were run on nothing stronger than tea or coffee), Olivia Robertson noticed a hush: 'Lennox Robinson, very long and thin, and Walter Starkey, small and plump, had begun a duel of wit . . . they cut and thrust verbally at one another, they backed, they feinted, thrust, parried, attacked and all the time the audience listened as connoisseurs . . . it was not the meaning that mattered, it was the technique. It was a work of art.'[21]

People were however becoming a little dissatisfied with these traditional styles. In August 1932 a new form of entertaining was introduced. The *Irish Tatler and Sketch* reported the introduction of the cocktail party by the Secretary to the American Legation. 'A most enjoyable affair', wrote the *Tatler*, 'and a new idea to Dublin. Cocktails with the accompaniment of chips and almonds, tiny onions, olives and sandwiches.'[22] In December *Model Housekeeping* suggested a simple supper party, which it said 'is always appreciated, especially on Sunday nights. For supper two courses are ample, or if a third is desired, soup in the winter is always welcome . . . the menu selected is lentil soup, chicken with tomato sauce, and green salad, trifle.'

Health was a constant worry. In the 1930s it was still thought of as a gift from God, easily destroyed (rather than a right, or even a duty, as now). The big killer was heart disease (a death rate of 1.9 per 1,000 in 1929), then tuberculosis (1.3) and cancer (1.06). In 1932 tuberculosis, though tragic because it so frequently struck the young, seemed to be waning in virulence. As a result of strenuous state efforts over the previous twenty-five years, rates per 1,000 had gone from 2.55 in 1907 to 1.25 in 1932. (When Noel Browne became Minister for Health in 1948 the rate was 1.04 per 1,000.) To many observers there seemed more cause for concern over the steadily mounting deaths from cancer, especially since, as the newly set up Hospitals Commission put it, 'the fight against cancer in Ireland has hitherto been carried on in a more or less desultory fashion'.[23]

For lesser ailments there were of course plenty of remedies. Wild claims were made for patent medicines such as Aspro, which was claimed to conquer rheumatism, gout, neuralgia, flu, sleeplessness and 'pains peculiar to women'. Both sexes suffered, so advertisements claimed, from ailments such as nerves, lazy glands, brain fag and other disabilities. Luckily these problems were easily removed by any number of tonics. Zam-buk, 'the grand herbal ointment', was particularly effective, at least according to the often quoted testimony of Mr T. Mullins of Feakle, who had severely cut his right leg with a scythe, and had been in terrible pain. Zam-buk, however, rapidly removed the pain and 'knitted the severed flesh'.

A combination of stodgy food and doubtful plumbing made constipation a favourite worry. An ad for Beecham's Powders claimed that as much as ninety per cent of poor health was caused by constipation. Plumbing was still an uncertain quantity, especially in older houses, and people were very familiar with the image of the ill-plumbed house exposing its inmates to typhoid and other diseases. There was a lurking fear by analogy that, as the Eno's ad put it, 'waste matter which is not dismissed properly and to time remains to create poisons'. Smokers with throat problems were urged to change to Craven A, 'made specially to prevent sore throats'.[24]

Personal appearance was as ever a fruitful area for quackery. Cosmetics had not long been customary for respectable women—when in June *Woman's Mirror* announced that 'every normal girl uses the powder puff, the lipstick and a soupçon of rouge', there was an element of proselytising in the comment.[25] So for advertisers the question was often not which cosmetic, but whether to use one at all. One frequently reproduced advertisement for a cosmetic showed a cartoon of daughter addressing a harassed mother—'Mother', her daughter was pictured as saying, 'why does Mrs S look so much younger than you? She's your age, but I think she uses some kind of skinfood.' 'What a difference that powder makes!', shrieked another regular advertiser over pictures of a spotty and lonely 'before' and a ravishing and husband-catching 'after'.

Wincarnis, in 'A Word to all Good Daughters', declared, 'Of course Mother is beginning to show her age . . .' before enthusing on the benefits of tonic wine, which the daughters were then supposed to buy for their mothers. On a different topic, the Veet hair-remover advertisements announced bluntly, 'Men detest superfluous hair. They never find a woman attractive who suffers from it.' Men themselves were urged to use Mutesco Hair Tonic, 'made in a monastery . . . by a well-known missionary priest'. (Clergymen were frequently used as authority figures to endorse products: one was quoted as writing to a manufacturer: 'I have been keeping my eyes open for years for the ideal toilet paper, and I have at last discovered it. It is Bronco.'[26])

Personal manners were another symbol, prized as much for what they revealed as for their content. Recognising their importance for the establishment of a new Ireland, the Christian Brothers wrote and published a little book of etiquette for their pupils, called *Christian Politeness*. The book was designed to be used in class, it being recommended that pupils should read a chapter a week, and be examined on their mastery of the subject matter. The boys were urged to put the principles of the book into practice, especially at recreation times, when, as the author put it, 'rudeness is so apt to betray itself'.[27]

'Nothing', the CBS pupils were told, 'contributes more to exterior dignity and propriety of manners than exactness in preserving the natural position and motions of the body.' (Children's posture was a constant parental worry: in March the *Irish Independent* urged mothers to take special steps to teach their daughters to walk gracefully, as it was a key aspect of personal beauty.)

On waking in the morning the pupils were told first to offer the day up to God, and then to rise and dress modestly—'the use of the daily bath has now become very general, and is highly to be commended'. Teeth are to be brushed every morning, and if possible at night—'an inexpensive mixture of bark and camphor, or soot and salt, or camphorated chalk may be used with safety and advantage as tooth powder'.

The next section deals with food, and the many traps of the dining table. The author states that 'it is vulgar to play with the salt cellar and spoon, knives, forks, etc.; to sponge up crumbs with your bread or to look curiously at the plates of others'. Other injunctions include loading the fork with large portions and filling the mouth ('excessively rude'), drinking tea from the saucer, handing your emptied plate to the servants, and holding the knife in the manner of a writing pen. One mustn't 'scrape up the last morsel as if cleaning the plate—indeed it is better to leave a little on your plate' (though not of course so much as to lead your hostess to think that you didn't like the food). At the end of the meal the ladies leave the room, and the gentlemen spend fifteen or twenty minutes over their cigars and wine (the decanter always being passed to the left).

The mysteries of afternoon visits are dealt with at some length ('while standing in the hall, it is exceedingly improper to hum a tune, speak loudly, finger the furniture, or gaze through the windows'). What to do with the hat, the umbrella ('invariably left in the hall') and the personal visiting cards, are all discussed. The guest enters the drawing room with the right hand ungloved, ready to greet the hostess, who advances a little way down the room for the purpose. Obvious conversational pitfalls such as wounding Christian modesty, discussing the faults of a clergyman, or mocking the physical defects of others, are prohibited. Less obviously, the pupils were warned against the use of irony, puns and the frequent introduction of proverbs. Slang—'objectionable and inelegant phrases such as "beastly dull", "rotten", "you bet", "all jolly rot"'—was of course deplored.

As with any book of etiquette, the detailed rules give an intolerably mincing, and probably out of date impression of daily life. Yet they were taken extremely seriously. The Church long maintained an interest in personal manners, both as part of its general campaign of civilising the Irish (as for instance in the suppression of such customs as the visits of Straw Boys to weddings), and in the interest of creating leaders in the local communities—a gentleman in every parish, as the Church of England used to claim.

Most clergymen took the view that class distinctions were natural and even beneficial—as Leo XIII had written, 'inequality is far from being disadvantageous either to the individual or to the community'.[28] Some went so far as to maintain these distinctions inside the church— Hugh Leonard, who was born in Dalkey in 1926, remembers the red ropes stretched across the aisle half-way down the local church, so that those who had put twopence on to the plate at the door couldn't sneak into the pews reserved for those contributing to the sixpenny plate. 'The quality and the Holy Marys sat near the altar; the cornerboys and the wasters stood at the back where they would be the first out, and the ordinary people sat between them.'[29]

The working out of these subtle rules, the clash of symbols and the distinctions between people that they implied, were important hidden issues in the battle fought at the beginning of the year in the general election.

Chapter Nine

Digging the Political Trenches

AT the start of 1932 William Cosgrave's Party, Cumann na nGaedheal, was in power, as it had been since 1922. In the previous election, the second in 1927, he had won 62 seats out of a total of 153; the next largest group was Fianna Fáil with 57. Six other groups held seats: Labour, Farmers, National League, Sinn Féin, Independent Republicans and Independents.

During his ten years in power Cosgrave had consolidated the economy and the institutions of the new state. His policies had been conservative, favouring free trade and the development of the export side of agriculture. The most radical departure had been the Shannon Scheme, for generating electricity by damming the Shannon. In the 1920s the country used 40 million units of electricity a year, all produced by private generating operations. Even in the cities supply was weak: only one-third of Dublin and a quarter of Cork had electrical power, and Sligo, Kilkenny, Drogheda, Tralee and Athlone had none. The new scheme was planned to provide 110 million units a year, two and a half times the existing consumption.[1] Critics said it was unnecessary, it was too costly and it infringed private property rights. When the scheme was accepted in 1927 by the Dublin Chamber of Commerce, then the mouthpiece of conservative Protestant business opinion, this last point became less sensitive. This vote was a critical statement of identification of that community with the new state.[2] At a time when public expenditure was only one-third of modern levels, the Scheme was certainly daring and costly. Total government expenditure in 1925 was £25 million; the Shannon Scheme was planned to cost one-fifth of that.

Cosgrave called the election early in 1932 so that the clamour of the hustings would not disturb the Eucharistic Congress in June. (A more cynical politician might have allowed the glow expected from that event to shine on him by leaving the election until the autumn.) The campaign began with the government party on the defensive. Cuts in government spending necessitated by the international situation (world trade had dropped thirty-three per cent in a year) had upset important groups of voters. Even during the election campaign, civil servants, teachers and Gardaí, natural supporters of the status quo and therefore fundamental parts of Cumann na nGaedheal's constituency, were threatened with wage cuts; ten years in power had made the Party a little arrogant.

Since the shooting of Kevin O'Higgins in 1927, Cosgrave had become obsessed with the idea that militant communists in the IRA presented a serious threat to the state, and had reacted with a security clamp-down, which was not popular among nationalists, smelling too much of coercion. The IRA was undoubtedly violent, active and dangerous. For years there had been a continuous series of shootings and attacks on police barracks, much as there is now in the North. Month after month judges, jurymen and police were attacked or intimidated. '1931 was notable', wrote one chronicler, 'for a remarkable upsurge in IRA activity, for killings, shootings and for continual seizures of arms and explosives by the police . . . the shootings of jurymen and police witnesses made it almost impossible to get a verdict in an ordinary court.'[3]

The Cumann na nGaedheal line in the election was a straightforward appeal to the conservative instinct. 'President Cosgrave and his government have stood with you', proclaimed one advertisement. 'In the darkest hours they did not falter. They led you through the welter and chaos of civil war. They made the country safe for you. They established peace and progress. Their task is not yet done. Stand by President Cosgrave.'[4] As the campaign wore on, they began to be more explicit. Previously bland and allusive statements became tinged with more vigorous scare tactics, exploiting the communistic leanings of the extreme IRA factions, and fears engendered by remarks such as Seán Lemass's comment a few years before that Fianna Fáil was a 'slightly constitutional party'. During the election Lemass developed his view that the Fianna Fáil policy was not communistic, but was the Irish equivalent of Communism, a remark which did not reassure all of his hearers.[5]

Fianna Fáil took a considerably more radical line than the government, developing the old Sinn Féin ideas of self-sufficiency. They would first of all clear the ground by abolishing the Oath, the Annuities and the Governor-Generalship. These symbols of the ancient enemy removed, they would settle down to revitalising the economy, not by developing exports, but by stimulating home industries to meet home demand.

Although de Valera and his followers had described the Oath as an empty formality since 1927, it was a formality they found humiliating.

Above. R. M. Smyllie, who became Editor of *The Irish Times* in 1934, enjoying a quiet pipe and a pint. *Below.* Puck Fair, Killorglin, 1932

The strength of their detestation naturally aroused a countervailing attachment to an Oath which not even the British cared much about. ('We don't care a damn about the Oath', said the wife of the President of the Board of Trade to Lemass at Ottawa later in the year, 'but we're not letting you away with the annuities.')[6] The Annuities were certainly another matter. They arose out of payments under various Land Acts by which British governments had financed the transfer of holdings from landlords to tenants. They and other connected payments amounted to £5 m, one-seventh of Irish merchandise exports, or one-fifth of annual tax revenue.[7] For Fianna Fáil there were economic, moral and legal reasons why they should no longer be paid. For their opponents the issue was one of international credibility—a new state should not renege on its agreements.

In a speech on 3 February de Valera quoted at great length a legal opinion provided by various eminent lawyers to the effect that in strict legal terms the Annuities could arguably be withheld. (This opinion was echoed by one given to the British Government later in the year, which partly explained their reluctance to go to independent international arbitration on the issue.) Having proved to his satisfaction that the Annuities shouldn't be paid to the British, he did not explain why the farmers should go on paying them to the legal successors of the British in power. Indeed some of the wilder Fianna Fáil orators let the farmers believe that they would not have to pay them at all.

More revealingly of the times, de Valera was not seriously asked, nor did he attempt to envisage, how the British might, in a time of economic depression and international unrest, react to the financial and imperial implications of withholding the Annuities. De Valera apparently felt that he only had to point out the rights of the case to the British, and they would honourably acquiesce. The political argument was almost totally on the question of the rights and wrongs of the Annuities, and hardly at all on the likely consequences of withholding them.

On this and other issues the Fianna Fáil candidates, from de Valera downwards, took full advantage of the freedom allowed to an opposition to fantasise about how much better the world would be if only they had been in power. At the beginning of the campaign, de Valera explained to a Thurles meeting that the abolition of the Annuities would enable the government to undertake schemes as big as the Shannon Scheme every year. At the hustings the Party proclaimed that by a programme of manufacturing in Ireland goods now unnecessarily imported, the Free State could employ 85,000 more people (unemployment was reckoned at anything between 80,000 and 100,000). Taxation would be reduced by £2 million.

By the end of January the election campaign began to hot up. Fianna Fáil took a large advertisement in the *Irish Independent* on 30 January describing 'The disastrous record of Cumann na nGaedheal, the greatest failure in Irish history!' One of de Valera's favourite lines was to attack the waste of tax revenues in the payment of high salaries to public servants. Cosgrave, as President of the Executive Council, had a salary of £2,500 at this time, and the ministers £1,700 each. These salaries, declared de Valera, would have to come down. A salary of £1,000—equivalent to nearly £30,000 a year after tax in 1990 terms—should be sufficient for any minister to meet his expenses and rear his family, and the same limit should apply to civil service salaries. One of the first acts of the new government was to reduce all ministerial salaries to £1,000; only de Valera's was fixed higher, at £1,500. These were half the levels obtaining in the Six Counties.[8]

As the election wore on, Fianna Fáil were clearly making inroads, despite the best efforts of the *Irish Independent* and *The Irish Times*, which always presented Cosgrave in the most flattering light, and as far as possible de Valera in the opposite. On 9 February, for instance, the *Independent* took great pleasure in reporting that Mr de Valera's speech in Feakle, Co. Clare had been loudly and frequently interrupted by the braying of an ass tethered to some railings. Despite this strong media support Cumann na nGaedheal were worried. De Valera was successfully tapping a disappointment felt at all levels that the social and economic renewal that people had expected from an independent Ireland had failed to materialise. Fianna Fáil had, as their advertisement put it, 'A Plan . . . to employ Irishmen in Ireland to grow our food, to make our clothes and our implements, to provide the materials for our houses, instead of getting that work done for us by foreigners in other countries.' This simple idea was deeply enticing to nationalists of all classes who knew that despite legislative independence, the country was neither rich, nor Gaelic speaking, nor united, nor even had the wound of emigration been staunched.

In the country de Valera strongly appealed to the thousands of small farmers who participated very little in the exchange economy. For many of them the years of waiting to inherit the farm, and the closeness of the rural community, had implanted above all a vigorous understanding of the evils of dependence. A programme based on self-sufficiency was therefore extremely attractive, and if it implied that the country would have to make do with the 'plain furniture of the cottage' as de Valera put it, in order to live within its means, so be it. For them, after all, there was little to lose.

In the cities it was clear that Protestant interests still held substantial ownership in the large companies, the banks and other financial institutions, and many Protestants made no secret of their continuing loyalty to Britain. The cultural freedom that had been hoped for was also proving elusive. Every sort of benefit had been expected from independence: in 1917 the writer, Brian Ó hUiginn, wrote in the introduction to a volume of his comic stories called *Fun o' the Forge*, 'God speed the day when the smutty wit of the Sasanach shall be heard no longer in our land, when the laughter of the open-hearted, clean-minded Gael shall ring from end to end of Eirinn, lighting every mind, lifting up every heart, and softening for all who have suffered the memory of those sadder days that they have known.' Such intense expectations were bound to fail, but it was natural to seek scapegoats.

The Freemasons were a favourite target. In many people's minds the Masons took something of the same position in Ireland as the Jews in Germany, as scapegoats for national disappointment. In the Sligo/Leitrim constituency, for instance, Fianna Fáiler Ben Maguire told the electors that the Cumann na nGaedheal Government had been the agents of the Freemasons and the ex-Unionists, who had always been England's tools in this country. (Soon after this speech Maguire had a motor accident, and his Cumann na nGaedheal opponent, Pat Reynolds, chivalrously announced that he would address no meetings in Maguire's territory of Carrick-on-Shannon until his opponent was back on his feet. This sporting gesture alas did Reynolds no good.) In Dun Laoghaire Sean Brady said that the reason for Cosgrave's failure to govern the Irish people lay in the shadow of Freemasonry. Lodge membership, he said, had grown from 21,000 in 1921 to 28,000 in 1928.[9] Two days before polling one of the Party's most senior men, Seán MacEntee, also attacked the Masons. The *Catholic Bulletin* developed the point in its usual vigorous style: 'The Mason stalks the land on imperial stilts. Tomorrow he will descend from those stilts to lay a grip on it that you will never release. Every diocese reeks with Masonic effluvia . . .'[10]

Whatever the cause, it was clear that Fianna Fáil was offering something new, while Cumann na nGaedheal was relying on the mixture as before, a policy of 'proven leadership, sound policies', combined with scare tactics. The difference in message was repeated in the physical appearance of the two leaders. Cosgrave was small and conventionally dapper, with a wing collar and a trim moustache—the epitome of bourgeois elegance. De Valera appeared at election meetings in the country, illuminated by rows of blazing tar-barrels in a great black cloak, riding a white horse—Emmet, Parnell and Pearse combined in one.[11]

It was not merely a matter of style; organisation was a key part. The Fianna Fáil campaign book went into elaborate detail— candidates were told, for instance, always to site the speaking platform for a meeting in the corner of the square, not in the middle, so as to maximise the effect of the audience. Cumann na nGaedheal on the other hand had very little organisation, and what they had was pulled together more or less unenthusiastically for the occasion. Desmond FitzGerald, Minister for Defence, complained to his civil servants what a bore it was to have to go to Sunday morning chapel meetings and stand on a ditch making speeches.[12] Unfortunately for Cumann na nGaedheal, politics was changing quickly. In UCD's L and H debating society, the political cradle of the next generation, students hinted at a new cynicism; in the elections for Auditor the winning candidate was later unseated for having paid his supporters' membership fees.[13]

For some, de Valera embodied Irish national aspirations, and he was the recipient of intense personal devotion. In his autobiography, Robert Briscoe, a TD who was later Lord Mayor of Dublin, described his own feelings. For him de Valera 'had the indomitable determination of a Washington; the militant faith of a St Paul and the moral grandeur of the prophet Elijah. It is remarkable that he also had a sense of humour which was noticeably lacking in these great men . . . well do I remember my first meeting with the "Chief". It was shortly after [he had] escaped from Lincoln jail . . . de Valera turned and looked down on me. Though I am not short, I felt small before him. He took my hand in a firm grip, and shook it silently. I was too awed to speak. Nor did I have to. Our eyes meeting for those few seconds said all that was needed; his the warm friendly look of a leader toward a trusted subordinate, mine a pledge of utter devotion to him and to the cause he served.'[14] No one felt that way about Cosgrave.

De Valera was not always taken quite so seriously. The outgoing Cumann na nGaedheal Minister for Agriculture, Patrick Hogan, told an audience that he would rather be ruled by Ghandi than de Valera— and just so that no one could misunderstand him, he added: 'and I cannot say much worse than that'.[15] One of the Cumann na nGaedheal advertisements listed the world leaders who had failed to bring unemployment down at all, let alone in the spectacular way Fianna Fáil were promising. The list included Hoover, Mussolini, Masaryk and Hindenburg; 'They can't have heard of De Valera—send him on a world tour—the world needs him more than you do!'

In an advertisement a few days before polling day, Cumann na nGaedheal struck a note of portentous scare-mongering:

> Mr de Valera has announced his intention to repeal the act which protects the People from the tyranny of the gunman and the Secret Society. He will abolish the Oath, which he knows to be nothing more than a promise to obey the Will of the People as expressed by their elected representatives . . . Mr de Valera could not have been more definite and precise in setting forth a policy which must inevitably result in the destruction of our State institutions . . . with your State institutions will disappear the Stability, Religious, Economic and Financial, which through ten years of State experience is becoming a characteristic of the Irish people. Its place will be taken by sporadic Revolution, Irreligion, Poverty and Chaos—the chief and well-known marks of those countries which experiment in Constituent Assemblies and changes of regime.

By 10 February the Government Party was shouting 'Sanity or Suicide?—a Vote for Fianna Fáil is a vote for national suicide.'[16]

Immediately before polling day, a sensational murder connected with the election took place in Leitrim. One of the sitting TDs for Leitrim, the chivalrous Pat Reynolds in fact, was murdered while canvassing; also shot was his bodyguard. An ex-RIC pensioner was immediately arrested. The story revealed at the inquest gives a vigorous insight into electioneering conditions of the time. The accused man, Joseph Leddy, was sitting down with his family to dinner on Sunday evening, when Reynolds knocked and walked into the room. He started the row straight away.

'You _ _ _ _,' he said, 'you're out canvassing against me.'

'I never went canvassing against you,' said Leddy, 'I always figured on giving you number one.'

Reynolds repeated what he had said, and took a swing at Leddy. He was clearly in a rage:

'I'll kill you, you _ _ _ _,' he roared.

The source of the row was Leddy's RIC pension. He had been in the RIC during the Troubles, and had claimed a pension on foot of his helping the national struggle. The extent of his help seems to have consisted of a little drilling of the boys, and lending his pistol when required. Reynolds claimed he had got the pension for Leddy—a helping hand he now regretted.

'You _ _ _ _,' he shouted from the street, 'I took a wrong oath to get you the pension, and by _ _ _ I'll see you broke of it.'

By this time Leddy was brandishing his shotgun, and Reynolds' bodyguard came in on the act, pointing out, 'There are more guns than yours.' Leddy then shot both the bodyguard and Reynolds with the shotgun; he calmly picked up the bodyguard's revolver to give it to a bystander and was arrested.

Irish Independent

IRELAND'S NATIONAL NEWSPAPER

DUBLIN, SATURDAY, FEBRUARY 13, 19??.   PRICE ONE PENNY.

Births, Marriages and Deaths
Financial News
Broadcasting

GIVE THE WORLD A CHANCE!

LOOK AT THIS DISASTROUS RECORD

		UNEMPLOYED 1931
Hoover couldn't do it!	United States of America	6,000,000
Hindenburg couldn't do it!	Germany	5,000,000
MacDonald couldn't do it!	United Kingdom	2,734,854
Mussolini couldn't do it!	Italy	909,234
The Mikado couldn't do it!	Japan	406,923
Pilsudski couldn't do it!	Poland	382,819
Masaryk couldn't do it!	Czecho Slovakia	336,874
Miklas couldn't do it!	Austria	120,694
Craigavon couldn't do it!	Northern Ireland	69,887

THEY CAN'T HAVE HEARD of DE VALERA ● **SEND HIM ON A WORLD TOUR**

HE SAYS HE CAN DO IT!

THE WORLD NEEDS HIM MORE THAN YOU DO

●

The Fianna Fail Party is not a party of harmless economic doctrinaires. It has a record of anarchy and war in the past, and its policy will lead to anarchy and war in the future.

Only last Wednesday night Mr. Sean T. O'Kelly said to the voters of North Dublin at Smithfield:—

"THE POLICY OF HIS PARTY WAS BEFORE ALL A REPUBLICAN ONE—HE WOULD NOT CONDEMN THE PRISONERS IN ARBOUR HILL WHO BELIEVED IN THE DOCTRINE OF GUN VIOLENCE."

BE FAIR TO YOURSELF

YOU CANNOT AFFORD TO TAKE A CHANCE!

WITH ANARCHY: Fianna Fail is pledged to repeal ALL Acts passed for the public safety. No clap-trap about coercion can hide the fact that this means a free hand for the so-called "I.R.A." and the Communist Organisation known as SAOR EIRE.

WITH COMMUNISM: The real danger of Communism in Ireland does not come from the Catholic unemployed, but from the alleged "Intellectuals" who have organised Saor Eire and enticed into it misguided country boys. It is to these mischievous propagators of violent revolution that Fianna Fail is pledged to give freedom from "Coercion."

WITH A BREACH OF THE TREATY: Abolition of the Oath of Allegiance, which Fianna Fail promises to please the "I.R.A." and the Communists, means, WITHOUT A SHADOW OF DOUBT, a breach of the Treaty. It will be construed as an unfriendly act by Great Britain. It will be followed, according to Mr. de Valera, by a period of NON-CO-OPERATION with Great Britain. This means FOR CERTAIN that a Fianna Fail Government cannot possibly conclude a Trade Agreement with our best customer.

WITH NATIONAL DISCREDIT Fianna Fail propose to seize the Land Annuities. SEIZURE by the Irish State of monies that do not belong to it would have a DISASTROUS EFFECT on all Irish securities and every form of Irish credit.

WITH A CONTINUANCE OF POLITICAL UNREST: All our energies for the next few years will be needed to develop our economic resources, to extend our markets, to improve the lot of our people. We cannot do this and keep up a needless and meaningless squabble about political formulas. Fianna Fail is the one party that has kept this squabble alive for the past ten years. THE BEST WAY TO GET ECONOMIC ADVANCEMENT IS TO DEFEAT FIANNA FAIL.

VOTE FOR the GOVERNMENT PARTY

Cumann na nGaedheal advertisement a few days before polling: the breadth of international reference no doubt amused their own voters.

In the event Fianna Fáil won 72 seats, five short of a majority, but with the support of the seven Labour TDs were able to form a government for the first time. The *Derry Journal* described the scene in the Dáil: 'it was a full hour before the people felt they could demonstrate without fear of repression or suppression . . . the gallery, excited and enthused, cheered and cheered'. Thus, noted the *Catholic Bulletin*, 'for the first time the artificial, imitation-British dignity of the Cosgrave ministry was swept aside'.[17] In Mullinarry Cross, Dr Ward (FF), to the accompaniment of four different bands, gloated over the fact that Cumann na nGaedeal had lost one of its two seats in Monaghan. The constituency, he announced, had 'struck a resounding blow against British imperialism, and when next they struck, they would knock it down'.[18]

Seán MacEntee calculated that at least 640,000 Catholics had voted for a change of government as against only 480,000 in favour of the government party: 'by a majority of one-third, the Catholics of the Twenty-Six Counties had rejected Cumann na nGaedheal'.[19] Although the source of these figures remained obscure, it was certainly likely that the Protestants had followed *The Irish Times* in supporting Cosgrave. (Not all did this enthusiastically—to some he was still the 'murderous potboy'.[20]) For the Anglo-Irish, the Empire and the royal connection were reassurances of ancient values. They could not bring themselves to believe anything would change, despite de Valera's clearly expressed views. Gregg, the Archbishop of Dublin, who was by no means a stupid man, wrote in the *Church of England Newspaper* ten days after the election, 'so far as Mr De Valera is concerned, a *coup d'état* need not be anticipated . . . it will be the King's Government . . . those who look for a prompt set-to with Great Britain on such questions as the oath for members of the Dáil, or the withholding of the annuities . . . will be disappointed'.[21]

De Valera and the new government, however, had other ideas, and immediately set about doing what they had promised. The first step was to promote the Bill to abolish the Oath. The next excitement came in Seán MacEntee's Budget, which imposed taxes and duties on a wide range of new items from silk underwear (90 per cent duty) to bachelors (whose income tax was doubled). Even then income tax was not particularly oppressive. A man with two children paid only £1 2s. 6d. at £400 and surtax now began at £1,501 (just £1 above the basic rate for the top civil servants).

New duties were imposed on all postal packages and on soap, newspapers, wooden furniture, sports equipment, paper bags, tea, bicycles, matches and many other products. Ireland was on its way from being one of the least protected economies in the world to one of the most, a situation which held good until 1958. The range and speed of introduction of the new duties seems to have taken the business community completely by surprise, and the *Irish Independent* took a gloomy delight in reporting for weeks afterwards how the customs posts at the border were in disarray because of the duties, and on the docks the package tax meant that every parcel had to be opened.

Political argument rumbled on for weeks, as interest groups of all sorts made their case to be exempt from the new duties. Thus at first all imported books and periodicals were to be taxed; later this was modified to a tax only on leather-bound books and entertainment magazines (which meant in effect largely those popular with women); at first all sporting occasions were to pay entertainment tax—then GAA games were exempted. Some of the taxes had not been well thought out. Mrs Collins-O'Driscoll (C na nG) pointed out in the Dáil that vital components of women's corsets came under the newly taxable heading of Manufactured Articles of Brass and Steel, a point that had evidently not occurred to the somewhat embarrassed minister, who promised to change the regulation.[22]

The next political excitement came in July, when, true to its electoral pledge, the government refused to pay to Britain the due instalment of the Annuities. Britain, rejecting arbitration, responded vigorously to this challenge and imposed a series of duties on Irish agricultural exports. As a result, by August cattle prices were at 1914 levels. Many farmers, remembering over-exuberant speeches by Fianna Fáil electoral candidates, refused to pay their share of the Annuities. Faced with this grim reality, Fianna Fáil deputies resorted to rhetoric. Frank Aiken announced that 'the Irish people have been producing food for John Bull to grow fat, but now the result will be that the Irish will grow fat on their own food . . . if they went down to the slums of Dublin they would find that the unemployed were damned glad of the situation brought about'.[23] In September Seán MacEntee, Minister for Finance, declared that 'retention of the Annuities would secure a prosperity and a standard of living here unparalleled in Europe, and far above that enjoyed in the Six Counties . . .'.[24] This cheerful view was not widely shared: on his return from the Imperial Economic Conference in Ottawa, Joseph Brennan, head of the Currency Commission, was confronted with an alarming radio message. 'Dublin situation so threatening British businessmen are preparing to evacuate with wives and children. Grave fear of clash between three bodies of definitely

"You'll have to go back, sir. You can't go through here."
"What's up? Political meeting?"
"No, Civil Service examination for ten vacancies!"

"I see in the papers that we'll never be able to consume all the food we produce."

Founded in 1922, *Dublin Opinion* was often sharp in its comments.

military cast: Irish Republican Army, Free State Army Comrades Association and a Communist organisation. Meanwhile managers of British establishments find shop windows placarded "Ban British goods".'[25]

An emergency vote of £2 million (the sum by which, before the election, Fianna Fáil had promised to reduce taxation) was passed. The inexperience of the new government showed in the handling of this. They announced that the assistance would be distributed to the country in proportion to the number out of work. In Ballina, it was later discovered, there were suddenly more registered unemployed than inhabitants. Dark suggestions were expressed that in some areas relief work was only available to those who joined the Fianna Fáil Party.[26]

Fianna Fáil was taken by surprise by the speed and vigour of the British Government's reaction to the refusal of the Annuities. Few had believed that so drastic a response was likely. Consciousness of this mistake and what it would mean for their hopes of a revived Ireland no doubt added bitterness to the exchanges in the Dáil, as Cumann na nGaedheal TDs hammered home their criticisms. In the Dáil exchanges became more ritualised and entrenched than they had been before. De Valera himself began to get rattled, most uncharacteristically accusing the ex-Minister of Agriculture, Patrick Hogan, of having been 'bought' by the British Government. In August he appealed for co-operation from the Cumann na nGhaedheal Party in the national crisis; he appealed to the opposition to 'give them a chance'. The very vigour of the British response had the effect of uniting the country behind de Valera—even the *Irish Independent*, mollified by his evidently statesmanlike performance at the League of Nations in Geneva, began to warm to him by the end of the year.[27]

In the Dáil and in the country the government's policies were presented as a continuation of the struggle against the old enemy. In that context opposition was merely treachery; Fianna Fáil deputies accused the opposition of 'playing the British game' and even of advising the British what to do. This was no light accusation, for the IRA were believed to be importing arms in great numbers, and the assassination of Kevin O'Higgins was fresh in the memory.[28] Frank Ryan of the IRA announced in November that 'while we have fists, hands and boots to use, and guns if necessary, we will not allow free speech to traitors'.[29]

Cosgrave's meetings were broken up in May and September (on the latter occasion with 'considerable pummelling' on both sides).[30]

Membership of the Army Comrades Association (later nick-named the Blueshirts) rocketed: numbers had reached 30,000 by September, and were expected to go to 100,000 by the following March.[31] The Association had been founded in February primarily as a pressure group to protect Army pensions which, rumours had it, were to be reduced by Fianna Fáil to pay for pensions for those who had fought on the Republican side in the Civil War. At first membership was confined to ex-members of the national army. It quickly took on a role as the protector of Cumann na nGaedheal meetings against attacks. At the same time its aims widened. To 'uphold the State' in the face of opposition from organisations such as the IRA (of whom Fianna Fáil was regarded as a mere front) became an important objective.

By the end of the year both import and export figures showed alarming declines, particularly in cattle; terms of trade were worsening, and the Economic War was joined in earnest. On the stock exchange, however, the tone was described at the end of the year as 'optimistic and supporting, despite the budget imposts, politics and tariff tangles'. Investment money was amply available for first-class propositions—the Revenue Commissioners noted that two-thirds of non-real property wealth left by estate duty payers was in stocks and shares, and as much as 17 per cent in cash; only 8 per cent was in trade assets and 3 per cent in household goods. A Dublin Corporation loan for £650,000 was five times oversubscribed within twenty-four hours at the end of the year.[32] This experience was repeated later in the decade: P. J. Carroll's flotation in 1935 was oversubscribed as much as ten times, largely by Irish investors who sold British shares for the purpose.[33]

Politically, the government's position was precarious. In November de Valera survived a vote of censure by five votes. The seven-member Labour Party, who were therefore essential to Fianna Fáil's majority, were however becoming restless, particularly in face of the rapidly increasing unemployment. There were also by-elections outstanding in Donegal, East Cork and Waterford, two of them likely wins by Cumann na nGaedheal. Rumours of an imminent general election were in the air. Important forces in Fianna Fáil were believed to favour an election in the spring, though de Valera himself was said not to have made up his mind.[34] He was toying with the idea of reducing the number of deputies to 100. In December a new national party was mooted, combining Cumann na nGaedheal, Farmers, Independents and possibly Labour interests, with a view to restoring trade relations with Britain. This group became the basis of the new Party, Fine Gael, in the new year.

Chapter Ten

The Kneeling City

THE increasing rancour of political exchanges concealed one profound matter that virtually all politicians had in common: as de Valera himself said at the 1931 Fianna Fáil Ard Fheis, 'if all comes to all, I am a Catholic first'.[1] His main opponent, Cosgrave, was also a devout man, who expected guests to join in the family rosary if they arrived while it was in progress.[2] Virtually the whole population believed in the immediacy of the spiritual sphere, many to a starkly dramatic extent. Austin Clarke recalls that he was taught to regard a tiny ringing in the ear as the howls of a soul in Purgatory, whose urgent and terrifying agony was muffled only by the vast distance.[3] More bearably, Chesterton quotes a working woman overheard during the great Eucharistic Congress—'Well', she said tartly, 'if it rains now, He'll have brought it on Himself.'[4]

The material sphere was envisaged as merely part, and not the most important part, of the real world. It was a darkling plain on which a mighty struggle was being fought out between the armies of Satan and the armies of Christ.[5] 'The preternatural genius displayed in organising this anti-God campaign', (referring to religious persecutions in Russia, Mexico and other places) declared a pastoral letter of the Scottish bishops late in 1932, 'makes it clear that the directing force is no mere human intellect.'[6]

Foremost in the armies of Satan were the Jews, who had infiltrated and corrupted the Freemasons, who in turn controlled the Protestants generally. In a typical outburst, the ultra *Catholic Bulletin* described 'the battle which the Catholic Church in Ireland fought for three centuries against England, that pitiless foe, combining the enmity of the Synagogue with the ferocity of the amphitheatre'. On Christ's side in this great contest were the angels, the saints, the Catholic Church (Militant as it was called, with no metaphoric intent) and the faithful.[7]

For Irish readers there was, added to this mighty scenario, a special national role. Just as in the dark ages Irish missionaries had come from the remote Catholic fastnesses in the North to bring Europe back to the Church, so now, with the new barbarians (that is Communists, liberals and Jews) pressing hard at the citadel, the uniquely Catholic Irish

Main news page, *Irish Independent*, 1 November 1932—Satan takes precedence over the tearful scenes in the Park as McNeill retires.

could again spread into the world and ultimately perhaps restore the glories of the thirteenth century. For some commentators even the otherwise deplored spread of English through Ireland and the continuing emigration could be seen as part of this divine contingency plan. For the Irish nation included also those living beyond the seas: 'when Ireland calls her sons to her', wrote the *Irish Press*, 'there is a stirring in every part of the Universe'.

The battle was fought not only in the world, but inside the soul of every individual: each person was pictured as infinitely precious to both sides. As in the Oceania of Orwell's *1984*, there was a state of constant war-alert; zealots, lay and clerical, made disciplined adherence to minor advices matters of major import. In his 1932 Lenten letter Bishop McKenna of Clogher struck a common theme: 'we are living in very dangerous times . . . the fight today is between an anti-Christian attitude towards life in all its relations, personal, domestic, social and civil on the one side and Catholicity on the other. The weapons being used for the propagation of anti-Christian ideals are chiefly of the intellectual and moral order, agencies such as the Press, theatre, cinema, radio and others. . . .' Other bishops agreed with him, and added their own glosses. Dr Morrisroe of Achonry was concerned with the 'abomination of the commercialised rural dance halls', which he described as 'sign posts on the road to infamy and shame'. Dr O'Kane of Derry was concerned about poteen, which he said 'had brought ruin to whole districts, encouraged lying and perjury in the courts, undermined self-respect, (and) is raising a race of degenerates . . .'[8]

Not only was the religious outlook all pervasive, it was also different in tone from the worship of pre-Famine times. From the middle of the nineteenth century the Irish hierarchy, led by Paul Cullen, had increasingly imposed a vigorous clerical discipline on both the clergy and people. In doing so many of the old devotional styles were overlaid by practices introduced from Britain and the Continent. 'From France, Belgium, Italy and elsewhere poured in new approaches, new ideas, new religious orders and groupings of one kind or another, each with its own brand of piety and accompanying badge . . . processions and sparkling shrines began to figure largely in the Irish spiritual diet as did jubilees, tridua, novenas, missions, Forty Hours, perpetual adorations, blessed altars, Benediction, stations of the cross, devotions to the Sacred Heart and to the Immaculate Conception, confraternities, sodalities of everything and anything and nothing, societies of many brands, Vincent de Paul, temperance, purgatorial. A host of back-up services also existed, providing scapulars, missals, prayer-books, holy pictures, Agnes Dei . . .'[9]

With this new approach came a casuistry and an obsession with legal forms. The pages of the *Irish Ecclesiastical Record*, which was in effect the official voice of the hierarchy, are full of detailed and technical queries to Maynooth theological experts, many obviously arising from the confessional.

This attitude was not exclusive to the Catholic clergy; the Church of Ireland Vicar of Sandymount, who was admittedly very 'high', was prosecuted and severely reprimanded in the 1930s for such offences as making the sign of the cross, saying a prayer with his back to the congregation, praying inaudibly, putting a Cross on the communion table and singing a non-authorised hymn.[10]

The 'devotional revolution', as it has been called, had been stunningly successful: in the half a century or so from 1830, Mass attendance rose from an estimated thirty per cent in rural districts to over ninety per cent.[11] But increased Mass-going was not the only arena for pious energy. Meetings, sodalities and prayer-groups were widespread. The 1932 Jesuit *Directory* lists as many as twenty-three separate and well-attended groups based on St Francis Xavier's in Upper Gardiner Street. These included the Confraternity of the Sacred Heart (separate branches for men and women), the Sodality of the Immaculate Conception (for young men,), the Sodality of Our Lady Help of Christians (for commercial men), the Night Workers' Sodality, the Conference of St Mobhi (for Irish speakers), and the Sodality of the Assumption of Our Lady and St Martin (for Civic Guards).[12] As well as these, there were outlets for pious activity in the Legion of Mary, the St Vincent de Paul, the Pioneers and other charitable organisations. A very high level of personal piety was common; serious-minded people were religious just as their counterparts later in the decade in England were anti-fascist. Many senior civil servants were daily Mass-goers, and some, such as the new Secretary of the Government, Sean Moynihan, devoted Legionnaires.

1932 was the fifteen hundredth anniversary of St Patrick's coming to Ireland, and the Catholic Church was determined to celebrate in style. There was plenty to celebrate. Barely a century after Emancipation, the present position of the Church in Ireland seemed to many commentators nothing short of a miracle. Time after time during the Eucharistic Congress foreign journalists marvelled at the sight of a nation, as it seemed, united in prayer. The celebrations were also an opportunity to copperfasten the identification of Irish and Catholic in a flood of rhetoric. The *Father Mathew Record* expressed the point thus: 'because of his sins the Jew is left outcast, a wanderer, nationless; for the virtues of his ancestors the Irishman has a country, not only fair and green but one of saints and scholars . . . Irish nationality is so bound up with the foundation of all true nobleness, the Catholic Church, that the words "Irish" and "Catholic" are linked constantly.'

Throughout the year writer after writer repeated the point. To be Irish meant to be Catholic; it was also to participate in some vague way in the ancient traditions of the Celtic way of life. (This despite the fact that many traditionally Irish styles of devotion such as holy wells were frowned on: 'the priests didn't like the Well, and tried to discourage the pilgrimages. They said it was a pagan well . . . the peasant folk didn't mind the priests. They believed that Saint Bridget washed her feet in it, not Finn MacCoole', as Patrick Kavanagh recalled,[13] and the custom of 'stations' (Mass held in rotation in the private houses of the parish) was an object of particular attack; the ancient traditions of holding baptisms, weddings and funerals from home were all banned.)

The Irish nation had left the British Empire, the greatest the world had ever seen, and joined a still greater army. As the *Catholic Bulletin* put it, 'it is the pardonable pride of our Irish exiles that they founded a spiritual Empire . . . more extensive than that of Rome, more inspiring than that of Greece, more durable than that of England'. The ancient pomp and dignity of the Church was at least as spectacular as anything the British could supply, and had the inestimable advantage of being on the right side of the fight for the soul of the world.

It was therefore particularly provocative for the Protestants, who still represented one in fourteen of the Free State's population, not to mention those in the North, to claim not only that theirs was the true Church, but that St Patrick had had no papal mandate for converting the Irish, and was in fact an early Protestant in spirit. This argument was somewhat weakened when someone pointed out that in practice Protestants very rarely called their sons Patrick.

The Eucharistic Congress of 1932, which was the focus of the celebrations, was the thirty-first in a series that had begun in Lille in 1881, and still goes on. The purpose of the Congress was to celebrate the Eucharist, as part of a long campaign by the Church to encourage frequent Communion. Pilgrims and learned men gathered from every Catholic nation to hear papers and sermons and to attend Masses and processions.

From the beginning of the year preparations of all sorts were in hand. In January the City Engineer worried in public about the water supply; usage had gone from 13 million gallons in 1907 to 17 million in 1932. The cause, he complained, was that people insisted on letting the hot water tap run to warm up before washing their hands, thereby wasting water. He feared, especially if the weather was fine, that the visitors to the Congress would have to be rationed. The commercial opportunities of the occasion were not neglected. In the newspapers small ads began to offer items such as the 'beautifully painted' Eucharistic lamp bulbs, complete with pious slogans and papal insignia (suitable for Shannon current, 40–60 watts, 2s. each). So great became the flood of souvenir items that the Managing Director of Clery's told his staff that 'clergy and nuns are objecting to Eucharistic emblems being put on drapery goods, carpets, linens etc.'—they were not to buy any more such items without consultation. Householders on the route of the procession were warned by the organisers to resist allowing advertising signs to be put up in their gardens. A few weeks later it was reported that Jury's had bought 190 cattle and 500 sheep in preparation for Congress week.

By May the preparations were in full swing. Nearly every day the *Irish Independent*, in an increasing fever of excitement, reported some further titbit. On 3 May, for instance, readers were told of the advanced state of preparation of the floodlighting for Dublin's public buildings; that 70,000 children were expected at the Children's Mass in the Park; that the government had sent out thousands of invitations for the official State Reception in Dublin Castle; that as many as eleven cardinals were expected in Dublin during the Congress. The following day readers learnt that the Corporation had arranged a special double shift of street cleaners for the week of the Congress, and that sixty wooden huts to serve as temporary public conveniences were to be erected in O'Connell Street and other places. On 5 May the main news page carried a story warning householders that the supply of suitable lamps and other decorations was running short. The abundance of these stories was not just a silly-season phenomenon. The new Fianna Fáil Government was providing a steady stream of exciting events: on 5 May, for instance, the Bill to abolish the Oath was passed, a levy and bounty on butter was imposed.

In the middle of May an encyclical from Pius XI reminded everyone what was at stake. 'Subversive factions', he told the faithful, 'taking advantage of the world-wide misery more and more brazenly unfurl their banners of wickedness and hatred of religion . . . formerly atheists were lost in the multitude, now they form a huge army that with the help of secret societies grows bolder every day.' His Holiness declared that never before in the history of the world had there been a crisis of such gigantic proportions as the present one, and he compared the danger of the situation to the time of Noah before the Flood.[14]

Above. Off to the Phoenix Park for the Children's Mass during the Eucharistic Congress.
Below. Dutch Girl Guides at the Garden Party saluting the Cardinal Legate

In the Dáil TDs discussed the new duties on trousers and tennis rackets; and Miss Amelia Earhart set out on her bid to become the first woman to fly solo across the Atlantic. Clery's announced that they still had some pre-budget stocks in, including corsets, for stout figures, usually 10/- now 5/9, ladies' walking shoes 8/11, tweed skirts 4/11, linen table-cloths 2/11. Special, fast, cheap excursion trains had been organised from Clonmel, Kilkenny and Enniskillen to enable shoppers to take advantage of the prices. The short-lived Irish magazine, *Woman's Mirror*, told its readers what to wear for the dances during Congress week. 'On the whole skirts are shorter, especially street frocks and suits. Garden party skirts sway just above the ankles and in the evening they clear the ground all the way round.'

Although the Papal Legate was not due to arrive until 20 June, the activities of the Congress began on 5 June, with a week-long retreat for women. 'The city's womenfolk', reported the *Independent*, 'crowded the churches for the opening of the special retreat in preparation for the Congress.' A week later the men's retreat started. As the excitement mounted, rehearsals were held in the Park, and pilgrims streamed into the city. Some lived in special camps such as that erected at Marino, or the Knights of Columbanus 1,000-tent encampment in Artane; others stayed on the numerous boats moored in Dublin Bay. The organisers arranged for 275 interpreters to be assigned to various churches, and a special Bill was rushed through the Dáil to allow vessels moored in the bay to serve drinks in their ballrooms.

In an era when all businesses were clearly either Catholic or Protestant, there was much curiosity about how the Protestant firms would react. 'Several Protestant firms', it was afterwards noted ominously, 'in response to the request of the Organising Committee, decorated their premises, but some firms, among them prominent concerns largely supported by Catholics and Catholic organisations and industries, absolutely refused to do so.'[15] The debate in the Arts Club was no doubt typical: the chairman, a Scots Presbyterian called Hill Tulloch (who was also senior partner of Craig Gardner) resisted, on grounds of expense, the flying of flags, while Catholic members of the committee urged that not only should the national and Congress flags be flown, but also the front should be painted, and flower-filled window-boxes be added to the façade.[16]

The Papal Legate, Cardinal Lauri, finally arrived at Dun Laoghaire at about 3 o'clock on 20 June, to be greeted by an enormous crowd of more than 50,000 people, headed by President de Valera and his government. The correspondent of the *Revue de Deux Mondes* noted that 'from Dun Laoghaire Harbour to the Pro-cathedral, a distance of ten kilometres, there was an unbroken mass of people, compact, deep, on both sides of the route. In the city the pavements and the squares were completely covered by the multitude.'[17]

The big events of the following day were a garden party in Blackrock College given by the Hierarchy, and a State Reception in Dublin Castle. Clerical dress for all these occasions was carefully prescribed. On ecclesiastical occasions bishops were to wear choir soutane (violet), cincture with tassels, rochet, pectoral cross, mantelata, zucchetta, biretta. Those celebrating Pontifical High Mass would require, in addition, mitre, dalmatic and tunicle (white), buskins and sandals, gloves.[18] There was no doubt that this was the *Roman* Church. In brilliant sunshine at least 12,000 people attended the garden party which had been organised by the President of Blackrock, the Rev. John Charles McQuaid. The grounds were open to anyone who cared to go, and everyone who was anyone did. Fashionables and politicals rubbed shoulders with archbishops and cardinals among the marquees and white-clothed tables.

Irish Independent readers were told that over 250 gallons of cream were consumed at the garden party, as well as 400 lb of slab cakes and 12,000 French fancies. A group of Dutch Catholic girl guides sang hymns (rounding off their performance with a fascist salute to the Cardinal Legate). There was Benediction, and then the proceedings were completed by full-throated and emotional renderings of Faith of Our Fathers and the Lourdes hymn, Ave Maria. It was, as a commentator put it, 'the most emotional moment of an emotional day'.[19]

In the evening the State Reception was a glittering occasion of another kind. Over 2,500 special invitations had been issued. The guests filed past a dais on which sat the Papal Legate, the Archbishop and de Valera, who gave a speech in Irish and Latin welcoming the Legate. Conspicuous by his absence was the Governor General, James MacNeill, who had deliberately not been invited. The formal proceedings of the Congress began on Wednesday 22 June, with a ceremony in the Pro-cathedral. Later that night all the city churches held Midnight Mass; extraordinary numbers attended. At St Andrew's, Westland Row, for instance, the correspondent of the *Revue des Deux Mondes* noticed a large crowd gathered in the street outside the church, all ten thousand of whom wanted to receive Holy Communion. A priest told him that it was three o'clock before the last left the altar rails; Mass ended as dawn broke.

For the next four days Dublin was in a happy, busy daze. 'There was', wrote Dr Deeny, down for the occasion from Lurgan, 'a spontaneous excitement of religion, carnival, achievement, fun, and a wonderful feeling of being all Irish together.'[20] The crush of people, the parties, the intense religious feeling made these memorable times. For some they were more significant than for others—in July 'Kitty from Clare' wrote to Nora of the *Woman's Mirror* asking her advice. Three years ago, she said, her sweetheart had gone to America promising to take her out with him within twelve months; but his letters had got less and less frequent, and she had more or less given him up. They met in Dublin during Congress week—at first they greeted each other awkwardly, but soon became sweethearts again. Nora decided that whatever she said Kitty should 'follow the dictates of her heart', but she would be surprised if she wasn't in Broadway before Christmas.

The whole city was turned into one great church by 400 loudspeakers, by constant ceremonies, and by the multitudes of foreign priests, 'Dublin the kneeling city, the city of the millions of candles, the worshipping town, Dublin the heart of the Catholic world', enthused the commentator of the Dutch paper, *De Tijd*. All the commentators, Catholic and Protestant, were struck by 'the spectacle of an entire nation, from its President to the poorest of the poor, in adoration before the Blessed Sacrament (*La Croix*, France). 'One felt', wrote *Figaro*, 'that one heart was beating in a whole nation.'

The Protestants, whose hearts were presumably beating to a different rhythm, mostly looked on with a kind of baffled admiration. Others took a less high-minded attitude, such as the three young Protestant clerks from Bray who were fined £5 each for uprooting several papal flags after returning late and the worse for drink from a dance.[21] In the North pilgrims coming down to Dublin were stoned and attacked in Lisburn, Ballymena, Belfast and Coleraine; in Larne a large mob attacked an old people's bus, hurling stones, lumps of coal and bottles through the windows.

It was estimated that over 5,000 priests took part in the Congress, not to mention 11 cardinals, 160 archbishops and bishops, and numerous abbots. Each day was taken up with meetings of various groups: on Friday, for instance, the programme began at 9.00 a.m. with separate sectional meetings of the Australian, Belgian, Czechoslovakian, Lithuanian, Polish and Scottish groups, at 11.00 a.m. there was Solemn Pontifical High Mass in the Pro-cathedral, followed by exposition of the Blessed Sacrament; at 3.00 p.m. more sectional meetings (American, Australian, Canadian, Dutch, English, French, German, Hungarian, Italian, New Zealand, Maltese, Oriental, Portuguese, Spanish, Uruguayan, Yugoslavian). At 8.00 p.m. the Women's Mass was held in the Park, which was attended by at least 250,000 women who braved the threatening rain. They were told by the Legate that 'daughters and sisters should be helpful to their parents and brothers. Wives should inspire their husbands with the sweet fragrance of their goodness and virtue and the gentle attractiveness of their example.'

For a few days Dublin became a truly cosmopolitan city. Exotics such as the Sioux priest wearing his traditional head-dress of feathers, or the Archbishop of Galilee, an African with a white beard, or the bishops of the oriental rites, such as the Bishop of Olympus (Byzantine–Slavonic Rite) or the Bishop of Lebedus (Ruthenian Rite) or the Indian Bishop of Kottayam became common sights. (The one thing that wasn't allowed was the Union Jack—a group of young men made the manager of the Shelbourne remove it from among his set of flags, a gesture that caused some resentment in England.)

The climax of the Congress was the huge Mass in the Phoenix Park on Sunday. When all were gathered, there were about a million people in the Park that morning, each in pre-ordained spaces, men separated from women, civic dignatories from men, priests from all. At the consecration, wrote the *Press* reporter, 'through that silence, so deep and perfect that if you closed your eyes you were alone, through that silence rang St Patrick's Bell . . . down to the ground those million people bowed, down in an ecstasy of adoration that the one voice of the bell called out into silence. From all that multitude as the Host was lifted up went an unspoken intensity of devotion that gave to the air itself a sweet happiness.'

Immediately after the Mass a procession was formed, which carried the Blessed Sacrament down to the final Benediction at a specially constructed altar on O'Connell Bridge. The order of this great procession, which took four hours to wind its way to O'Connell Street, was, like so much else of this great gathering, meticulously planned.

After the final Benediction at the specially prepared altar on O'Connell Bridge, the Congress was at an end. The following days were somewhat anti-climactic as the pilgrims prepared to leave (there were more stonings in Belfast) and the decorations began to be taken down.

Life slowly returned to normal. General O'Duffy congratulated the Guards on their handling of the occasion and gave them a day off. A correspondent claimed that the mayfly season had been the best for twenty years; another noted that women had a weakness for beige, despite its being a difficult colour to carry off. Guinness put its famous dray horses on the market; holidays in the Isle of Man for 8s. 6d. a week full board (about £15 in 1990 terms) were advertised in the small

The last scene of the Eucharistic Congress: O'Connell Street during the final Benediction

First came a detachment of cavalry, followed by the Banner of the Blessed Sacrament; then:

60,000 men by parish;
Cross bearers and acolytes;
Reverend Brothers;
Canons Regular—in this order: Canons Regular of the Lateran, Premonstratensians, Canons Regular of the Holy Cross;
Monks—Benedictines, Cistercians, Basilians;
Mendicant Orders—Dominicans, Franciscans (1. Friars Minor, 2. Conventuals, 3. Capuchins), Augustinians, Carmelites (1. Calced, 2. Discalced), Trinitarians, Servites.
Clerics Regular—Theatines, Barnabites, Jesuits.
Ecclesiastical Congregations: Oratorians, Vincentians, Sulpicians, Fathers of the Society of Foreign Missions of Paris, Fathers of the Holy Ghost, Passionists, Redemptorists, Fathers of the Sacred Heart, Oblates, Marists, Fathers of Charity, Eudists, Assumptionists, Fathers of the Blessed Sacrament, Salesians.
Torch bearers
Blessed Sacrament
Cardinals
Archbishops
Bishops
Members of the Permanent Committee for Eucharistic Congresses
Other Prelates
Ministers of State
Judges
Foreign Ministers
Members of the Dáil and Seanad
Bearers of Papal Titles
Dublin Corporation
Representative Persons from the Six Counties, Corporations, County Councillors, Harbour Boards, Vocational Councils, Urban District Councils, Boards of Public Assistance, National University representatives, others;
Distinguished and representative women;
Female singers;
Women.

ads. The Senate passed a much amended version of the Oath Bill, and the Tailteann Games opened.

Chapter Eleven

The Sweep

HIGH on the list of the Irish public's daily concerns was sport, particularly those sports that offered the chance of a bet. Horse-racing, dog-racing and coursing were all followed with avid attention. The *Irish Independent* reported an extraordinary range of sports every day, and not in perfunctory detail. In the first week of January, for instance, there were full articles describing athletics, badminton, coursing, camogie, rugby, boxing, lacrosse, association and Gaelic football, table tennis, hockey, golf, handball, cricket and horse-racing. Sporting heroes were public personalities—in June Clery's arranged to have one of the boxing champions of the day visit the store, where he was mobbed by autograph hunters.

The big home event of the 1932 sporting calendar was the Tailteann Games. These were an Irish version of the Olympics, and like the Olympics, mimicked an ancient practice, the Oenach Tailten, whose history can be traced back to the eighth century. The Games were intended to be, as the *Independent* put it in the high-flown language reserved for such things, 'a racial re-union for the scattered children of the Gael'. They had first been revived in 1924, and again in 1928.

In those years the Tailteann Games had been held just before the Olympic Games, and so many international athletes with Irish backgrounds from America, Australia and elsewhere were already in Europe. This had made the competition extremely fierce. This year the Olympic Games were in Los Angeles, so the outstanding athletes from other countries were not available. The 'feast of manly competition' would be an Irish event, except, that is, for the Ulster boxers. Because the tricolour flew over Croke Park, the Ulster Council of the Amateur Boxing Association refused to allow their boxers to take part. Not that this worried the organisers; as they said in the programme, the Games 'showed the national and definitely anti-foreign direction taken in Irish social life in the past few years'. The 1932 Games started with Queen Maeve and her courtiers, complete with wolfhounds, parading around Croke Park—the contrast between the intensely felt ceremonial of the recently completed Eucharistic Congress and this costume drama was marked.

There were other sporting events of course: Shamrock Rovers beat Dolphin Park in the soccer final; three Irishmen won gold medals in the Los Angeles Olympics; Kerry beat Mayo in the All-Ireland football final, and Kilkenny beat Clare in the hurling final; in August de Valera and thousands of other Irish people attended the Horse Show. But by far the biggest sporting and betting story of the decade was the establishment as a world phenomenon of the Irish Hospital Sweepstakes.

At the end of the 1920s the Dublin hospital system was in trouble. There were twelve general hospitals, thirteen special hospitals and four nursing homes, serving a population in the Greater Dublin area of 420,000. Most of the hospitals were small, with 150 beds or less. They were also largely in need of repair and of considerable investment in new equipment. Before the First World War a surgeon had needed little more than a table and a peg to hang his blood-soaked operating-coat. Many operations had been performed in the patient's home, so a hospital needed no more than one theatre. By 1932, a self-respecting hospital needed six or eight theatres, as well as X-ray machines, pathology laboratories, physiotherapy apparatus and so on.[1] There were three maternity hospitals, the Rotunda, the Coombe and Holles Street; they provided 169 maternity beds and 85 gynaecological beds. Less than half of the deliveries in the Greater Dublin area were in hospital, compared to over eighty per cent in American and European cities. The richer patients went to nursing and maternity homes, the poorer gave birth at home. There was a steadily growing trend towards hospital births, however, with the number increasing by one-third between 1925 and 1933.

For years the main source of income for all hospitals had been the subscriptions of the rich. Unfortunately a combination of the increasing capital costs of equipment and facilities, and the fact that the most generous of the rich had either removed themselves to England or lost much of their money as a result of the Troubles, left most of the city's hospitals struggling to make ends meet. Even the best-endowed hospital for its size in the city, the all-Protestant Adelaide, in 1933 had an income of £16,500 and an expenditure of £19,000. Without the contribution from the Sweep, the three maternity hospitals would have lost £7,500 in that year, which represented nearly a third of their income.[2] The state certainly had no money to spare, so when it appeared that the National Maternity Hospital in Holles Street might have to close its doors for lack of finance, the government reluctantly agreed to authorise a lottery to raise funds for hospitals generally.

Thus was born the Irish Hospitals Sweepstakes. The idea was not a new one. Governments had supplemented their finances by lotteries for hundreds of years before the efficiency of income tax and the abuses surrounding the lottery persuaded the British Government to abolish them in 1826. Since then they had been illegal, although winked at on a parish scale. In 1918 an extremely successful lottery had been organised to compensate the victims of the *Leinster*, a mailboat sunk by German U-boats in 1918. The organiser of this lottery was a forty-year-old bookmaker called Richard Duggan, whose racetrack slogan was, 'What Duggan lays, he pays.'[3]

Ten years later Richard Duggan was one of the three organisers of the Sweepstakes. His partners in the scheme were Joe McGrath, the political contact, who had been in the IRA and also a Minister in the Cosgrave Government, but had resigned after the Army mutiny in 1924; and Spencer Freeman, an engineer who had spent the War in the British Army organising munitions and supplies. Duggan designed the gamble, McGrath saw to the sales, using his wide connections in government and out, and Freeman looked after the organisation and publicity. The ultra-respectable firm of accountants, Craig Gardner, where both McGrath and his brother had briefly worked, was appointed to perform the treasury and audit functions.

Hospitals Trust Ltd set up offices in 13 Earlsfort Terrace, and the staff began to organise the first Sweep, which was based on the November Handicap of 1930. Basing the gamble on English races such as the Grand National and the Derby, rather than Irish equivalents, ensured both that there would be large fields, and also the race itself would be widely publicised. The English media gave the Sweepstake widespread coverage until they were prohibited from doing so. The operation was from the beginning very well thought out in this as in other aspects. Rather than a simple lottery, which only allows one bite of the publicity cherry for each draw, the partners had decided on a sweepstake. This meant that there were two phases of excitement: firstly when the tickets were drawn against the horses, and then the race itself. Each ticket cost 10s. (about £16 in 1990 spending terms). Every purchaser received a receipt from head office, a system which had three advantages: it inhibited fraud and forgery by agents, it encouraged purchasers to feel a direct link with the Sweep that stimulated them to buy year after year, and it provided work for hundreds and then thousands of Dublin women.

From the beginning the venture was a success. The promoters had promised a prize fund of £25,000, based on projected ticket sales of £100,000; they privately hoped for sales of £125,000. The actual sales were an unbelievable £658,000, or £21.7 m. in 1990 terms. This gave the hospitals an addition to their budgets of the extraordinary sum of £132,000, or one quarter of the total expenditure of all the hospitals in the country.

The three promoters received the seven per cent allowed in the enabling legislation, which came to £46,000 between them. This sum in itself was more than the total annual expenditure of all the maternity hospitals in the country. For the next Sweep, on the Grand National of 1931, the sales receipts nearly trebled to £1.7 m. and the hospitals got £439,000. The promoters' share had been reduced to two per cent, which worked out at £42,000. By the Grand National Sweep of March 1932 more than six million tickets were sold, worth £3.3 m. (over £100 m. in 1990 terms).[4]

The Sweep was (like the Congress) a superb feat of organisation. The tickets were sold in books of twelve, two of which represented the agent's commission. The enormous clerical task of supplying receipts meant that the Sweep quickly became a major employer in Dublin. With money coming into the office in more than forty currencies, 1,000 people worked in the Foreign Department alone. By 1932 over four thousand were permanently employed, compared to 19,000 in the civil service. In a world where female employment was hard to come by, this alone made the Sweep a welcome addition to Dublin life. Women in the cities generally worked in domestic service, in the clothing industry and as commercial and clerical employees. Most women left work when they married, and even if they didn't marry, job security was not high. In November Arnott's, reacting to the depression, dismissed two women who had been with them for twenty-five years—they were, said the firm, 'too old' at 40.[5]

There were jobs to be had elsewhere too. In the United States McGrath used the smuggling network of the IRA as a machine for selling lottery tickets. Their physical skills also came in handy for deterring the Mafia and others who saw the cash potential in the Sweep. 'Some of the ablest executive brains' abandoned the struggle for Irish freedom, dropped out of Clann na Gael, and 'devoted themselves more to ticket-pushing than to revolution.'[6] At this time only about one in twelve of the tickets was sold in America; the bulk, nearly three-quarters, went to the United Kingdom. Since the Sweep was also illegal there, tickets had to be smuggled into the country in various unofficial ways, and many people were involved in travelling to and fro with tickets. Special trains had to be laid on from Euston just before the Sweep closed to accommodate the hundreds of people coming from Britain with large sums of money to bet. The stewards on

HOLYHEAD CONTRETEMPS.

Many a middle class budget was supplemented by judicious trips to friends in England with Sweep tickets to sell on commission.

the mail-boats and the Liverpool ferries were notoriously ingenious about smuggling large quantities of tickets (on one occasion inside a coffin). Many a middle-class housewife supplemented her dress money by judicious trips to friends in England with a handbagful of tickets.

> Once the tickets were sold and the receipts dispatched, the six million or more counterfoils had to be taken to where the draw took place. In 1932 this was the Plaza dancing and billiards hall in Middle Abbey Street. Three times a year throughout the 1930s, a parade was organised through Dublin, with hundreds of the employees dressed in fancy costumes. For the Derby Sweep of 1932, 8.2 million tickets were escorted through the city in their boxes by 200 male and female jockeys, some on horseback. In other years inventive panache came up with other themes: one year a Haroun al Raschid theme, complete with real camels and asses; another, Trojan slaves with a wooden horse; another, 'rare and strange fish'; another, opera characters—200 Brunnhildes, Madame Butterflys, Titanias and so on.[7]
>
> The sheer physical task of ensuring that the millions of tickets were fairly mixed taxed Captain Freeman's ingenuity to the hilt. By 1932 he had devised a massive wind blowing machine, which was set up in the Plaza. After being thoroughly tumbled, the counterfoils were conducted on a miniature railway, escorted by the jockeys, Brunnhildes or Trojans, to the great eighteen-foot cylinder with six little doors from which they would be drawn. At the first Sweep blind orphan lads had been used to draw the tickets, but by 1932 it was felt that nurses were more in keeping with the spirit of the enterprise. The draw was conducted with maximum razz-a-matazz in front of an audience; one year over two hundred foreign journalists attended to witness this phenomenon, including Edgar Wallace.
>
> The enormous sums of money involved in the draw always provided tremendous excitement. 'The whole town', wrote the diarist of the *Irish Independent*, 'had a holiday atmosphere this week. The number of people from every part of the country and from England and Scotland who find the draw a business which entails their presence in Dublin is extraordinary. The hotels and restaurants were working at a hectic rate, the streets were packed with motor cars and thronged with visitors. All the folk in and around Dublin who are always looking for things to fill in their leisured days were having the time of their lives sitting in the Plaza for hours on end, then meeting for luncheon and seeing everybody else they knew lunching too, then returning to the draw and sitting for more hours on end; and doing exactly the same thing for three days running.'[8]

The record sale of over eight million tickets for June 1932 meant that the prize fund was divided into 28 units. Twenty-eight drawers of tickets for the winning horse would each get £30,000 (£1.65 m. in 1990 terms); the second horse tickets £15,000, the third £10,000. In addition there were the drawers of horses not scratched, and 100 cash prizes. The draw was a lengthy business, since over 3,500 tickets had to be pulled from the drum. The sweep organisers had originally started with a single winner, but when an Italian café owner in Battersea,

London, won £354,000 (equal in purchasing power to over £11 m. in 1990) with a single ticket, it was clear that individual winnings on that outrageous scale would jeopardise the future of the Sweep. Also the publicity value of a win of £10 m. is not ten times that of £1 m. So the organisers divided the receipts into units of £100,000. The more units, the more chances people felt they had.

The organisers were always conscious that not everyone approved of the Sweep: not only were four out of five tickets sold in countries where lotteries were illegal, but even at home there were doubters. In a rare (if not unique) burst of unanimity the *Catholic Bulletin* agreed with Archbishop Gregg in deploring the operation. Gregg thought that 'it would be hard to find anything more cynically callous than this trading upon greed and profiting by the losses of others. The most repellent part is that the sweepstakes are for our hospitals.'[9] For the *Bulletin* the Sweep was 'a great international scandal, a malignant menace, a putrid pool, a giant evil'.[10]

The draw, like all the Sweep's operations, was conducted with maximum panache. The hall was decorated by the Harry Clarke Studios, and elaborate precautions were set up to prevent the possibility of fraud. The operations were conducted by the publicity-loving General O'Duffy, the chief of police. 'In a glare of stage lighting six nurses seat themselves on the stage immediately in front of the slowly and almost noiselessly revolving drum', wrote the feature writer of the *Irish Independent*, describing the scene in June 1932.

'They sit sideways to the cylinder . . . another nurse sits directly facing the audience behind the little glass container which contains the names of the horses and which is spun by man power.

"One", snaps General O'Duffy, like the crack of a whip. Six bare left arms open the six portholes as the drum comes to a standstill, and six bare right arms are held aloft with open palms. "Two", comes the sharp military command, and six right hands are inserted through the portholes to emerge a moment later with six tiny slips of paper, which are held aloft for all to see.

"Three"—the nurses slam the portholes shut with their left hands, while General O'Duffy walks across the stage and takes the counterfoils from their right hands. A male attendant in a green and white jockey uniform tests all the little golden doors to make certain that they are securely fastened, and the cylinder of fate begins to revolve once more.

Meantime, a horse has been drawn from the glass container after innumerable hefty spins, and its name announced by Mr O'Sheehan, now in his customary seat behind the golden shute, which, continually revolving, carries the precious slips down to the quarter-hundred officials, assistant officials, linguists, typists, recorders and others who sit at a long table where the orchestra would be. After the freshly-drawn counterfoils have been stamped and noted by the group of auditors on the stage, Mr O'Sheehan reads the names or *nom de plumes* and the addresses and the loud speakers make his words audible even at the back of the hall. Irish winners, North and South are always applauded.'

Less than eight per cent of prizes went to Ireland as a whole, and just over five per cent went to the Free State. None the less the Irish people managed to buy (for themselves or for others) over 370,000 tickets each time at £16 each. Virtually every household had an interest in the outcome; world-wide, it was estimated that over thirty million people were involved.

The real value of the Sweep to the Irish economy, however, lay in what was not distributed as prizes. We can calculate at least the magnitude of this. Assuming that prizes were distributed in direct proportion to purchases, the total ticket sales for the three Sweeps of 1932 were £11.1 m., of which three-quarters came from Britain and Northern Ireland. Sales in the United Kingdom in 1932 amounted to £8.2 m. and £5.5 m. was returned in prizes. This annual donation from Britain to Ireland of £2.7 m. (the Annuities were reckoned to be £5 m.) was enough to oblige the British Government to set up a Royal Commission to prevent the sale of Sweep tickets. This hit sales for a period, so that it wasn't until the 1950s that the record 1932 level was fully recovered.

Distribution of 1932 Sweep receipts*

	£ m.	1988 Equivalent £ m.	1988 National Lottery £ m.
Gross Income	11.12	378	110.4
Prizes	7.40	253	51.1
Available for expenses	3.70	125	59.0
Less			
Contribution by IFS citizens (Expenditure less prizes)	0.20		
Net Irish income	3.50		
Expenditure			
Available to beneficiaries	2.80	94.0	36.8
Wages to employees	0.34		
Expenses	0.32	30.6	22.5
Promoters' share	0.24		

*Based on the accounts audited and presented to the Dáil by Craig Gardner; as permitted by the Act 'certain sales expenses' were excluded from the accounts. It is therefore likely that they understate the benefits to the country of the informal channels necessitated by the illegality of the Sweep in its major markets. The National Lottery information is from Davy Kelleher McCarthy, *Assessment of the Economic Impact of the National Lottery* (Dublin 1989) 6.

For the Sweep as a whole, the net income to Ireland in 1932, after deducting overseas prizes, was £3.5 m.—somewhat more than the government's receipts from income tax. The effect of this inflow on employment and the national economy must have been enormous. Certainly the hospital system was transformed as James Deeny, the Department of Health's Chief Medical Adviser, describes: 'Starting with forty county hospitals . . . we carried out a formidable programme. We built regional and teaching hospitals, regional sanatoria, mental hospitals, county hospitals, specialist hospitals, clinics, dispensaries and other health institutions. All in all between 1940 and 1965 more than two hundred hospitals were built, and another large number reconstructed.'[11] This formidable flow of money into the country continued, with a break during the war years, right through the 1960s, only faltering in the 1970s, when certain states in the US, which was by then the major customer, began to organise their own lotteries.

Even in the 1960s over £37 m. (at least £400 m. in 1990 terms) was given to the hospital development programme. By then the moulds that had established themselves in the 1930s were beginning to crack. For thirty years the country had been conservative and protectionist in cultural, economic and religious terms. Locked behind the walls of tariffs, censorship and religion, the country stagnated.

By 1963, however, each of these barriers had been breached. De Valera had retired from active politics, and his successor, Lemass, had seized his chance to turn economic policy on its head; the Catholic Church was undergoing the great upheaval caused by the Vatican Council; even censorship had undergone a change since 1957—the board now, as its historian put it, 'regarded their task much as a British or French board would have regarded it: that of making it difficult for the average person to read books which were pornographic and had no literary merit'.[12]

Part 3
1963

Chapter Twelve

Melting

Life was never better than in nineteen sixty-three . . .
between the end of the Chatterley ban
and the Beatles' first LP.

SO wrote Philip Larkin. Certainly this was true in Ireland, where the effects of the western world's post-war boom were just being felt. It has been said that few societies have changed more rapidly and more radically than Ireland since the 1960s. In 1963 this process had well begun, and things looked rosy. Even in the North the professional antipapist, Brookeborough, who had held the Unionist line since 1940, was reluctantly giving way to new blood.

For the previous thirty or more years the country had steadily become poorer and more isolated. The intention and effect of de Valera's policies had been to insulate the country from rough winds overseas. 'It would be a fine thing for us in this country', he once said, 'if we could shut ourselves off from the rest of the world and get back to the simple life I knew as a boy in Bruree.' From inside, the country had been seen increasingly as the last bastion of real Catholicism and of the ancient traditions of the Celtic race. From outside it was largely regarded as quaint and irrelevant. The Economic War, emigration, neutrality, protectionism, the 'sore-thumb' policy in relation to the North, had each added to this effect. This isolation, and the willingness of other countries to accept Irish emigrants, reinforced the conditions that created it, as one researcher discovered. 'Minister', said a middle-aged man, 'the Irish have the answer to any social problem that might come up. It might not be the best answer, but it is the one we have come to use—out! Thousands do it every year. I like it here, but the youngsters don't seem to, so they move. Why get all involved for someone who is going to leave the country just as soon as they can anyway?'[1] In the event eighty per cent of the generation born between 1931 and 1941 emigrated.

De Valera had begun his long period of dominance of Irish parliamentary politics with a ringing statement of intent. He declared that 'if we fail to make the radical changes obviously necessary to provide for all our citizens so that everyone may be at least reasonably housed,

Two views of Dublin in the late 1950s: (*top*) Thomas Street, (*bottom*) Stephen's Green

clothed and fed, we shall be failing in our duty, and failing cruelly and disastrously'. In the 1950s 400,000 Irish citizens out of just under three million decided that de Valera's idea of reasonable comfort was not theirs.

De Valera's now nostalgically remembered country comfort was often simply squalor by modern standards. Alice Taylor described the once in six years clean-up before the Stations in one country farmhouse. 'Dunghills disappeared from the yard . . . loose sheets of galvanised iron were nailed down and missing slates replaced . . . Mice and spiders who had nested comfortably in the house for months [were swept away] . . . Broken window panes patched with bits of old timber were replaced.' In a neighbour's house the milk sat on the table in a bucket, hens nested under the table, and mice infested the linen box.[2] The 1961 Census revealed that at least half of all houses outside the urban areas simply had no fixed lavatory facilities whatsoever, indoors or out. In Longford, for instance, there were only 1,600 indoor lavatories in the whole county of 30,000 people. Commentators spoke of 'threadbare villages, half ruins and half tacky shops, almost as dreary as ghost towns . . . rank country towns spreading out and out like spilt drink'.[3]

Perhaps de Valera, who after all lived in Blackrock, not Bruree, hadn't been wholehearted about the economic values. He was, however, deeply concerned with the other objectives of his Party, notably the reinvigorating of the Irish language and the reunification of the national territory. To the end of his life he was said to regard the preservation of the Irish language as more important than combating unemployment or emigration. Few in the 1960s, even in Fianna Fáil agreed with him. The objective of putting more people to work on the land had also failed: the very opposite had occurred. Emigrants from all classes left as soon as their education was complete. It was easier to get an overdraft from the bank for a church than for a factory.

Yet the fact that his major policy aims had failed so conspicuously seemed not to upset the voters at all. His magic lay in his great personal charm, and in allowing the people to feel good about themselves, without their actually having to do very much. In a rough postcolonial world it was undoubtedly comfortable to be regularly reminded, as one writer put it, of 'the aristocratic stamp of the Irish, their innate refinement, delicacy of feeling, artistic sense, their interest in culture and learning, their strong spirituality . . . and side by side with these their manliness, physical vigour and courage'.[4] If things went wrong, there was always the English to blame.

Popular history, which dealt almost exclusively with the heroic Irish struggle against the English, was never far from people's minds, reinforced by anniversaries, centenaries and chance discoveries. In May 1963, for instance, 'at Kilmahunna, four miles from Banaher, a number of skeletons buried two feet below the top face of a gravel pit were found. The civic guard who investigated found skeletons of what appeared to be an adult and child buried close together and another adult buried about six feet away. It is believed that they were victims buried during the famine of 1847.'[5]

By 1963, however, this excuse had begun to wear a bit thin. *Hibernia* quoted an old man's story about how he and a friend had left Clare as young men to make their fortunes in Liverpool. Amid the customary lamentations they set out, and after great travelling they arrived at the great city, where to their disgust, though not to their surprise, very few people seemed able to speak Irish. Exhausted by the trip they lodged for the night in a cheap hotel. When they awoke they found that all their possessions—packed into suitcases—had been stolen. It was just the kind of thing to be expected when one ventured into ruthless pagan England. The writer said that he could well understand that such a traumatic experience could cause a profound and life-long hatred for the English, particularly since it had been English economic policy that had driven him out of the West in the first place. 'And there was worse to it than that', continued the old man, 'later in the day we found that after all that travelling we hadn't got to Liverpool at all, and the place we were in was Dublin!'

By 1963, however, after a miraculously successful switch in economic policy, the Irish economy was growing faster than any in Europe. For most of the old men in power, however, this new warmth was a mixed blessing.

Prominent among these was the 68-year-old Archbishop John Charles McQuaid, who had been Archbishop of Dublin since 1940. McQuaid, like so many of his priests, was a countryman—he had been born in Cootehill, Co. Cavan. Educated as a Holy Ghost Father in the traditions of Frs Cahill and Fahey, it was widely believed that his flinty public image concealed acts of private generosity. For him, the scholastic philosophers of the middle ages had moulded Europe into a civilised unit of social, juridical and religious culture. In this imaginary world kings and emperors bowed to the Church; there were no Protestants, Freemasons, Liberals or Communists; Jews were kept in ghettos; heretics firmly dealt with.

The problem was how to recover that glory in modern conditions. It was certainly not likely that mere economic success would do it, and neither would ecumenism. McQuaid had after all been instrumental in closing down perhaps naive Legion of Mary attempts to draw Jews and Protestants into the Church by debate and discussion.[6] The Church's discipline, which included its control of education, offered the best opportunity. McQuaid's two preparatory suggestions to the great Vatican Council which started in October 1962 were typical of his approach. Firstly, he asked that religious orders be no longer exempted from the power of the local bishop; and secondly, that Our Lady be declared Mediatrix of All Graces—almost a co-redemptrix—a counterpart of Jesus. This position was of course extremely unpopular with Pope John's 'separated brethren', the Protestants.[7]

In common with many Irish bishops McQuaid mistook the importance of the Second Vatican Council, which in the event completely changed the face of Catholicism. They regarded it as merely finishing off the abruptly terminated business of the Council of 1870. At least one member from a southern diocese attempted to stay at home rather than attend, and there was a general expectation that, as McQuaid famously announced, 'no change will worry the tranquillity of your Christian lives'. Dr Lucey, Bishop of Cork, assured his people in his Lenten message in 1963 that 'nothing sensational will emerge from the Council'. Throughout the debates McQuaid held grimly to his conservative position against a rising tide of reform. Xavier Rynne, the contemporary chronicler of the Council, reported that in the discussion on the development of the Mass, 'Archbishop McQuaid came out once more against any thought of change.' He was at least listened to. Cardinal Browne, the Irish Dominican, suffered the indignity of the fathers retreating to the nearby coffee shop as he 'droned on' about St Thomas Aquinas.[8]

This complacency stemmed from a deep assurance of being right, reinforced by the position the Church held in the esteem of the Irish people. In research done in 1963/4 the American Jesuit, B. F. Biever, found that nearly ninety per cent of his sample agreed with the proposition that 'the Church is the greatest force for good in Ireland today'.[9] Biever describes 'ostensible signs of respect, men tipping their hats to clergymen on the street, women bowing or crossing themselves, policemen stopping the traffic at a busy crossing so that the good father may cross without delay'. In the libraries of University College Dublin virtually all the students stood for the Angelus at 12 o'clock and 6 o'clock. The American Jesuit describes how he joined a queue to make a telephone call, 'when to his chagrin the person in the booth, who was already in the middle of her call, hung up, came out and surrendered the booth to him. He protested, but the reply was simple: "No priest should be standing in line waiting for the likes of me."' (During 1963 one chancer took advantage of this attitude. He telephoned various married women, posing as a priestly social researcher and asking 'the most intimate questions about their relationships with their husbands within the marriage'. It was only after they had honestly answered the question that the women smelt a rat.)[10]

There was no great popular pressure for change: eighty-eight per cent of the sample refused to declare the Church 'out of date'—Fr Biever's respondents declared complacently: 'when you've got the truth, lad, you don't worry about keeping up with the times', and 'I wouldn't change a thing the Church is doing; it keeps the society here in Ireland a God-fearing one, and in the end there is nothing else worth doing. The Church may not be getting us jobs, but it is keeping our people happy and with their feet on the ground.'

There were cracks even in this relationship. Among those with more than twelve years of education, four out of five disagreed strongly with the Church's dominance, feeling that (as one respondent put it) 'the world is too complex today for a clerical state, and that is what we have in Ireland. What do priests know about politics, except that it leads to socialism?' These thoughts had been tentatively voiced by both priests and lay people in print, particularly in the late 1950s, in journals such as *The Furrow* and *Doctrine and Life*. Business people were more cynical: 'If you aren't a good Catholic here', said one, 'you'd be blackballed by the hierarchy and you'd lose your shirt. There is nothing like attending Mass with your wife and kids, making sure to be seen of course, to help the business.'

The clergy agreed with the great majority in thinking of themselves as natural leaders. One priest told Fr Biever, 'no one questions our authority. How can they? We have more education, thank God, and with that education comes responsibility to lead.' Another commented, 'I look at Ireland and I say to myself—who else could lead? The politicians are new at the game, we have few economists, our professional people leave. Who stays? We do.' Of course they were conscious of some criticism: 'some of your smart intellectuals have forgotten that it was the Church that never deserted the people when they needed help and guidance the most. We deserve the place we have in the nation, and we do not intend to give it up. What has made Ireland unique is the Catholic Church, and nothing else.'

Whatever its claims to leadership, the Church could do little to stop the changes brought in on the tail of economic growth. In the five years since the publication in 1958 of *Economic Development*, wage rates had gone up thirty-two per cent in Dublin (and slightly less in the country). People felt rich; for the first time since the early 1930s it was reasonable to feel cheerful about Ireland's future. In Shannon Michael Viney noted 'the sweet tang of optimism . . . like an aura of aftershave applied freshly every morning'.[11] Visitors noted the reduction in public drunkenness. 'There was', wrote one returned emigrant, 'an unaccustomed briskness about the way Dubliners moved, and a freshness of complexion I had not noticed before . . . Even the grumbles were indicative. There were complaints about all the money being spent on jet airlines and luxury hotels, and it was annoying that the upsurge in car ownership meant that the Irish would now have to take examinations for driving licences.'[12]

In January Lemass proposed a break with republican tradition: that there should be an Irish honours list. *Hibernia*'s readers were asked by the editor (then Basil Clancy) to nominate suitable recipients. The list provides an insight into the great and the good of the day, at least as perceived by that magazine's thoughtful but conservative readership. Seventy per cent voted for de Valera; the next most popular name was Micheál Mac Liammóir with 43 per cent. After him came William T. Cosgrave and Seán Lemass; then Sean T. O'Kelly, General M. J. Costello of the Sugar Company, Cardinal Michael Browne and F. H. Boland. Then, with 27 per cent voting for him, came Frank Duff, the founder of the Legion of Mary, and Sean McEoin. Other names mentioned were Siobhán McKenna, Ronnie Delaney, Christy Ring, Rev. Dr Lucey, Rev. Dr Philbin, Mother Mary Martin, J. A. Costello, Sean O'Casey and Brendan Behan. In summary, politicians comfortably led the field, with six names out of nineteen. Next came religion with five names (John Charles McQuaid notably not featuring); two each for sports, acting and writing; one businessman (state-sponsored) and one civil servant. The range of possible stars was not wide.

Despite the rapid changes, the older, rougher Ireland was not quite dead. In February *The Irish Times* reported that a heifer being walked to the slaughterhouse had escaped and jumped through someone's front window in Dun Laoghaire. The beast was recaptured, but only after causing considerable damage. Two women were admitted to hospital with shock and head injuries. On the Feast of St Blaise twenty-two priests blessed the throats of the thousands of people who attended the Franciscan church in Merchants Quay for the purpose. The minimum marriage age for girls was still only twelve: in May the Church of Ireland Synod heard that between 1957 and 1959 four girls

Left. William T. Cosgrave (1880–1965). *Top*. President Eamon de Valera (1882–1975)

Melting

aged fourteen had married and sixty girls and one boy had married aged fifteen.[13] In June two elderly people died when their house in Bolton Street, Dublin, collapsed; three weeks later the Corporation, in a panic, had evacuated 520 families from 156 dangerous houses. One of these families reported that they had been buying a tin of rat poison every day. Also in June small retailers began to pressurise the Dáil to vote against the turnover tax (an early form of VAT). One TD found a .303 bullet in his post and the anonymous message: 'This is for you if you vote in favour' . . . another was threatened with kidnapping.[14]

During the Dáil debate on the Turnover Tax, Oliver J. Flanagan, the Fine Gael TD from Leix-Offaly, compared Taoiseach Sean Lemass to an Irish Khrushchev or Castro. He also accused two independent TDs of having sold their votes to Fianna Fáil for £3,500 each. In the mêlée during this speech Flanagan was called a perjurer and the dirtiest mouth in Irish politics. References were made to the Locke's Distillery case of 1948, to the Civil War, to the seventy-seven, and, of course, to the Blueshirts. Much of this came from the young Brian Lenihan, then Parliamentary Secretary for Lands, who followed up with: 'Is this tout to be allowed to make such statements? . . . The gas chamber is the place for you . . . you are good manure, that is all you are.'[15]

The Beatles came to the Adelphi in Dublin in November and teenagers rampaged in O'Connell Street. Sean Moore, the Lord Mayor, a Fianna Fáil TD, couldn't understand what he described as 'a display of moronic barbarity after a performance by a cross-channel theatrical group'. In December ex-boxing champion, Garda 'Lugs' Branigan became a sergeant. His technique of quieting trouble-makers by what he called 'a few taps' from his formidable fists had made him a local character.

New American-style high office buildings began to rise above Dublin's natural four-storey skyline, to the disgust of the refined. Liberty Hall, O'Connell Bridge House and Hawkins House were the most conspicuous of these. The controversy over the ESB's houses in Fitzwilliam Street was just getting under way. For most people these developments were a welcome sign of prosperity. There was also satisfaction in the idea that at last the ascendancy's Georgian buildings had come to the end of their useful life, and could now be replaced with something truly Irish. There was, alas, a certain philistinism in the air. For instance, the Dáil heard in February that despite the increase in the city's population, twenty per cent fewer people visited the National Gallery than in George Bernard Shaw's time. The Corporation had a plan to fill in the Grand Canal with concrete to build a sewer and a car park.

DUBLIN OPINION

ONE SHILLING
OCTOBER 1963

The National Humorous Journal of Ireland

"An opulent and luxurious monument to Labour, Joe, but it seems to be leaning a bit to the right."

Dubliners tended to be more impressed than annoyed by the new buildings springing up in the 1960s.

Intellectual life flickered but scarcely flared in the pubs near the offices of *The Irish Times*, in small theatres and publishing groups. The quality of public debate on social and political issues was not high. Those from the non-possessing classes who might in another country have challenged the system either emigrated or were sucked into the civil service or the Church. From there, like Myles na Gopaleen, they conducted private sniping campaigns against their paymasters. Even in the universities the market for ideas was not lively. In general a university degree was looked on as a qualification leading to a career, rather than a search for enlightenment. The choice of a course of study was governed by the student's vocational aspirations, or those of the parents. Not surprisingly, half of Irish students reported feeling little or no enthusiasm for their studies.[16] For their seniors, the 'enervating minutiae' of university politics were more eagerly addressed than the national condition.[17]

On the other hand, the censorship laws, which had been since 1929 the favourite battleground of philistine and anti-philistine, were slowly beginning to lose their grip. In the peak year of the 1950s over a thousand books had been banned—in 1963 the number was 454. These, however, included important titles such as Sylvia Plath's *The Bell Jar*, James Baldwin's *Another Country*, Jack Kerouac's *Dharma Bums*, and a paperback edition of Simone de Beauvoir's *The Second Sex*. There was also Barbara Cartland's *Husbands and Wives*, and a good sprinkling of books about orgies, eager mistresses, nymphs, forbidden ecstasy and the like. The previous year had seen Joseph Heller's *Catch-22*, Iris Murdoch's *A Severed Head* and Edna O'Brien's *Girl with Green Eyes* and *The Lonely Girl* banned. In practice, official censorship was only part of the problem. At St Patrick's teacher training college in Dublin in the 1950s, John McGahern recalls that 'even though we were 18 to 20 year olds, there was still supervised study every evening, and we were only to read what was prescribed. If you were caught reading T. S. Eliot, for instance, you were biffed across the back of the head.[18] When Brendan Behan wanted a copy of the Penguin edition of Plato's *Symposium*, a bookseller told him, 'we saw a slight run on it, and the same sort of people looking for it, so we just took it out of circulation ourselves. After all we don't have to be made decent minded by Act of Dáil. We have our own way of detecting smut, however ancient.'[19]

It was notably a paperback that stimulated this remark. The huge increase in paperback publishing in the late 1950s and early 1960s, as *The Irish Times* commented at the time, 'made the task of the Censorship of Publications Board almost impossible. Not only has the number of publications increased, but the paperback industry has made available to the many books which hitherto had been within the grasp of the few.'[20] The Lady Chatterley trial in 1960 had pushed back the barriers of outspokenness, and in Britain 75 million paperbacks of all sorts were being produced and snapped up every year.

Paradoxically, the country's isolation from the world for a generation or more had produced an almost neurotic obsession with what the world thought about Ireland. This was the international version of 'what will the neighbours say?', the social and moral sanction of daily life that stifled so much spontaneity. Visitors' opinions were eagerly sought. In May, *The Irish Times* devoted half a column to the thoughts of Miss Norma Lynn Knobel, a high school teacher of American and world history at Richardson, Texas. 'The Irish', she announced, 'are a fun-loving but deeply religious people.'

International success for anyone remotely Irish (especially if Catholic as well) was very important to national self-esteem. They were widely discussed, perhaps as an antidote to self-doubt, in public and in private. Kennedy, as President of the United States, was of course in a class of his own, but when the British Variety Club marked Peter O'Toole as Best Actor for his role in *Lawrence of Arabia*, the Irishman's Diary called it 'a bit of a score for Irish performers'—that O'Toole had been rejected by the Abbey some years before on the grounds that he spoke no Irish did not appear.[21] When Seán MacBride became Secretary General of the International Commission of Jurists in November, *Hibernia* became quite lyrical. 'The appointment . . . is a compliment not alone to a distinguished Irishman, but to Ireland as a nation. It marks our position in the family of nations in a special way. It recognises that this ancient people has a special role to play in the community of peoples. It says in effect that we are called upon to serve the cause of freedom everywhere . . .'

Serving the cause of freedom was as usual easier said than done, as the Irish Army had already found in the Congo. The international stage was dominated by two large and self-righteously aggressive coalitions. On one side of the Cold War lay the Western alliance dominated by the United States—the Free World, as it was called. On the other side were the Russians and their allies.

The most dramatic point of confrontation was Berlin, where the infamous Wall was now two years old. Marxist/Leninist ideology told the Soviets that in due course history would bury the West, as the Russian leader Mr Khrushchev regularly pointed out to Western leaders. The Reds, as the press called them (as in one *Sunday Press* headline: 'Red kids eat more cabbage'), were not content simply to let history take its course. In May *Hibernia*'s special correspondent noted the dangers to Ireland of Russian paratroopers. 'The Russians are adept at falling free for 100 seconds. The reason that they jump from this great height—20,000 feet—is that the sound of their planes will not be detected. This tactic is obviously planned only against countries which have no radar defences, like Ireland. There would be definite advantages for Russia (no need to set them down) in occupying Ireland. If that should happen here, we should wake up one morning to find the country in Russian hands.' In April the editor of *The Distributive Worker* warned his fellow trade unionists of the growth of Communism in Ireland. 'The number of card-carrying members is less than one hundred, but its influence is immense . . . obviously there is no time for smug complacency. If these facts awaken Irishmen to the true nature and extent of the danger of Russian influence in our country, they will have served their purpose.'[22]

If history was to bury the West (and the East too very likely), it was more generally expected that it would come through what was called 'the unthinkable'—global thermo-nuclear war. Far from it being unthinkable, in practice millions of roubles, dollars, pounds and every other currency were spent brooding on its consequences. By accident or design, it was thought, a nuclear exchange might occur any day.

Books and newspaper articles told readers in detail what this would mean. The blast from a twenty-megaton bomb exploded over the GPO in O'Connell Street would leave a 600-foot-deep crater stretching from the North Circular Road to Trinity College and the Four Courts. This would instantly fill with scalding water from the Liffey. Children playing in Crumlin, Ranelagh and Glasnevin would be incinerated; people seeking refuge from the overpowering heat in the Dodder or the Tolka would be boiled alive; seminarians walking to Mass in Maynooth would find their soutanes bursting into flames; a massive fire-storm would sweep the city, worse by far than Dresden or Hamburg; virtually every building between Kippure and Donabate would collapse. After this would come radiation sickness, and then panic and disease.[23]

The Irish Times, in common with most Irish people, took a blandly optimistic view; 'our civil service is probably right in assuming that it wouldn't have to deal with more than one or two misguided missiles in the 10 or 20 megaton range'.[24] The prevailing winds, it was felt, would blow any fall-out from Britain away to the north-east. So

TURN YOUR BACK TO THE FLASH.

Turn your back to the flash. Hands in front of body.

Above. What to do if caught in the open by a nuclear blast (Irish Civil Defence pamphlet, *Bás Beatha*). *Below*. The pub: a retreat for the breadwinner from priests and women

common indeed was this feeling that the rich from Europe and beyond were buying up property in the west at an alarming rate. Oliver J. Flanagan raised the matter in the Dáil—'If we go on as we are', he said, 'rural Ireland will be stripped of its population.' This was, he claimed, 'a new invasion by a new type of landlord. The land-buying was often caused by Germans and others looking for a bolt-hole in the event of nuclear war.'—what was the Minister going to do about it?[25]

One entrepreneur tried to cash in on fears of nuclear war by launching an anti-fall-out sweet. This product, which came in three flavours—barley-sugar, butter mint and fruit drop—filled 'the body's reservoir with minerals such as potassium or carbohydrate complexes; radioactive materials are absorbed in these and are passed straight out . . .' The spokesman of the Irish Association of Sweet Manufacturers was not amused.[26]

There was plenty of international news to distract one from the strains of 'living in the shadow of the Bomb', as the phrase went. England had long been Ireland's model (whether to follow or reject); in the 1960s swinging London became the centre of world attention. Macmillan was still Prime Minister, and Harold Wilson had just come to the leadership of the Labour Party, and promised to replace the tired, corrupt Tory regime with the white heat of technological revolution. It was the era of 'you've never had it so good'—'England swings like a pendulum do' went the song. There was *Private Eye* and 'That Was The Week That Was', Wimpy bars, Vespa scooters, Jean Shrimpton and Julie Christie, John le Carré, the Liverpool sound, bright plastic whatnots in primary colours, pop art, the twist, Sunday colour sections, Minis (the car, not yet the skirt). Even Hollywood stars such as Elizabeth Taylor and Richard Burton turned out to be British.

In the spring an extraordinary crop of rumours broke out: one of them told how a member of the British Cabinet had served dinner at a private party stark naked except for a mask and a small lace apron. Quite soon it became clear that behind these rumours there was at least one substantial scandal. The Secretary of State for War, John Profumo, had been sharing a mistress with a naval attaché of the Russian embassy. Profumo initially denied any impropriety with Christine Keeler. However as stories of naked romps round the pool at Cliveden, obscure intermediaries connected with MI5, slum landlords and other seedy characters became public, he could not sustain this line. Irish readers snapped up *The Daily Telegraph* to relish the sight of the British establishment, from Macmillan to Lords Hailsham and Denning, making fools of themselves.

In August another unexpected insight into the new British character was revealed. The Great Train Robbery was a brilliantly organised theft of some two and half million pounds of used notes from a mail-train. Although the engine driver was clubbed on the head with an iron bar and permanently disabled, it was quickly clear that that British public regarded the train robbers not as violent thugs, but as folk heroes. Students of Southampton University elected the crime's organiser an honorary member of the Union.

The best-known Irish criminal of 1963, Shan Mohangi, was not so lucky. Mohangi was a South African Indian medical student who became engaged to a 16-year-old Hazel Mullen. On 17 August she called at the Green Turreen restaurant in Harcourt Street where he worked as a part-time chef and told him that she was seeing someone else. In a fit of jealous rage he strangled her. In between 'helping' the distraught Mullen family to find Hazel, he dismembered the body in the restaurant's basement; he later attempted to burn the remains, but the smell he created attracted the attention of the fire brigade. Eventually he confessed to the murder, and was convicted first of murder, then of manslaughter.

In the early 1960s Ireland was, as we shall see, like an icebound lake to which spring had come later than to countries south and east. The country resounded with noises of long set structures—economic, social, political, religious—creaking and crackling as the ice melted. Garret FitzGerald wrote at the time, 'the outlook of the people has changed gradually, but radically, from one of cynicism and near despair to one of confidence and self-assurance. This psychological breakthrough is of far greater importance than any purely economic achievements.'[27] In the February issue of *Creation*, under the heading 'Super living in the super sixties', journalist Caroline Mitchell enthused: 'this country is on the way up. We are going up financially, industrially and artistically . . . the first whiffs of outside air have been stimulating, enabling us to see ourselves more clearly as others see us, and in many cases for the first time.'

Chapter Thirteen

Getting and Spending in 1963

THE Irish economy was thriving at the beginning of 1963. The growth rate was certainly much greater than the planned 2 per cent, and a massive wage hike of 10–12 per cent in the previous year had not resulted in serious inflationary consequences, though Lemass was much concerned about the long-term effects of uncontrolled wage bargaining. Increased taxes on alcohol and cigarettes had absorbed some of the purchasing power, and new wage rates brought more people into the income tax net. Income tax receipts on the new PAYE system introduced only three years before, were some 20 per cent up on the previous year.[1]

New motor car sales in 1962, at 31,700, were up 11 per cent on the previous year. (In 1932, the total number of cars on the road had been only 32,000—by 1963 this had risen to 230,000.) The ESB pumped out 50 per cent more electricity in 1963 than had been used in 1958. Manufacturing output was up 30 per cent or more on the levels of 1958, and the stock exchange had shot up from an index of 94 at the beginning of 1958 to 210 at the end of 1962—by May 1963 the index had reached 252.

People had no trouble increasing expenditure to meet and overtake new income levels. There was, as usual, a gap to fill. In Dublin that meant finding and keeping a job. The first problem was, for half the population at least, that they were female. The civil service, the local authorities and many large companies operated the marriage bar, which meant that they neither recruited nor retained married women. On getting married women simply left the workforce. As a result only one in twenty married women actually went out to work. This extraordinary custom was justified as reinforcing the family, according to Article 41:2 of the Constitution. Those mothers who might be tempted to work were discouraged by moral persuasion. As Angela MacNamara put it, 'the grown man or woman who speaks with love, gratitude and reverence of his mother is rarely found to be the child of a "working mother" . . . much of the disappointment, failure and heartbreak in the world today is the direct result of the mother's neglect of her vocation'.[2]

In practice the marriage bar simply obliged women to choose between a career and a family, a choice that men did not have to make. The

Women and children, men and cattle: street scenes from Dublin of the early 1960s

looming fact of this choice deeply influenced attitudes to the education of women, and the likelihood of their getting any serious job. The typical social pattern was therefore the breadwinner father model, with a dependent wife at home and several children. Few wives were able to add to the family income except perhaps by taking in lodgers; this involved offering bed, breakfast and usually an evening meal for rural migrants (in the civil service and the banks), students and foreigners.[3]

For men the impetus given to manufacturing opened out a new range of possibilities. Of those born between 1936 and 1941, 40 per cent of those not emigrating worked in some form of family employment.[4] In the space of a few years after 1958 the Ireland of the family farm, the family firm and the family shop was to be replaced. Real wages (that is, excluding inflation) were up 28 per cent since 1953, though unions were concerned that productivity per worker (up 32 per cent since 1953) was increasing considerably faster than employment (up 17 per cent since 1953). The boom in manufacturing had, as a result, produced only 8,000 new jobs.[5] The significant point, for the urban middle class at least, was that the jobs were to be allocated on the basis of education and skill.

All sorts of new opportunities were being explored. When C. S. Andrews' son Christopher married in October, he and his new wife honeymooned in Palm Beach, Florida—the 'man of no property' himself had had to be content with France. Patricia Boylan had some fun in *Hibernia* at the launch of a new biscuit. This was organised by the 'dynamic' Frankie Byrne, 'one of the first and best-known PR people in Ireland', who had opened her own agency in February. Described as 'the most new important biscuit since the birth of the cream cracker in 1885', the Gye biscuit was made by Jacobs and Guinness. At the launch party, 'fine big fellows with moustaches and buttonholes and glasses in big hairy fists miminied to each other over the subtlety of the flavour, the appeal of its suntanned colour, its texture and tactile strength and its resistance to damp, not to mention its viability. Some of them congratulated others who looked so sweet and so modest as they tried to minimise their parts in the hard protracted negotiations that had gone on for months.'[6]

Daily life was dominated, as ever in Ireland, by one's position in the social pecking order. Nearly everything you did throughout the day was a function of this: especially where you worked, how much you earned, and where you lived. It was of course bad form to say so; indeed there was judicial authority for the view that class distinctions were almost entirely absent in Ireland. Judge Barra O'Brien made this announcement in Limerick, while refusing to accept counsel's argument that there was a class difference between farmers and farm labourers.[7] The author Ulick O'Connor agreed: in Ireland, he said, 'we have an aristocracy of personality. There is a kind of classlessness in Irish society because we are more interested in a man's mind and personality than his title or income.'[8]

The only place in Ireland where this classlessness actually operated was the pub, that men-only haven from the rigours of life, where neither women nor priests penetrated to bring reminders of diurnal or eternal reality, and where consequently all sorts of comfortable myths could flourish. In Dublin there were some 640 pubs, each comfortably supported by an average of less than four hundred male drinkers. It was estimated that some 15 per cent of income was spent on drink. (Young women were beginning to be seen more and more in pubs, but they were still not a common sight. Men would only very reluctantly allow a woman to buy a drink.[9])

Over the the last few generations most of the old Protestant ascendancy class had been bought out, had died out or had quietly left. The newly dominant Catholic middle class rather disingenuously disclaimed any intention of replacing them. One bank director and owner of a large business got himself into a revealing muddle when he was described as upper class: 'I'm amazed,' he said, 'at your use of upper, middle and lower class. We are quite ordinary people. We do not consider ourselves in any way an upper class. We think of ourselves as ordinary middle-class people and we don't have any activities that are associated with upper-class people. There are really only two classes here—a working class and a middle class, although you might say there is an upper and a lower level in that middle class.'[10]

This ordinary middle-class bloke was almost certainly a prominent member of a key group which held the reins of modern Ireland's economy. One hundred or so families, by interlocking shareholdings and directorships, controlled virtually all the large companies and financial institutions of the country. A mere ten families have been identified as the inner circle of this group.[11]

His wife would not have been so hypocritical. Jane Beaumont, writing in the *Sunday Review*, described the rampant snobbery in south Dublin. 'Girls are sent to college not to broaden their education but to meet the right people and to mix with their own class.' (Or, as a contemporary Mercier author put it, 'women . . . are actually capable of being educated, but the kind of education suited to their nature is of a different order; they are not inferior to men in their capacities, but these are suited to other fields of life'.[12])

Daughters' boyfriends were another source of snobbery.

> Mothers like to be able to announce that they're at university, or failing this, well up the ladder of success in the business world. For daughters, jobs where beauty and appearance are important count the most . . . At social functions, tuppence ha'penny must never be asked to rub shoulders with tuppence. In two suburban areas in County Dublin where residents' associations have held dances, I have been told that it was found necessary to hold two separate functions, one for the teens from the better-class houses and one for the more democratic youngsters from the cheaper housing estates.[13]

In the towns of Ireland, the same snobbery applied. Monica Barnes recalled Kingscourt, Co. Cavan in the 1950s.

> The small-town snob system was remarkably complex, very subtle. It rarely came out into the open, but everyone knew their place. . . . It was most visible at the reading out in church of the annual collection. Each year the ledger of contributions was read sonorously from the altar, confirming the relative social standing of each Kingscourt citizen. The names were read according to the amount each gave. Prosperous shopkeepers and professionals first; they gave a pound. Less prosperous shopkeepers and business people gave fifteen shillings; then the ten shillings, the fives and then all the plebs who gave half-a-crown. And if you paid beyond your amount, people talked about you getting beyond your station.[14]

The truth was that the status of most families was dependent on the status of the head of the family, a man, and his status was largely dependent on that of his father. One might move up or down one class between generations, but the high mobility implied by classlessness was non-existent. 'The son of an unskilled manual worker had a negligible chance of reaching managerial grade', wrote the statistician, Roy Geary. Even his grandsons had only one-fifth the chance of reaching professional status (the highest class) that they might have had in a perfectly mobile society.[15] These conclusions were based on a study of the actual life experiences of a large sample of men born and bred in

Dublin. For those coming into Dublin from the country, entry to the better jobs was relatively easy, and a high proportion of the new professional and administrative jobs was filled by non-Dubliners. It was actually harder for skilled and semi-skilled workers to break in.

The key requirement became secondary and third-level education. This was a speciality of the middle classes, who were therefore poised to take advantage of the new opportunities. Secondary education was not free at this time, and so only about one-third of those who might have done took advantage of it. For the children of professional and managerial parents, the participation was considerably higher.

The real crunch came in third-level education, where one in three of student-age men and women from the higher professional group attended, while the children of semi-skilled, unskilled workers and agricultural labourers achieved an attendance of less than one in two hundred. One in four children of the lower professional, managerial and executive class attended. Although these figures refer to both sexes, in practice a woman's chance of going to university was even more biased by social origin than a man's. In the light of the marriage bar, it is not surprising that less well-off families decided not to encourage their daughters to go. Fees in UCD, for instance, went up in May to £65 a year for arts courses and £100 a year for medical students; Trinity arts degrees cost £70 a year. This was one-eighth of the average industrial annual wage.

Many employers had ceased to enquire about an applicant's religion—the question was, could he or she do the job? In March Senator J. N. Ross told the pupils of Christ Church Cathedral School that there was no need to emigrate: 'There was a time', he said, 'when many Protestants felt that unless they could get work in a Protestant firm, they might not get work easily. But people no longer worried about whether one was a Protestant or not. If a job was well done, one would not be prejudiced against by being a Protestant.'[16] Not everyone thought that way. Fr Biever was told: 'Religion and business might not mix in some areas, but here in Dublin they are one and the same thing. I'd starve if I had to rely on the Protestant customer, so how can being a good Catholic hurt me?' For some (about half of his sample) religion was still a significant factor in making ordinary commercial purchasing decisions: 'I think we ought to keep our money among our own. God knows that they [the Protestants] tried to keep it away from us long enough.'

Some professional firms were quickly sensitive to the changing mood. In the accountancy firm, Craig Gardner, which then employed about two hundred staff, a committee of partners was established with a view to assessing the suitability of applicants. The old paternalist style of partners introducing whoever they liked was abandoned. The premium had been abolished in 1957. The firm cut back on its employment of the older type of unqualified clerks, and took a vigorous interest in the exam progress of young articled clerks. Articled clerks were expected to pass at least one exam every year; increments were not paid to those who did not. Graduates made up a quarter of the articled clerks.

As in the other years described, there was a wide range of earnings. Top of the heap were the few businessmen making large sums from property—it is of course impossible to guess at their takings. As a group, the professionals continued to do well. The 1956 *Irish Independent Guide to Careers* noted that 'the maximum income any barrister can hope to earn in this country is about £6,000 a year'. (£6,000 in 1956 was equivalent to about £80,000 in 1990.) The same publication commented that 'it is doubtful if the incomes of those few at the very top of the [medical] profession exceed £5,000 a year'. At this time the Secretary of a Government Department earned about £3,000. The *Irish Independent Guide*, however, remarked that although Saturday mornings were still worked, 'it may be safely assumed that work in the Civil Service is not unduly arduous . . .'

In 1963, when the average industrial wage was £541, the twelve partners of Craig Gardner averaged £6,000 each (the equivalent of some £66,000 in 1990); eight of the firm's staff earned more than £1,500, fifty-four between £900 and £1,500, and the rest (mostly clerks, trainees and typists) less than £900 (under £10,000 in 1990).[17] These were good salaries, as might be expected in such a firm. Other positions were less handsomely rewarded. Seán Lemass, as Taoiseach, for instance, got £4,000; the Secretary of the Department of Finance much the same. The newly appointed Director General of Telefís Éireann, Kevin McCourt, got £5,000, and General Costello, head of the Sugar Company, got £4,500;[18] an advertisement in *The Irish Times* (7 March) sought a new Director-General of the Irish Management Institute and offered £3,000.[19] In February Dublin Corporation advertised for a senior consultant engineer at £1,000–£1,300; a junior would get £800–£1,000.[20] The standard tax rate was 6s. 4d. (32p) in the £; surtax began with a taxable income of £2,500. In 1962/3 there were 7,520 payers with an average taxable income of £3,500 each (some £38,000 in 1990).[21] One of these was Gay Byrne, as he frankly, and perhaps proudly, admitted.

Down the scale, the two editions of the *Irish Independent Guide to Careers*, published in 1956 and 1967, give an idea of the range of salaries paid by various posts, and the rapid and general increase in real earnings between the two years.

Salaries for various jobs, 1956 and 1967. (These salaries are the levels for a married man at the top of scale but excluding allowances such as rent, children, overtime etc.)

	1956	1967	% increase
Retail Price Index (1953=100)	107	153	42
Average industrial wage	364	744	104
Printer	500	900	80
Creamery manager	526	1,275	142
National schoolteacher	800	1,490	86
Architect (Dublin Grade 1)	950	2,350	147
Bank manager	1,050	2,225	119
ESB engineer (basic grade)	1,070	1,900	78
Company secretary	1,200	2,200	83
Public relations officer	1,500	3,000	100
Assistant Principal	1,612	2,435	51
Senior Pilot Captain	1,950	6,253	220
Successful junior counsel	2,500	5,000	100

It is striking to compare the 1963 figures with those of previous years examined in this book. The cost of living in that year was approximately three times what it had been thirty years before. The average industrial wage, however, went from £126 a year to £541, a rise of more than 400 per cent. The top civil servants on the other hand earned (excluding children's allowances) £1,500 in 1932 and £3,375 in 1963, a rise of 225 per cent. The enormous range between the highest and lowest earnings had levelled considerably, and at the relative expense of the higher earners. In 1907 the top civil service salaries were £2,000, and a skilled labourer might expect £80 a year, a ratio of twenty-five to one. In 1932 a senior civil servant had earned twelve times the average industrial wage; by 1963 he earned in practice six and a half times the equivalent wage.

To see how people lived on a more ordinary level of earnings, we can quote the case of 'Liam Sheehan' as he was called in the Time-Life book on *Ireland* (published in 1964). Liam earned £1,375 in his job as a personnel supervisor in a Dublin factory. He was 42, and he and his wife Maureen had six children. Although 'Irish Government economists' pointed out that the best sirloin steak was only 4s. 6d. a pound in Dublin, and salmon 12s. a pound, that the best seats in the Abbey or

The new supermarkets, and domestic electrical goods such as fridges and televisions, made a real impact on family lives in the 1960s.

the Gate were only 10s. 6d. and that membership of the best golf club cost £20 a year, Liam Sheehan was not impressed. 'I assure you, that when you're supporting a wife and six children on a salary like mine, you eat precious little sirloin steak . . .'[22] The Sheehans had a small car (a four-cylinder Fiat), a television, but no telephone. At this time the telephone directory for the entire country was still in one volume—there were only 66 telephones per 1,000 inhabitants across the country.

The car and the television were very likely being bought on hire-purchase. Between 1958 and 1963 the amount of hire-purchase and credit purchases shot up threefold. Much of this expenditure was on cars—up to four times, and radio and television—up five times. Domestic electrical appliances were another great source of credit purchases.[23] In the fifties hire-purchase had been used for cars and for machinery. In the self-confident sixties consumers felt happy to increase their indebtedness well beyond the rate of their earnings increase to buy more frivolous items.

Liam Sheehan came home every lunch-time to his big meat-and-potatoes meal of the day at home. Not only was this cheaper, but the commercial provision of ordinary meals during the day was not extensive. In February the barmen of Dublin protested against a plan to serve cooked meals in pubs. 'We have no objection to cold foods, snacks, sandwiches, Bovril and soup, but the serving of heavy four- or five-course meals is out!', announced their leaders.[24] Maureen spent around £10 a week on food and milk, leaving £15 a week for all other expenses. These included rates at £50 a year, two packets of cigarettes a day (the average adult still smoked seven a day), and the secondary education of two of the girls at £15 each. The girls' school clothes would have cost as much. One mother complained bitterly in *Hibernia* about the costs of kitting out her daughter, which included a winter coat, a beret, three blouses, an English tweed pinafore dress and a blazer—total cost £17 8s. 5d. (just over £80 in 1990 terms). Health could be dear. People earning more than £800 a year had to pay for everything themselves, except school health, tuberculosis and infectious disease services. The average fee for a surgery call was 10s., or 15s. if the doctor called to the home; drugs were getting expensive, so people were tending to go straight to hospitals to get them free.[25]

Liam and Maureen lived in a six-roomed house near the Phoenix Park for which they paid £73 a year. A slightly grander house, such as a three-bedroom, two reception in Stillorgan was advertised for £4,100; one in Rathgar, five bedrooms, three reception, for £6,000, and a five-bedroom house on one-third of an acre in Foxrock for £8,500.[26] This was about two and a half times the taxable income of the average surtax payer. In all Dubliners spent only ten per cent of their income on housing, which was less than they spent on drink and tobacco.

The daily patterns of another household, this time in the up-market suburb of Rathgar, has been preserved in a series of household expenditure notebooks.[27] (Rathgar, like Foxrock, was famous for its upper-class pretentions and special accent. Girls from Rathgar, as the current joke had it, thought sex was what coal came in.) The family is unusual in having only one child, a daughter, but in other respects was no doubt typical.

The wife kept meticulous records of her expenditure of £7 or £8 a week (including on one occasion 1*d*. for the toilet when in town). During the week there would be daily purchases. On Sundays it might be: church 7*d*., V de P (St Vincent de Paul Society) 4*d*., *Irish Catholic* 4*d*., papers 11*d*. Food was bought virtually every day; in January 1963 for instance there were only three days in the entire month when no food was purchased. Typical items include: chops, chicken, 'meat', ham, corned beef, potatoes, peas, onions, cabbage, bananas, spaghetti, Nescafé, sugar, butter—with the exception of spaghetti, the staples of the not very adventurous Irish diet of the day.

Typically Irish men gave their wives a household allowance (in cash) plus an allowance for presents, clothes and anything personal. If more was needed, it was negotiated—'a frilly nightdress', suggested an *Irish Housewife*, 'will get better results than browbeating . . . Show me a man who will refuse anything when approached in the right manner by a one lightly perfumed and lightly clad.'[28] If the husband got a rise, a percentage of that went to the household expenditure. With little chance to earn money themselves, women were dependent. They were not helpless however: Austin Clarke told the story of one of his mother's friends, a seamstress who had toiled night and day at her sewing to help keep her husband and family. The husband was given a rise, but he didn't tell her, keeping the money for his weekend drinking. When she found out a year later, she was appalled by his meanness. She looked after him for the rest of her life, but neither spoke to him nor slept with him again, despite all the admonitions of the clergy.[29]

The pattern of food-buying was changing. Although the country was dotted with shops of all kinds (actually one for every sixty-five adults or so), most of these were very small. Of the 26,000 retail establishments, a quarter were pubs or groceries with pubs attached. The biggest category was the simple grocery, in which 8,400 establishments employed 20,000 people, with an average turnover of less than £10,000. Many of these small local shops offered bad value, bad presentation and a narrow range of goods: 'a pack of robbers they are', thought the *Irish Housewife*. Supermarkets, which had an average turnover of £300,000, were springing up in city and country, being blamed indeed for the rise in shoplifting.

'Today's housewife no longer buys just for one day', said the upmarket *Creation* magazine, 'but can buy her goods in bulk, to plan ahead for a week or more. Much of this food is of a comparatively perishable nature and consequently the need for proper storage is underlined. This is where refrigeration comes in. Refrigerators are now within the reach of most families, and this is a good thing, because they are essential for keeping food fresh, tasty and healthy . . . what few people seem to realise is that a fridge is not just a seasonal necessity . . . the spread of central heating in many homes in the country is another reason—yet only slightly over 30,000 homes have fridges, while one without a television set is exceptional!' (The author exaggerates slightly: only one in three households had TV in 1963.) The cost of an AEI fridge giving 5 cubic feet of storage space was 60 guineas. A similar fridge today would cost one-fifth of that price in real terms.

Bread and milk were delivered daily to the Rathgar family, and paid for once a week. The general category 'groceries' appeared on fifteen days in the month, meat on ten, fish on six—the family was especially fond of kippers. Other frequent purchases included pork chops and eggs (frequently duck eggs). Cheese was not noted in January, but it was in February, so perhaps it was not bought often. Items such as stamps, newspapers, clothes from Switzers and Colette Modes, and charities appear regularly.

For ordinary transport the housewife had her Humber bicycle, which had to be repaired during the year; otherwise she took the bus. The family went to Mass regularly, and attended sodality meetings as well as making charitable payments to the St Vincent de Paul and the Little Sisters of Charity. Other religious expenditure included the Easter dues and the regular purchase of the *Irish Catholic*. Expenditure on books is recorded once a month, and the cinema about six times during the year; the theatre is more of an occasion, however. Only one visit is recorded, and this is preceded by a special visit to the hairdresser. Other items included the monthly rent, wages to the servant—Bridie left during the year and this resulted in a lot of expensive newspaper advertising for her replacement, May, who arrived some time later. In *The Irish Times* around this time 'A capable general' was sought for a modern house in the Ranelagh district, and was offered £4–5 a week all found.[30]

Her daughter was allowed 1s. a week pocket money, and money for the Girl Guides and dancing classes. In May the purchase of a hat for 18s. 9d. is recorded, perhaps in preparation for President Kennedy's visit.

The Household Budget Enquiry of 1965/6 reveals that expenditure proportions had changed somewhat since the Civil Service enquiry of 1932. Thus the top-earning group in 1965/6 spent 24 per cent of its disposable income on food; in 1932 the top group spent 29 per cent.

The most revealing conclusion to be drawn from the 1965/6 survey, however, is how for urban dwellers expenditure on food is correlated with social status. Social group 5 (unskilled workers), for instance, spent nearly twice as much as social group 1 (higher professionals) on white bread. The classes between spent progressively less as they got higher. For milk the progression went in the opposite direction: social group 1 spent most, social group 5 least; the other groups according to their rank in between (barring in this case, the families of skilled workers, who spent nearly as much as the higher professionals). This scaling of expenditure applies to most food products; on eggs, cheese, steak, lamb, chicken, tomatoes, fruit and spirits, social group 1 spent most, and the others ranked below in order. For butter (to go with all that white bread), bacon, potatoes, cabbage, tea and cigarettes, social group 5 spent the most and the rest progressively less as they rose up the scale.[31]

The Irish were generally well nourished—indeed the government boasted that according to United Nations figures, consumption of calories per head was the highest in the world.[32] Quantity was not the same as quality. In theory, of course, Jammets, like the Ritz, was open to all. In practice what one ate depended on what one earned, which in turn depended largely on what one's father had earned in his time.

Chapter Fourteen

Daily Lives in 1963

IT was an affluent age, everyone agreed. It was also an age when the Irish seemed to be taking control of their own destinies, even in the previously disappointing economic field. For the first time for generations the adventurous young did not feel they had to go overseas to invent a future for themselves. It was, or at least it might be, possible to do it in Ireland. Not that the old tunes were totally silenced. The ultra-Catholic publication, *The Word*, still hammered on about Freemasonry, international Jewry, Marxism and Communist dupes; the Department of Foreign Affairs (under Frank Aiken) produced *Facts about Ireland* which described the foundation and coming to power of Fianna Fáil, but failed to mention any other party.

People got married and had babies in the old way too. Because of the late marriage age, half the births in Dublin in 1963 were to women over thirty. (In England and Wales seventy per cent of births were to women under thirty.) Despite the current belief that there was an abnormal birth-rate nine months after St Patrick's Day, in fact the peak month was May, with nearly two hundred births per day. These babies could look forward to between 62 and 67 years of life, depending on sex and whether they lived in town or country. Country people lived longer than townees, and women were expected to live two or three years longer than men. In 1932 the expectation for both sexes was about 57 years, with women living a mere six months longer.

The causes of death had changed somewhat from 1932. The old scourge, tuberculosis, was down to one per cent of deaths. Pneumonia ('the old man's friend, as it was called) and bronchitis made up eight per cent; the big killers were heart attacks, strokes and cancer, which together accounted for over forty per cent of deaths.

During their upbringing children would have noticed a sharp difference between the way boys and girls were treated. Boys were nearly always exempted from household chores, while girls were expected to help with everything. In extreme cases they cleaned the boys' shoes and vacated favourite chairs when they came into the room.[1] The marriage bar and other prevailing attitudes reinforced the sense of separate castes: while boys were to be toughened into breadwinners, girls were already undergoing apprenticeships before becoming homemakers. The intense relationship that resulted between mother and son was proverbial. 'Only a mother knows the taste of salty tears', one woman was told as she wept after her son's curly locks had first been cut. 'The first haircut, the first day at school, they go to work, maybe across the sea and get married. You keep breaking your heart from the minute they are born—you never lose them though, you will always be their mother'.[2] Daughters had to learn to put up with this favouritism with wry resignation. Only when a mother-in-law attempted to continue the relationship with her son after his marriage was there likely to be serious tension.

Two books of etiquette published in the 1960s are aimed at the future (male) breadwinner. Martin Molloy justifies his *Book of Irish Courtesy*[3] on the grounds that 'social assets have a very solid market value, and the young man who possesses them is usually assured of a buyer . . . in the next few years this market value is certain to rise at a very rapid rate as Ireland draws nearer to entering the Common Market'. In their little etiquette book published in 1962, the successor to *Christian Politeness*, the Christian Brothers stick to rather higher motives. For them Christian Courtesy 'is the fulfilling of the Divine precept, "As you would that men should do to you, do you also to them in like manner."'[4]

Both books were in practice aimed at boys and young men, and their message is clear. As Molloy puts it: 'there are few social activities more revealing of the individual than his table manners. In normal society they are always interpreted as a pointer to one's upbringing and education . . . no one with ambition to succeed in life can afford to risk having them called into question.' In other words, if you want to get on, you must have, or pretend to have, middle-class manners, and the earlier you start the better.

There was also of course a little unease about the genre. After all, was there not what Martin Molloy called 'the aristocratic temper of the Irish mind'. 'This', he wrote, 'is very much in evidence. Despite their long years of hardship, the Irish never became bourgeois: their minds were too fine, too sensitive. They have an inordinate respect for good breeding, not in any class-conscious sense but in their regard for the integrity and other personal qualities which they rightly associate with members of the Old Stock. This aristocratic stamp is very clearly exemplified in the average Irish countryman, than whom there is no finer gentleman to be found anywhere; and no shrewder judge of what constitutes a true gentleman.'

Having got over this hump, the books concentrate on laying down a set of basic rules for various circumstances. For the table, we are told: don't play with the knife and fork, don't dip bread into the soup, don't put your knife in your mouth, don't stuff your mouth with food or pile your plate mountain high, don't reach over others to get the salt, don't speak with your mouth full, shut your mouth while chewing.

F. X. Carty remembers his etiquette lessons in the Holy Ghost Seminary around this time. The lessons were given every Monday by the Sub-Master, who solemnly took his place at the speaker's rostrum complete with napkin, knife, fork, spoon and perhaps boiled egg, as he prepared to teach these future missionaries the niceties of table manners. For instance, 'bread was to be cut into eight pieces and each piece buttered separately. Butter was to be placed on the side of the plate . . . under no circumstances was butter to be spread over the whole slice together . . . twenty-eight chews per moderate mouthful was the ideal. This would make us more like Christ, showing that we had control over the things of the flesh.'[5] One absolute rule was never to talk about food; to enjoy eating as such was unbecoming to a serious person.

In St Patrick's teacher training college in Dublin, John McGahern had experienced a different regime in the 1950s: 'Things were pretty savage really. One fellow got badly beaten by the authorities over an egg. There was a crew of students from the Gaeltacht who had come through special preparatory schools and really they were still savage. Rations were very small, so if you had any table manners at all you starved. This fellow, anyway, complained that he hadn't got his boiled egg, so he was called up and given a battering in front of the whole refectory. Likewise, if you didn't go to daily Mass, you could be expelled.'[6]

Much Irish food, certainly that supplied in institutions, was perhaps best forgotten. Cooking in Ireland, as an American commentator put it, was 'a necessary chore rather than an artistic ceremony, and the Irishman will usually eat anything put in front of him without bothering overmuch about its flavour or seasoning.'[7] In restaurants, nine out of ten ordered 'steak, every time, and seven men out of ten will order chips with it!'[8] It was a vicious circle: dully cooked food reinforced the idea that to like food was somehow perverse. Monica Sheridan, who had a popular Telefís Éireann cookery programme, 'Monica's Kitchen', told the story of her young sister, fresh from her honeymoon, who made an omelette for her new husband. He looked at her coldly across the table, turning the omelette over with a searching fork. 'If I must have eggs', he said with finality, 'I'd rather have them boiled.'[9]

Right. Modern cookers may have revolutionised the kitchens, as this advertisement claimed, but it took longer to revolutionise the eaters.
Below. The Haugheys at home (1962)

Things were beginning to change, slowly. In February *The Irish Times* noted that 'to judge by the crowded tables at the foreign restaurants in town, more and more Irish people are discovering the delights of new dishes . . . from the piquant flavour of prawns in tomato sauce, to the spicy sting of a good curry, the juicy succulence of chow mein, the exotic extravagance of paella, to the solid worth of Boeuf au Bourgogne . . .' There was still a self-consciousness about some places, however. A lawyer told Fr Biever that he had never been to Jammets, the most famous eating place in Dublin at the time—'it was a place for the Protestant country club set and American tourists. An Irishman wouldn't know what to do in a place like that!'

If you were invited to a small dinner party (for six to eight people) at the home of Charles Haughey, the thrusting new Minister for Justice, his wife Maureen (so the up-market women's magazine *Creation* told its readers in April) would very likely offer you their 'special favourite, Steak Fondue. Small cubes of very tender raw steak, well seasoned, are placed on a platter. Then each guest, using a special two-pronged fork selects his pieces of steak and cooks them at the table exactly to his taste, in hot melted butter [sic] in the chafing dish. A variety of sauces and a tossed salad complement the dish.' 'Their guests', commented *Creation*, 'find Steak Fondue a very amusing novelty.'

Novelty it certainly was, though later it became so popular that hardly a wedding present list was complete without its fondue set. *Creation* made a brave attempt to stimulate its readers: 'You might think', it wrote in February, 'that Chinese food is too exotic to be attempted in the kitchen, but this is not so.' (Thirty years before, *Model Housekeeping* had made a similar remark about omelettes and soufflés.) Breda Ryan, the wife of the businessman Mayor of Galway preferred a chicken dish with a very rich sauce, *Creation* readers were told in March, with fresh salmon or oysters for the fish course, and always a soufflé or fresh fruit to follow.

As with table manners, a chap's dress would unwittingly reveal his origins, and more. 'Dress is often a reliable pointer', wrote Martin Molloy, 'not alone to personality but also to character. It is the mark of a mature and balanced person that he does not follow every fad.' In practice Molloy recommended that his readers concentrate on the all-purpose lounge suit. 'This is the correct dress in Ireland for: informal dinners, cocktail parties, funerals, receptions, christenings, opera, ballet, race meetings, openings of Churches and Schools. On all of these occasions it is bad taste to appear in sports clothes.'

The wearing of hats was no longer *de rigueur*, but if they were worn, correct hatmanship must be shown. 'Greeting a lady in the street, a gentleman who is wearing head-dress raises it with the hand farther away from the lady . . .' The Christian Brothers expected boys wearing caps to be particularly alert.

In general dress at all levels was sober and dull. 'The variety and eccentricity of modern fashion' so much deplored by Martin Molloy was hardly in evidence. One returning emigrant, going for a stroll in a short-sleeved shirt and sunglasses on a fine Sunday morning in Dublin was embarrassed to find himself the only one so casually attired. Everyone else was formally dressed: 'the men in dark going-to-Mass suits and the women looking most refined in their carefully ironed dresses, veiled hats and white gloves'.[10] Even students dressed quite dully. Suits, grey flannels and dull sports jackets were the style.

Women, of course, were driven by a much more exacting code. They were, for instance, forbidden to wear trousers inside UCD; they covered their heads in church. 'Keep away from pants and jeans'; advised the author of *Dating without Tears* (a book in which there is a sympathetic postscript for the over twenty-fives), 'unless you have slim hips and a very flat tummy *and* long legs . . . whatever you've chosen, you must be wearing the right size and shape of girdle and brassiere underneath.' For a Christmas party the thirteen-year-old Caroline Walsh wore 'the woollen red skirt I wasn't so sure about but which the lady in the shop had deemed ideal, the little blouse, the inevitable black patent shoes, and—oh thrilling moment—my brand new, first-time-ever suspender belt and nylons'.[11]

To help women undergraduates to conform, a modelling and beauty class was organised for Trinity students. Run by Mrs Zoe Weinman, who owned a modelling agency in Dublin, it included daily classes in deportment, clothes co-ordination, colour sense, make-up and hair. In her preliminary talk on 'The Secret of Attraction', Mrs Weinman 'stressed the need to shock girls into realising that people were commenting on their general sloppiness'.[12] There were in fact eight modelling agencies in the city, several offering 'improvement courses'. A young woman who had taken such a course told the *Sunday Press*: 'I had worn no make-up except lipstick until then, and the beauty woman told me I would have to take care of my skin—that meant the purchase not only of cold cream and face powder but of skin tonic, nourishing cream, tinted foundation, eye make-up and face packs. After the course I felt very glam., all those deportment exercises made me feel two inches taller. I knew how to pluck my eyebrows the right way.' Her boyfriend was less enthusiastic—he 'said the course made me look less like a model than ever'.[13]

No doubt the same woman read with interest beauty consultant Bronwyn Conroy's interviews with TV personalities, Gay Byrne and Terry Wogan. They were asked what they were looking for in a girl: Gay Byrne thought he liked femininity, intelligence, a nice voice and figure, good legs in dark stockings, blonde hair, brown eyes and sensible clothes. Wogan was more interested in a sense of humour, good dress sense and grooming, and his pet hate was bad make-up. Both were keen on how a girl walked, and her general deportment.[14]

Boots and trousers for women were the new thing. 'Boots, boots, boots and more boots', commanded *Vogue*: in Paris Saint Laurent concentrated on 'showing women how to dress for their boots'. One of his models was shown with alligator boots shockingly high up her thighs. The rule for 1963 was: legs first. If they weren't in boots, they were in knitted stockings, in paisley, cable knits, rugger socks, diamonds, tartans.[15]

Women's trousers, depressingly called 'slacks', were a favourite source of scorn to the old-fashioned. Admittedly their tailoring was not yet very sophisticated, but they hardly merited the vehemence that 'Cherchez la Femme' displayed. During the great freeze in the early months of 1963, when there was skating on the pond in Dublin Zoo for the first time since 1947, he wrote to the *Sunday Press* complaining : 'It is rare these cold days to see a woman under forty wearing a skirt while out shopping. The streets are full of muffled, duffled and betrousered travesties of womanhood . . . come on girls, let's have some glamour to brighten up the streets!' And S. Ó Cuanac agreed with him: 'The masculine clad female', he considered, 'is one of the most revolting sights for mankind to behold.' The readers of the *Sunday Press* would not have won prizes for feminist thinking: in March another complained about having to pay when he took a girl out: 'It takes a brave man', he wrote, 'to take out one of these painted, trousered, fashion ladies of today. These painted ladies are not worth a smoke to any man.'[16]

Although they might have been more graceful, the *Sunday Press* readers could be excused for not being feminists; Betty Friedan's path-finding book, *The Feminine Mystique*, was only just published. Val Mulkerns, reviewing it in *The Irish Times*, wasn't much impressed: 'she forgets that the full life of the mind only works if there is a mind there in the first place. . . It is my belief that if the cage doors were suddenly opened, the prisoners would scuttle back to the kitchen at the earliest possible chance.'[17] In the month that this review was published, Dublin

"*Just look at that poor girl with no boots on her feet!*"

Two views of fashion: the craze for boots, and working class underwear on washday

was reading less challenging matter: top of the fiction bestsellers was Ian Fleming's *On Her Majesty's Secret Service*, then Daphne du Maurier's *The Glassblowers* and Monica Dickens's *Cobbler's Dream*. Top of the non-fiction list was Cecil Woodham-Smith's *The Great Hunger*, then Mac Liammóir's T*he Importance of being Oscar*, Cardinal Suenens' *The Nun in the World*, and Kevin Danaher's *Ireland Long Ago*.[18] Others, such as June Levine, also had trouble with *The Feminine Mystique* when it first came out: 'how could she really know what life was like for a girl like me? I was twenty-nine years old and had three children, and still did not call myself a woman . . .'[19] Women were discouraged in various ways from thinking of themselves—in some households even saying 'I' was frowned on. Later in May the Chief Justice, Cearbhall Ó Dálaigh, told the Irish Housewives Association that 'the women of this country had equal rights with men six years before the women of Britain'.[20] (He meant of course voting rights. This is a nice example of the deeply embedded Britain-as-model thinking that affected so many Dublin circles from the radical chic to the higher civil service.)

A more realistic estimate of relative positions even in middle-class Dublin was revealed by a Ballsbridge housewife who wrote to *The Irish Times* in January complaining bitterly about an architect's proposed scheme of three-storey houses. 'No woman', she declared, 'will single-handedly take on a three-storey house . . . This is not prejudice or obstinacy, but working knowledge gained seven days a week winter and summer, most days doing at least fourteen hours. Can I really manage to carry my sick husband's breakfast tray, the week's washing, the parcel from the cleaners, and the toddler's damp mattress down the stairs all at once, and without letting the baby slip out from under my arm? . . . Naturally while she nurses four consecutive cases of measles on the third floor, the good housewife finds time to organise neat piles at the front door for the milkman and the breadman, the notes and the key for the ESB or the gasman, the key at the back door for the coalman, not to mention the procession of beggars, sales folk, children next door and, dear oh dear, not another beastly friend calling in? Of course reliable, consistent help from a loving husband would be fairly useful, but so many men seem to have an "anti-attitude" to running up and down stairs on messages for their wives.'[21] Since the husband would have been exempted by his mother from any contribution to housework since he was a boy, it is not surprising that he took that view.

One great solvent to so many of these attitudes was to be television. Telefís Éireann (TE) had been launched with great fanfares at the end of 1961. It was given the contradictory task of making money, while at the same time 'bearing constantly in mind the national aims of restoring the Irish language and preserving and developing the national culture'.[22] Despite constant carping from critics, the first aim tended to predominate.

Television had become a fact of Irish life by 1963, broadcasting five or six hours a day, of which fifty-five per cent were programmes brought in from abroad, mainly America. The average set was switched on for nearly three hours every day of the week. When Maureen Haughey advertised for a nanny (£5 a week), she was careful to stress that both central heating and television were available.[23] Pundits began to worry about the effects on family life: 'only at mealtimes does a family meet with a common object in view . . . those homes where meals are eaten on a tip and run basis, with one eye on the clock or the TV are missing something irreplaceable'.[24] Television was by no means universal, however, perhaps because it was seen primarily as entertainment. As Frank Duff resignedly admitted, 'we had better face up to the fact that amusement is one of the special purposes to be served by TE'.[25]

Favourite programmes included (from America): 'Sergeant Bilko', 'Bat Masterson', 'Have Gun will Travel', 'Dr Kildare' and the 'Jack Benny Show'; locally made programmes with high TAM ratings included the 'Showband Show', the News, 'Country Style', 'Jackpot' and 'O'Dea's Your Man'. English TV, for those who could get it, included 'Sunday Night at the London Palladium', '6.5 Special' and 'Emergency Ward 10'. The bright young names were Terry Wogan, Bunny Carr, then a continuity announcer but later to compere a long-running quiz show, and Gay Byrne. Byrne had just completed his first season of the 'Late Late Show' to some acclaim, but he was taking no chances. He was at this time also working four days a week in England for Granada and BBC Manchester. 'This is a peculiar job', he told an interviewer, 'you earn a lot of money, but you wonder how long it will continue. Five years maybe.'[26]

Although the News as such was always high in the ratings, audiences for home-produced public affairs programmes, which tended to be straightforward studio discussions, were not large. There was the curious fact that, as Maxwell Sweeney put it, 'there has been less inhibition in discussions on television than on the radio'. This phenomenon was to become more marked as the 'Late Late Show' got into its stride. People as news conscious as journalists did not necessarily possess a set. F. X. Carty recalls that his father, then editor

Top. Eamonn Andrews, first Chairman of the RTE Authority, Edward G. Roth, first Director General and Archbishop John Charles McQuaid at the opening and blessing of RTE in 1961.
Bottom. 'The Showband Show', one of the most popular locally made programmes on television

of the bestselling newspaper in the country, the *Sunday Press*, only bought one in the middle of 1963.[27]

Just as the Eucharistic Congress had stimulated radio purchase, the great events of 1963, in particular Kennedy's visit and the election of Pope Paul VI, stimulated TV sales. By then one house in three had a licenced TV set. There was, of course, active and persistent licence evasion: in 1962, 11,000 people were prosecuted for not having radio or TV licences.[28] The slow acceptance of TV in rural areas surprised local pundits, but by the end of the sixties three-quarters of homes had TV.[29]

It took a little time to get used to the reality presented by television. It was still, for instance, usual to watch the black and white screen in a darkened room. The broadcasting of religious services such as Benediction caused problems. They were often at awkward hours, just when the children were being put to bed, or the family tea was in progress. The viewer was puzzled how to react with proper reverence—should domestic chores be stopped, should one kneel, or put out cigarettes?

Television was the flashy medium of the sixties. Advertisers echoed its jargon: 'I guess I'm tuned in to the wrong channel—I'm right out of the picture', ran one Colgate ad. In her list of 'What's In', journalist Brid Mahon included: two button suits (for men); doing the Bossa Nova; going to an island for your holiday; calling your son Sean and your daughter something old-fashioned like Sarah, Miriam or Deborah; serving Irish stew or pigs' feet, bacon and cabbage for your party; and listening to TW3 [not yet watching, note]. This last was the BBC satire programme 'That Was The Week That Was' which infuriated the staid with skits such as a Consumer Guide to Religions. 'Cheap smart alec superficiality', ranted *The Irish Times*' TV critic, John McDonnell. 'Satire sounds smart, but it covers prejudice, cruelty and sheer bad taste.'[30]

Daily life in urban Ireland was becoming more and more open to the world—not only to the 'great moral laxness of Britain', as Angela MacNamara put it, on the television screens, but also to the exciting possibilities for a country that could produce such men as the President of the United States. Kennedy was, for many in Ireland, the symbol of the potential of a new, successful, dynamic Ireland. No wonder so many took him to their hearts during his extraordinarily successful visit in June 1963.

Chapter Fifteen

The Moral Irish

THE Irish were always a remarkably moral people. Everyone knew this—it had been a source of frequent self-congratulation since the days of the Gaelic League. By comparison with European countries, writers pointed out, the morals of the country were almost irreproachable. This was usually ascribed to the intense loyalty of lay people to the Church. 'Look at our morality in Ireland', said one of Fr Biever's interviewees, 'we are better off than most if not all countries in the world. How can you say the Church is behind the times?'

The European country everyone had in mind particularly was, of course, pagan England. Worryingly, the increasingly outspoken British media, so eagerly consumed at least in the populous eastern fringe, was beginning a new assault. 'The strong moral tradition of the country . . . can no longer be counted on, as so many corrupting forces are in direct competition with it', wrote *Hibernia* in March 1963. The Bishop of Tuam agreed: writing in his Lenten pastoral of advancing secularism and attacks on chastity, he feared that 'even in this country there had crept in a certain looseness, a spirit of laxity . . .'[1]

However crime rates are still low, and the police solved a very high proportion—of the 885 crimes against the person reported in 1962, 830 were detected. Fourteen thousand offences against property were reported, of which two-thirds were detected (twenty years later, 86,000 such crimes were reported, with just over one-third detected). One hopes that Mrs Mary Roberts of Fairview was one of the lucky ones. She was robbed of her handbag containing her life savings (£120) while she stopped in O'Connell Street to buy her two-year-old grandson an ice-cream. She carried the money around with her, she said, because there 'had been so many cases of house-breaking recently that [she] thought the money would be safer in her bag than in the house'.[2] To some extent the low rate of crime was because, as a contemporary report put it, 'Irishmen of criminal tendencies invariably went to England and improved their criminal skills there, encouraged in this by the Irish police.'[3] Crime rates were one-third those of Britain.

The most spectacular evidence of high morality was the famous Irish chastity. The Irish were so chaste indeed that demographers have speculated on some kind of racial loss of libido as a result of the Famine. Nearly one man in three never married, and very likely had no sexual experience beyond the bleak masturbations described by Patrick Kavanagh. Those who did marry did so late and reluctantly—the national average age at marriage was thirty for men and twenty-six for women, and in the country, four years older still. Illegitimate births were less than two per cent of the total, though this figure was widely believed, like the equally low suicide rate, to conceal more than it showed. Pregnant but unmarried women were usually exported, like the criminals, to England.

One hundred years of repression by lay enthusiasts and clergy alike had swept the likelihood of sexual joy vigorously under the carpet. In September a group of young Italian tourists complained bitterly to the *Sunday Press* about this; 'If we hold hands in the street, people look askance at us; if we kiss in a public place such as a café, we are immediately put out.'[4] Marital sex was often not much more enthusiastically approached. 'I'm lucky, I don't mind it' or 'He's very good, he doesn't want it very often', were remarks that Dorinne Rohan heard from her women friends in the 1960s. One man said to her, 'We're all animals after all, aren't we? I don't believe in all this spirituality lark about sex.'[5] A husband told the Jesuit researcher, Alexander Humphries: 'back of everybody's mind is the notion that there is something wrong with it, something bad. It is deeply ingrained in us. I know that is true of myself and of most of the people I know.'[6] This feeling of 'badness' often led to prurience. When a newly married housewife proudly showed off her garden planted with all sorts of cheerful flowers, 'one old moth one day had the audacity to say to me: "One should not have a Madonna Lily so near a Red Hot Poker—it is vulgar."'[7]

Even jokes, the classic escape route for submerged thoughts, were not sexual in Ireland. Fr Biever was amazed to discover 'that the so-called dirty joke is not really connected with sex as such at all; rather it is scatological, bathroom humour, earthy, bawdy perhaps, but not obscene'. 'There was', as the egregious Oliver J. Flanagan pointed out, 'no sex in Ireland before the "Late Late Show".' Everyone knew what he meant. Actually by Ireland he meant the Republic. The Six Counties, where, as Angela MacNamara remarked, 'the instance of teenage immorality is so great', clearly partook of the atmosphere of pagan England.[8]

Not surprisingly there has been very little written about Irish sexual experience, at least until recently. Censorship thoroughly discouraged writers from addressing the question, and there was perhaps an awareness, especially in the absence of public discussion, that generalisations about sexual experience were not so much reliable statements of sociological fact as the expression of hopes or the venting of criticisms or attempts at propaganda. For generations the most vocal source of information about sex was the clergy. Having set the standards in the pulpit, they were in a unique position to discover (in the confessional) how far the rules were being kept. Since the pious and the scrupulous would be inclined to make much of normal sexual temptation, this process must have strongly reinforced an impression of a cauldron of illegitimate desire bubbling out of sight.

'I have never heard a priest talk about the beauty of marriage and the sex act', Fr Biever learnt. 'All we hear is that adultery and fornication and prostitution and illegitimate babies are bad, bad, bad! Nothing else seems to matter to them . . .' 'What are the chief dangers to chastity?', ran the *New Catechism*. 'The chief dangers to chastity are: idleness, intemperance, bad companions, improper dances, immodest dress, company-keeping and indecent conversation, books, plays and pictures.'[9] Company-keeping (by which was meant ordinary courting activities between man and woman) was apparently unqualifiedly bad, and the natural companion of indecent conversation. Books, plays and pictures, as such, were equally risky.

Mostly the Church was against sex, or at least taking pleasure in it. Sexual pleasure was associated with propagating the species; it was for the good of the species, not the individual. All direct, willed sexual pleasure was therefore, apart from legitimate matrimonial intercourse, intrinsically wrong, and an abuse of the order of nature.[10] The Church further took the view that marriages were made in heaven, and that any attempt to interfere with the process on earth was to be deplored.

The long attack on company-keeping and dancing went on throughout the de Valera era. Dancing was the moral equivalent of fornication, so zealous clergymen smashed dancing platforms, threw instruments into the ditch and roared condemnations from the pulpit. By the 1960s a more tolerant atmosphere had emerged: clergy had ceased to think of marriage as 'the shame-faced sacrament'. At Maynooth they laughed rather than fulminated at the story of a Galway priest who had noticed a young women from his parish sprawled on a beach wearing a very brief bikini. The priest sent the woman a note, asking her to wear a one-piece bathing suit. She returned a quick reply: 'Which piece do you want me to take off?'[11]

Dance-halls (the ballrooms of romance) sprang up all over the country. In many a country place the gaunt barn of the ballroom, which could often fit two or three thousand people, was the biggest building and the most profitable enterprise in the area. They were dominated by the new-style showbands, eight or ten musicians with set routines and neat suits who mostly played versions of the latest British and American pop songs. There were as many as 600 showbands, such as Dickie Rock and the Miami Showband, the Royal, and the Capitol Showband, plying the roads of Ireland. Huge crowds flocked to them night after night to hear songs written to appeal to Liverpool or small-town America.

Top of the list were the Beatles, then just hitting the first peak of their career (with 'Please, Please Me', 'She Loves You', 'I Wanna Hold Your Hand'). Others included Gerry and the Pacemakers ('How do you do it'), Adam Faith ('What do you Want'), Del Shannon ('Little Town Flirt'), Bobby Vee ('The Night has a Thousand Eyes') and the Beach Boys ('Surfin' USA'). Their lyrics were a long way from the Church's preferred style: 'I wanna be your lover, baby/I wanna be your man/ Love me like no other baby/like no other can', sang the Beatles. The dance-halls were regularly condemned, particularly for encouraging late hours, but they could not be stopped.

It was in 1963 that Michael O'Beirne bravely set up his matrimonial introduction agency in Ely Place. His first discovery was that none of the national newspapers would take his very discreet advertisements. To overcome this problem he visited the Catholic Welfare Bureau, and was gently but firmly discouraged. 'Life provides its own introductions', said the Monsignor, 'buying a packet of cigarettes is an introduction to the girl behind the counter.' This was not much consolation to the million or so unmarried people in the country at the time.

The most striking difficulty, O'Beirne believed, was the different expectations and aspirations between the sexes. The men were stuck in the country because of their farms, but the women wanted nothing of the drudgery their mothers had known. 'The average Irish woman', wrote O'Beirne, 'sees the average Irish man as under-educated, lacking in financial stability, deficient in ambition and initiative, careless and slovenly in dress and grooming. Their manners are boorish, and, to sum it all up the men are lacking in maturity . . . . [As a result] the women have left the country in their thousands, hurrying to the towns where they imagine all the supermen were to be found.'[12] In public of course these things were not said. When an article appeared in the Manchester *Guardian*, criticising Irish men, the normally cool and critical Brid Mahon leapt to their defence: 'we Irishwomen are quite pleased with our menfolk . . . they may not be madly demonstrative in public, but oddly enough we prefer privacy and loyalty . . . We do not consider ourselves downtrodden. The Church upholds the worth and dignity of a woman, and we don't lose out as a result, but then maybe we're old-fashioned enough to appreciate respect.'[13]

Among themselves the clergy discussed sexual and other matters in a peculiar and distancing jargon, shown in full flower in the pages of their 'trade journal', the *Irish Ecclesiastical Record*. For them, to make love to your spouse was 'use of marriage', kisses were *actus impudicitiae* (which might be *decenta*, but were probably not) and contraception was 'onanism'. This monthly journal was, as its masthead proudly proclaimed, published under Episcopal Sanction, and may therefore be taken as an authoritative statement of current views. An important part of the journal was the response to moral and technical questions sent in by readers. In the 1940s and 1950s this part of the journal was conducted by Canon McCarthy of Maynooth, who in 1960 published a two-volume collection of his answers to these queries.

'I have heard it stated', asks one of McCarthy's questioners, 'that the vast majority of modern dances are seriously immoral and suggestive, and therefore are to be regarded as a dangerous occasion of grave sin.' To which the Canon agreed that some modern dances, though not all, were seriously suggestive of sexual intercourse. On another occasion he was asked about the morality of kissing. He answered that 'indulgence in these acts will often be fraught with some danger, and they will therefore often be at least venially sinful'. The danger he had in mind was of course that of 'arousing or giving consent to venereal pleasure'—the slightest possibility of the latter was to be deplored. In a lengthy reply to Rusticus, the good Canon declares that 'the use of internal vaginal tampons can easily be a grave source of temptation . . . For this reason also their use must be regarded as morally suspect and indeed as definitely unlawful.' It is curious, and repellent, to imagine celibates up and down the country brooding thus about the morality of tampons.

Faced with this barrage, the Irish countryman, encouraged by his mother, retreated into the pub, from which he emerged only reluctantly. Sean O Faolain described a thirty-eight-year-old Irish countryman's approach to marriage 'Next September, or the September after, I will take a holiday with an object at Lisdoonvarna, County Clare. I will inform some of the priests on holiday that I am on the look-out, and that I am a bachelor of some substance who requires a wife with a dowry of a certain minimum figure. The good priests will pass the word around. In due course a girl will be selected and the wooing will proceed on a sane plane. At Christmas my people will visit her people, and her people will investigate my background, credentials and relatives. I will meet the young lady again on some such occasion as the Rugby International in Dublin the following Easter. In due course the nuptials will take place. If I marry at 40 on the lines I have indicated I will guarantee that at 60 my wife and myself will be fonder of one another than any couple of the same age who married in their youth for what Hollywood miscalls love, but which is in fact lustful infatuation.'[14]

The students at UCD lived in a different world to this ardent lover. They went on dates, did lines with particular friends, discussed love, marriage and kissing quite freely, both with boys and girls. 'Met J. and N. on the way to College', wrote a UCD student in her diary for 25 November 1963. She was then in her second year studying economics. 'We were discussing boys and girls, etc. They asked me did I ever turn down invitations. Said yes. They were horrified. "Some poor guy after weeks of effort finally works up enough courage to ask you out and then you turn him down!" I was saying how different it was for girls. You have a good run maybe going out with 3 or 4 different boys at the same time (they thought this was fantastic) and then there might be a month where you'd be going out with nobody. N. said there was always someone keen on you and all you had to do was to be extra nice to him—give him a big smile etc.'

More intimate details were for girl-talk only: 'coffee in the DBC with S., who was looking for advice on what to do when boys make advances. Personally I think it is quite alright to kiss a boy when you're keen on him. S. was being very vague . . . she gave me the impression that I was awful even to contemplate kissing someone before I was engaged to him.' The next day she meets another friend for lunch in the Annexe in UCD. 'J. said she had done it [that is, kissing] with V. . . . was amazed, but realise we can talk really frankly, which is great.'[15]

This was not a climate in which people knew or talked much of sex—Angela MacNamara believed that eighty per cent of the young girls who wrote to her would not even mention the word to their mothers. Many a middle-class girl, as a result, was shocked and terrified by her first period. Children grew to maturity with only the vaguest ideas of their own physiology, let alone that of the opposite sex. Angela MacNamara, who was just starting her long career as an adviser in these matters, noted that when she offered to write a series of articles for a popular newspaper, the editor told her that 'Ireland is not yet ready for the frank, open approach . . . the word "womb" is considered objectionable by some.'[16] Many a doctor treated with gentle

Meeting the opposite sex: (*top*) Twistin' the night away at the Hunt Ball; (*right*) 'Getting a bar', or perhaps more safely a ride on the back of a moped

advice childless couples who had been concentrating on the navel or other areas for insemination. Even the well educated could be surprisingly ignorant: Sean O Faolain in his autobiography, *Vive Moi!*, recalls how when at University College Cork in the 1920s, he wrote a poem with a line about 'Mother Ireland's teeming navel', and was put right—with a few skilful anatomical drawings—by a medical student friend.

F. X. Carty, who had entered the Holy Ghost Seminary after Blackrock in the late 1950s, remembered 'it was only when I already had taken a vow of chastity for three years and was preparing to take it for life that it dawned on me that there was such a thing as sexual intercourse . . . I had always imagined that men and women went to bed together and fell asleep and that eventually God, if he so willed it, sent them a child.' He was twenty-one at the time. With some embarrassment he consulted an older priest, who assured him that 'in humans it normally took place as in monkeys'.[17]

Once the dangers of the company-keeping period were over, there was marriage itself. 'Christian love, including sexual love, must be virginal', wrote one magazine author. 'The essence of virginity does not consist merely in abstention from sexual intercourse . . . If our love here (including married love) is based on faith, it is already in substance the virginal love of the life to come.'[18] Marriage, wrote Canon McCarthy, had 'as its primary purpose, not the personal perfection of the parties, but the procreation and education of offspring'. Anything which interfered with that purpose was anathema. Even 'to confine the use of marriage to the sterile days and thus avoid offspring' was doubtfully legitimate. The purpose of marriage was, after all, to fill first the churches and then heaven with new souls. The clergy themselves had, of course, left this duty to others, without much reluctance if the marriage rate of their brothers and sisters is a guide, and embraced the comfort, respect and security of the Irish priest's celibate life. No doubt they were aware, at least unconsciously, that a full church was as good as a pension to them.

Priests were advised not to make knowledge of the rhythm method widespread: 'indiscriminate diffusion of knowledge of the "safe period" could easily lead to its indiscriminate use—a situation fraught with calamitous social consequences'.[19] Other forms of contraception were, of course, grave sins. The use of condoms (always called 'artificial onanism') was nearly as bad as sodomy, and should be resisted by the wife as violently as 'a virgin would resist rape'. Only grave reasons such as 'the serious threat of desertion, cruelty, adultery, non-Catholic education of children would . . . justify a wife in co-operating materially with an act of natural onanism'. Despite this, in practice, *coitus interruptus*, combined with the rhythm method and stout-induced incapacity, were the only widespread contraceptive techniques.

In the urban Ireland of the 1960s matters were somewhat different, though not all that different. The Church's views of sex were not unpopular. Nor was it, despite what more worldly Continental churches might do, without warrant. Did not St Paul write, 'It is good for a man not to touch a woman . . .' (1 Cor 7)—did not a leader of the early Church suggest that Christians should allow the bishops to arrange their marriages, so that they might be 'according to the Lord, and not according to lust'?[20] Four-fifths of Fr Biever's sample rejected the idea that the Church's views on sex were out of date. For the young Bunny Carr, despite great theoretical interest in women: 'It never occurred to us actually, really, to sleep with a girl . . . Hell was real and sex was its close bedfellow.'[21] Not everyone was quite so innocent.

Rare flashes of anecdotal evidence, like lightning in a night sky, suggest the existence of an unofficial sexual world. In March 1963 it was reported that six dead babies had been abandoned in various parts of Dublin in recent months.[22] In his autobiography Bob Geldof remembers his school-days in the mid-sixties, and describes watching a woman masturbating in a shelter of the sea-wall, and how Mrs Armstrong from down the road seduced him at the age of thirteen. His schoolboy friends at Blackrock boasted to each other, as explicitly and as truthfully as soldiers, about their sexual exploits with the local girls after the dances at the Stella.[23] At the Church of Ireland Synod, a speaker deplored this attitude. 'If premarital sex relations were to be treated as a source of pleasure . . . the stability of married life would be undermined. Men looking for wives', he warned, 'are not looking for soiled goods, a fact that young girls should keep in mind.'[24]

Other types of sexual experience are even less documented. Most women certainly encountered sexual harassment, if only a fumbling self-exposure on the banks of the Dodder. There were also unknown quantities of incest and child-abuse: June Levine describes a sickening encounter in her childhood with a white-headed old neighbour who had a grand, Protestant accent. One day he put his hands into the pockets of her dress and rubbed her budding breasts: '"Nice little pocket", he said, and I felt very strange . . .'[25] Joyce, Kavanagh, O Faolain and McGahern all describe boyhood sexual encounters with men. Who can say how much more of this, and worse, there was?

Homosexuality was simply never mentioned. Typically, it was from the BBC that David Norris discovered the existence of other gays.

Then he became aware of 'hints of a dark subterranean world populated by balding old men, who were probably alcoholics, lived in greasy raincoats, hung around public lavatories, or the Phoenix Park, and tried to lure small boys into bushes with Smarties'.[26] In the late 1930s the historian, Richard Cobb, then twenty-one, went, as he thought, for a walk with Brendan, an eighteen-year-old Garda, handsome, with fair curly hair, very bright eyes and a rather beautiful figure. They marched purposefully along Killiney Hill (Brendan crossing himself piously as they passed a church). Eventually they reached a secluded spot, where to Cobb's embarrassment, Brendan got down to business. 'Was I not a *fairy*, too', he asked. Cobb, heterosexual by inclination, was, like most of his contemporaries, completely inexperienced. He now found himself about to start his sexual life with an unknown Irish policeman on the top of a cliff. He demurred, and offered the policeman £5 for his trouble. This was accepted in a way which led Cobb to believe that the handsome Brendan was in the habit of receiving tips for services of this sort.[27] Can Austin Clarke be right when he suggests that the closing down of the brothels of the Monto in the early 1920s led to 'several serious outbreaks of what used to be called unnatural vice'?[28]

Although the Church's most spectacular (and lovingly reported) denunciations related to sex, this subject by no means exhausted its practical moral concerns. McCarthy's *Problems in Theology*, for example, contains 1,000 pages in two volumes, of which only 160 are about sexual matters. The rest deal with an enormous range of issues, from suicide to the duties of landladies, from the legitimacy of the hydrogen bomb to the obligation to respect the legal price of tea, and from the morality of strikes, boycotts or smuggling to the payment of betting debts—the whole range of social and moral problems thrown up by Irish society in the 1940s and 1950s. It is particularly interesting to see the interplay between moral and economic imperatives. For instance, when asked about the custom of saving hay on Sundays, the answer is: Saving of hay is clearly servile work, and therefore forbidden. There is no such general custom allowing it always in Ireland. However, the farmer may be excused in broken weather, since otherwise loss or injury to the crop may be suffered. Ideally the parish priest would announce a general excusation from the pulpit.

The question always is: what precisely is the law? The law referred to was not the law of the state, but the universal God-given moral law promulgated by the Catholic Church. So calmly does McCarthy discuss the problems that it is difficult sometimes to remember that when he designates an offence as 'grave', what he literally means is that, unless expiated, this sin condemns the sinner to the eternal punishment of unquenchable fire, where the worm does not die and the fire is not extinguished (Mk. 9: 44–5).[29]

Although the individual judgment of conscience was important, in the end there were many activities, ranging from solitary sexual sin to murder, and from depriving one of the necessities of life to fraudulent bankruptcy, that were absolutely forbidden. Since the calculus was so obscure (literally, as most of the treatises were in Latin), and the stakes so high, it was always better to err on the safe side. As a result the boundaries of the sinful constantly tended to expand to a bizarre scrupulosity, unleavened by common sense. Many priests claimed, for instance, that it was a mortal sin for a young man to be in a lonely place with a girl. Tender consciences worried about whether it was a sin to knit or sew on Sundays, or to swallow a mite of water (while washing one's teeth) before communion. There was a satisfaction in this too, not only in the comfort and security of a known moral code, but also, for some, the intellectual satisfaction of discussing cases.

One was subject first to God's law, and then, if not contradictory, to the state's law. The best-known example of this was where the seal of the confessional overrode the civil duty not to act as an accessory after a crime. The authority of the Oireachtas and the political system in general cannot have been enhanced by this belief. Since the 'real' law came from a different system, perhaps it is not surprising that politicians sank to being messenger-boys bearing benefits.

Questions posed to the *Irish Ecclesiastical Record* by its wide readership ranged from the trivial to the grave. They very often appear to have arisen in the confessional or in discussion groups of local clergy. For instance (both questions and answers have been considerably abbreviated):

Question: How much do you have to steal to make the matter grave (i.e. a mortal rather than a venial sin)?

Answer: The question is complicated by the rising cost of living: in 1877 £1 was regarded as grave; by 1914 that standard had risen to £2, which would lead to the conclusion that for a working man, the absolute level now is probably about £8 or £9, or one week's wages.

Question: To get a job in a Protestant factory, may a Catholic applicant claim to have gone to a non-Catholic school?

Answer: If the school took only non-Catholic pupils, this amounts to an implicit denial of the true Faith, and is gravely wrong. However, since the appointment board has no right to intrude its bigotry and make religion an issue in appointments, the applicant may make an evasive answer that would conceal his faith and so deceive the board.

Question: May a priest urge the boycotting of non-Catholic traders?

Answer: Yes, assuming the boycott is for a morally good purpose. Catholics who combine in this way do not infringe any right of non-Catholic merchants . . . 'There is no obligation, even in charity, to confer an advantage or benefit on one's neighbour unless he is in some degree of grave need.'

Question: May Catholics vote for non-Christian (i.e. Jewish) candidates? [This question was asked in 1948.]

Answer: It is not desirable, but not unlawful to do so, providing the Jew agrees to act in accordance with Christian principles.

Question: As a means of protecting our young people from moral dangers (mixed marriages, etc.), it is thought that the emigration of girls under 21 should be forbidden by the State.

Answer: This would be morally inadmissible. 'For the sake of our Christian heritage, let us . . . resist, with all our vigour, any attempt of the State to intrude itself into the inviolable sphere of natural parental and individual rights.'

Underlying all McCarthy's answers there was a profound and arrogant certainty that the Church was right, and that the moral arithmetic developed during the Counter-Reformation had the answers. He was asked: Is it lawful that a Protestant minister, a Jewish rabbi and a Catholic priest appear on the same platform in Ireland as they have done in America? His answer was unequivocal. 'We Catholics cannot forget that truth is one, and that we have the truth. We cannot tolerate any doctrine other than our own, for such doctrine is false . . . We cannot see any appreciable advantages would result to the Catholic cause in a country like our own.'

Chapter Sixteen

The Nice Man Cometh

THE new note of the sixties was youth. The children of the post-war baby boom in the western world came bumptiously into their own, demanding new services and products. Entrepreneurs, from record companies to clothes manufacturers, tumbled over themselves to supply this market. For the first time to be young was not a sign of unstable immaturity, but a positive value. Fashions became informal; young designers fresh from art college, such as Mary Quant, made clothes they themselves liked to wear, and the fiercely expensive fashions of Paris took a back seat. Even in Ireland this was felt. At Lady's Day at Punchestown *The Irish Times* noticed that 'informality rather than high fashion was the keynote . . . one of the most interesting evolutions over the last two or three years is the equalising of fashion'.

The country's bestselling newspaper, the *Sunday Press*, regularly reported the doings of UCD's *jeunesse dorée* at the L & H. People who have since made their mark in Ireland were getting their first airing in the newspapers: there was Liam Hourican facetiously regretting de Valera's departure from the Dáil on the grounds that speeches were now dull and boring. There was Anthony Clare in a debate on the motion that the government and the leading opposition parties were becoming increasingly contemptible to the Irish people, complaining that politicians thought students cynical but never bother to ask why. More serious politicians such as Gerry Collins were getting their hands dirty organising the students' union.

In general, politics was in the hands of the old men whose original claims had been staked between 1916 and 1922. Although Lemass's Government contained the 'men in mohair suits', O'Malley, Lenihan and Haughey, who were in their thirties, their attitudes were not exactly youthful. 'I am not one of those', remarked Mr Haughey (aged 38), 'who think that the young of today are to be despaired of . . .'[1] By contrast, a large part of President Kennedy's attraction for so many people was that he was young: a mere 45. 'To the rest of us who still have old men at the top', wrote Mary Holland in *Vogue*, Kennedy's 'youth, vitality and firecracker energy made them seem like tired

Victorians.'[2] His wife Jacqueline also brought a whole new style and fashion consciousness to the White House. She wore bouffant hair-dos and tight-fitting tailored Pucci trousers. She had once won a People I Wish I Had Known contest by naming Baudelaire, Oscar Wilde and Diaghilev. It was difficult to imagine Mrs Eisenhower, Mrs Macmillan or Mrs Lemass coming up with these names.

The tense moments of the Cuba crisis, when it had seemed that nuclear war was imminent, had given the world a new view of John F. Kennedy. Not only was he young and photogenic, with a fine line in rhetoric (his declaration 'Ask not what your country can do for you, but what you can do for your country', thrilled more than American hearts), he was also a defender of the Free World—Gary Cooper in 'High Noon', played with real guns. In October 1962 the world had come very near to realising the worst fears of the nuclear doomwatchers.

At this time Russia had 300 strategic nuclear warheads as against 5,000 owned by the United States.[3] The Russian leaders under Khrushchev, basing their opinions on the Bay of Pigs disaster, decided that the American president was weak, and an important geographical advantage could be wrested from him. Over a period of weeks they stealthily built up an arsenal of missiles in Cuba, a mere hundred miles from the coast of Florida. These weapons could destroy any US city they chose in minutes.

Although US bases in Turkey were in a similar position in respect to the USSR, the American military were appalled when this build-up was suddenly revealed. Kennedy was faced with five options: to do nothing; to invade Cuba; to bomb the installations; to deliver an ultimatum to Russia and hope they would withdraw; to blockade the island. He chose the last.

On 23 October *The Irish Times* reported a grim-faced Kennedy's announcement that the US regarded the Russian activity in Cuba as unfriendly and a violation of the status quo. None of the ships then carrying military equipment towards Cuba would be allowed near the island. He called on Chairman Khrushchev 'to halt and eliminate this clandestine, reckless and provocative threat to world peace . . .' Twenty thousand US troops and forty ships, mobilised with remarkable speed, began to exercise in the Caribbean. A US newspaper headline ran 'Capitol preparing public opinion for possibility of war.' On 24 October the Russians announced that if the Americans sank any of their fleet of ships then moving to Cuba, 'there would be war. If interfered with, the USSR would deliver a most powerful answering blow.' Red armies were put on the highest state of alert.

The Soviet ships moved steadily towards Cuba. On 24 October American's NATO allies backed the US blockade. That weekend the Irish Civil Defence laid on a survival demonstration. Twenty-six volunteers built impromptu ovens out of dustbin lids and bricks. They then cooked and served 'potato and onion soup, roast shoulder of lamb, peas and potatoes, apple tart and custard, and tea' to guests. 'The project', wrote *The Irish Times*, 'demonstrated how expert these people have become at making improvised kitchens from all kinds of scrap materials and producing hot meals on a large scale without any fuss.'[4] In Tipperary a local councillor refused to vote for any increase in the civil defence budget on the grounds that 'we are anticipating something that will never happen', and that even if there were a big explosion anywhere in the world, 'it wouldn't affect us for a thousand years'.

Not everyone believed this. As tension mounted, with the American ships surrounding the island, and the Soviets steaming slowly towards it, confessionals throughout the country did record business. Many people felt that the world was nearer war than at any time since 1939. In Dublin Noel Browne and fifty other demonstrators were for appeasement, chanting 'No War, Mr Kennedy' and 'Hands off Cuba' outside the US Embassy (there being no USSR embassy in Ireland at the time). The police quite unnecessarily set dogs on them, and Browne lost some buttons. Other demonstrators were more seriously bitten. Always a favourite of the newspapers, Browne successfully turned public attention from a world crisis to the state of his overcoat.

Still the Soviet ships moved steadily towards the awaiting cordon. In the UN, Frank Aiken, Minister for Foreign Affairs, shrewdly asked 'why it should have been regarded as wise and prudent in the present state of world affairs to establish new military installations of this striking power in a small country in such close proximity to the American continent?' The Department of Local Government carried out tests on the possible effects of radioactive fall-out on water and sewage systems. The well-known British anti-nuclear campaigner, Pat Arrowsmith, arrived in Ireland with a friend to escape the coming war.

In the end, after several days of tension, the Soviet ships peeled away from their course and returned to harbour. Khrushchev announced the withdrawal of the missiles. The world relaxed, noting an increased respect for President Kennedy's nerve. The headlines went back to reporting the Chinese invasion of Tibet and Kashmir. This, as a letter writer to *The Irish Times* pointed out, had not stimulated any protest from Noel Browne. To be fair, the full horrors of the internal regime in

China were yet to be discovered by the world. Mao was to remain a hero to fashionable radicals for some years.

The Irish view of Kennedy was wholly approving. It was not always very knowledgeable. In a comment after his visit to Ireland in June 1963 *Hibernia* wrote in its July issue: 'Whatever hostile historians may do to the political record of John Kennedy, his status as the model head of a perfectly natural family is above assault. Kennedy's impregnable personal position, buttressed by private wealth and a truly Christian family life is of prime value to the nation he leads . . .' His visit gave a tremendous boost to national self-confidence. Here after all was one of our own who had 'fled from the famine-ravaged potato fields' to achieve the most powerful office on earth. He gave a kind of presidential seal of approval to the nation's new look, and incidentally put the old enemy in its place. Reviewing a just-published book, *The Great Hunger*, John Connell wrote: 'from the embattled Kennedys and Fitzgeralds and Curleys would one day spring a President of the United States who would be the leader of the Western world and who would spell out in a friendly way the end of Britain as a great Power. It would be a foolish Irishman who will rejoice at the eclipse of Britain in this age; our economies are too closely linked. But he would be a poor Irishman also who did not recognise that we have in us the power to be a greater people . . . truly the Irish are a great people. We are a great people, for within one hundred years of this appalling Famine we came back strong enough to challenge a great empire and win.'[5]

During his three-day stay, Kennedy visited Dublin, Wexford, Cork, Limerick and Galway. At every stage there was a curious compound of large measures of rhetoric with equally large measures of affection on both sides. His visit was a great excuse for a party: 'off to Clonliffe Road to see Kennedy', wrote one diarist. 'Scrumptious tea laid out and almost entire family there . . . Flags waving, music over loudspeakers, we all got up on the wall . . . the President arrived at last, looking young and fit and bronzed, smiling. Buses and cars full of security and press men all American looking.'[6] (This was Kennedy's fourth visit to Ireland. On his previous visit in 1957, just three years before he became President, Jacqueline Kennedy rang the *Irish Independent* from the Shelbourne to offer an interview, but the journalist decided to take the details over the telephone. It was Sunday, as he said, and 'three fellows are waiting for me on the golf course . . .'[7])

Kennedy himself seemed genuinely to enjoy the visit, perhaps because in Ireland he could get away for a time from the enormous

The Kennedy visit: (*top*) at home with his cousins in Wexford; (*bottom*) the ecstatic welcome in O'Connell Street

problems he was facing. He had left an America that was on the brink of racial explosion. Led by Martin Luther King, Blacks had begun to assert their right to eat at downtown lunch counters, to ride on buses, to go to university, to vote. As King fought his battle of wits and courage against the dogs and fire hoses of police chief Eugene 'Bull' Connor in Birmingham, Alabama, many were waiting for New York, Chicago, Philadelphia and other cities to explode with riots. Just before his arrival in Dublin, Kennedy had been in Berlin, the most sensitive theatre of the Cold War.

On his arrival at Dublin, he was greeted with no such tensions. De Valera addressed him in Irish, 'our native language, the language of your ancestors, the language that was spoken by the great Kennedy clan of the Dal gChais who, under the mighty King Brian Boru, smashed the invader and broke the Norse power for ever . . .' Kennedy himself played vigorously to this audience, reaching back to a rhetoric that had in many Irish ears begun to sound a little hollow. In his speech to the Oireachtas he spoke glowingly of Irish progress and rising living standards. 'Other nations in the world in whom Ireland has long invested her people and her children are now investing their capital as well as their vacations in Ireland . . . this revolution is not over yet.'[8] The description of a hundred and fifty years of Irish emigration as the nation 'investing her people' was certainly tactful.

In Wexford he was shown 'documentary proof of the rebel blood of his ancestors'. These were the prison records of a distant cousin who once spent two months in hard labour in Wexford Jail in 1888 for resisting arrest and obstructing the sheriff. As the *Sunday Press* put it, 'the hatred of oppression, the belief in the God-given freedom of man that are so much a characteristic of President Kennedy may have come down from the rebel blood which coursed through the veins of his ancestor James Kennedy who preferred jail to submission to an injustice'. At Galway the Mayor spoke his words of welcome entirely in Irish and Kennedy matched the moment. He 'rounded off his address by telling the crowd that if they ever went to Washington and told the man at the gate that they were from Galway, there would be a Cead Mile Failte for them'.

After the visit was over, Patrick O'Donovan wrote in the *Observer* that 'in Irish history this was the first wholly satisfactory act of nationhood. All of the others, even to the gaining of independence, have been compromises and less than the best that was available. This, with a Catholic president from the Irish diaspora singing her praises and taking time off from the brutal realities of power, was the real thing . . .

Ireland never showed herself to greater advantage, never demonstrated more clearly her individuality and maturity, and there was not a trace of shamrockery in sight.'[9]

Some showed greater maturity than others. On his return from New Ross, where his distant cousins had given him tea and cake in a smiling and informal atmosphere, there was a Garden Party in Aras an Uachtaráin. Two thousand had been invited, and for weeks beforehand fashion writers had been worrying about What To Wear. Simple, well-tailored clothes recommended one, no chiffon or silks. Hats were essential—by 26 June a leading milliner reported that she hadn't a hat left in the shop, everything from thirty shillings to thirty guineas had walked out of the door.

On the big day, ministers' wives favoured chic blue and white, and wild silk two-piece suits were also popular. Since it rained, the most useful accessory spotted by fashion writer Ida Grehan was a plastic parasol decorated with bright red flowers. When the President came out of the Aras, the guests surged forward. An obviously distraught de Valera tried to motion the pressing crowd back with his hands, but to little avail. 'Especially the elegantly dressed women wanted to shake hands with the smiling young president', wrote *The Irish Times* reporter. 'Toes were trampled on, high heels sank into the lawn, shoes were lost, beautiful hats were crumpled, guests fell over chairs . . . all the while Kennedy shook as many of the grasping hands as possible, including the white gloved hand of a woman who shouted and waved frantically over the heaving shoulders of the security men. "Jack, Jack, my hand, shake my hand!" When he did she turned away and adjusted her hat, expressing utter satisfaction to her friends and the others on whom she had trampled.'

Politely ignoring this display by the great and the good of the nation, the *Sunday Press* summed up the visit positively, 'In three short days this young man of destiny, great grandson of an Irish emigrant and leader of a mighty nation had written his own footnote in our history. He has given us a new pride in our heritage, won his way into our hearts and touched the very core of our being by honouring our patriot dead. They were three days of crowded incident, of welcome, of civic function and national honour for this boyish-looking statesman. But for the Irish people who gave their hearts it was a mighty period of burning pride, affection and esteem. . . For many the most lasting memory of President Kennedy will be his moments with the little schoolgirls outside the Ryan homestead. Watching their shyness melt away and seeing them whisper excitedly into his ear was a heartstopping business.'

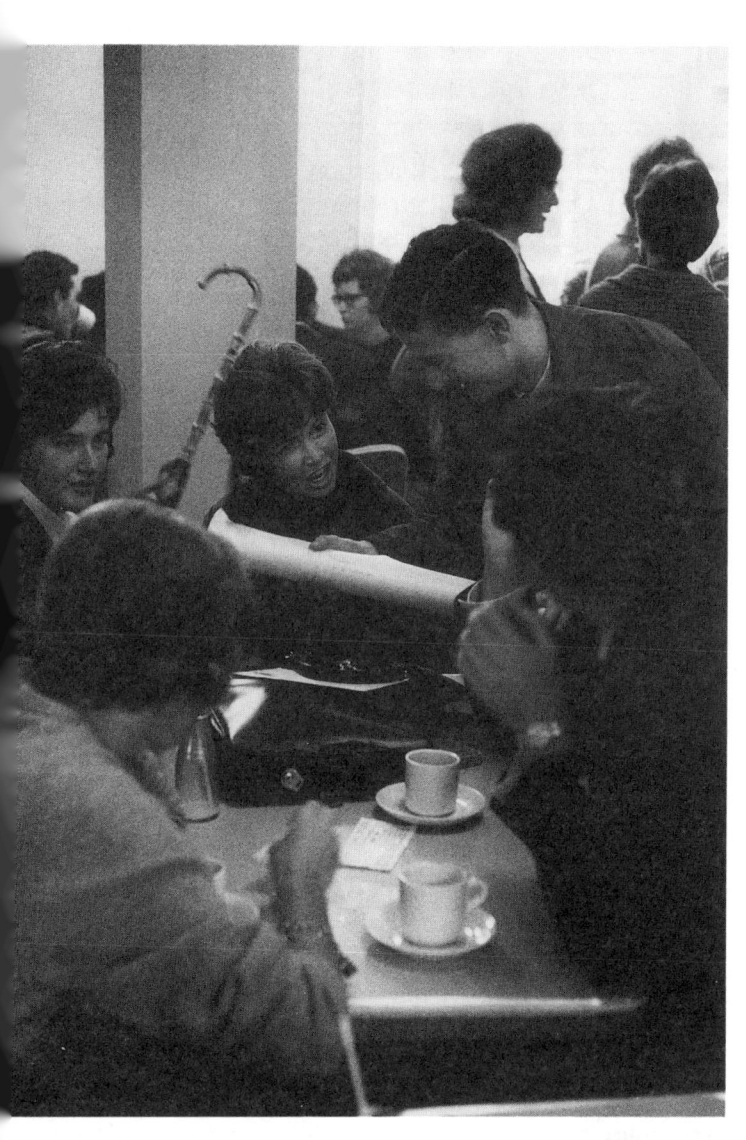

Below. 'Jack, Jack, my hand, shake my hand.' Kennedy, who was no doubt familiar with such scenes, and de Valera, who was not, being mobbed by the great and the good
Left. Lively argument in the UCD Annexe in the basement of Earlsfort Terrace

Kennedy left promising to come back as soon as possible. But five months later he was dead. On Friday 22 November, in Dallas, Texas, he was assassinated—an act that broke the sixties in two. The shock was felt across the world, but nowhere so deeply as in Ireland. One diarist records fulfilling a theatre engagement ('A Man for All Seasons'), but leaving at the interval: 'I was shocked all through.' And on Saturday only the one-line entry, 'still dreadfully upset by Kennedy'; on Sunday 'watched news on TV all day. Dead hopeless feeling. B. rang, but I didn't go out.'[10] Many sports fixtures were cancelled on the Saturday, and normal Saturday night activities came to a standstill. In a letter to an American diplomat friend, Garret FitzGerald summed up his feelings and those of most Irish people:

> I wanted to say simply how shattered we are at Kennedy's death. No one here realised how much he meant to us until he died. All have felt a sense of loss that normally arises only on the death of some near relative.
> For once Irish cynicism was silent, and even the most hardbitten Dubliners have been moved. Had you been here I think you would have been moved yourself at the reaction of the whole Irish people to this tragedy. Even now, a week later, we have not recovered. Many people have indeed been physically shaken by the news. The priest in All Hallows who is a friend of Jacqueline Kennedy's suffered a stroke on hearing the news—a mild one fortunately—and our doctor told us that he had had an abnormally busy weekend because of the number of people who were physically affected by the emotional shock.
> The whole affair was handled by the papers and especially by the radio and television in a manner that could not be faulted. The radio and television service suspended their normal programmes within minutes of the news and mounted a special programme culminating in a tribute by de Valera. The funeral was transmitted on both channels with of course the Telstar relay. Michael O'Hehir did an excellent commentary and Sean Egan's broadcasts from Washington were most moving.

During Kennedy's visit in June he had attended a ceremony at Arbour Hill, and had been deeply impressed by the drilling of the army cadets. In a gesture that went instantly to all Irish hearts, Jacqueline Kennedy requested the presence of a contingent of Irish cadets at the funeral. Twenty-four cadets, in superfine Army cadet uniform, complete with white epaulettes, white cap bands and FN rifles, went. Thus by proxy the Irish people attended the funeral. 'You can imagine', continued Garret FitzGerald, 'that the request for the presence of the cadets was well received here. This gesture meant much to us all and seemed an appropriate culmination to the work that Kennedy had done to build up Ireland and to add to its stature as a nation.

I am more than ever glad that I had the opportunity of being in the Dáil that day to hear him speak, and that I brought the children to see him passing by. This letter does not express my feelings because they cannot readily be put on paper. I felt simply that I must try to convey something of the feelings that have submerged us here in Ireland since last Friday night . . .'[11]

The day of the funeral, Tuesday 26 November, was virtually a national day of mourning: 30,000 civil servants received special leave to attend masses for the repose of his soul. A wave of sorrow swept the country. Many public engagements were cancelled. Student life, however, could not be repressed so easily. 'Commerce party out in Portmarnock', recorded Anna Boylan. 'M. gave me a lift out . . . N. a bit drunk, very talkative, danced . . . home with M., talking about Kennedy.'[12] Kennedy's murder was a national emotional experience, comparable to the death in 1960 of nine soldiers in the Congo on a UN mission, or, at the other end of the decade, Bloody Sunday in Derry. The death during the year of the much-loved Pope John was hardly felt by comparison.

Ireland, however, soon went back to the heady business of increasing the size of the economic cake. The economy was driven more and more by urban industrial concerns as the flight from the land continued. Over the twenty years or so following 1963, de Valera's idyll of rural Ireland finally dissolved. For the first time in history, one commentator has written, the Irish farmers' attachment to the land was broken. They began to measure their lives against those available elsewhere, and found them wanting.[13] Thirty years of Fianna Fáil rule had done what neither Cromwell nor the Famine could achieve. Country people lost their self-confidence and became defensive. As the farmers sat gloomily in the pubs, their wives and daughters read magazines and watched 'the box', sucking in urban aspirations, urban attitudes and urban values. Extraordinarily outspoken discussions of religion, sex and politics went on, without thunderbolts striking anyone.

The shock when Brian Trevaskis called a bishop a moron on live television later in the decade is still remembered. British and American programmes showed different ways of living with a new vividness. With the aid of television, the aspirations of the Dublin middle classes were to become (with some lags) the aspirations of the country as a whole. In the past, urban children had learnt Irish through tales of reaping and sowing, harrowing and winnowing. Now country children were to learn the language through images of pop stars, boxing matches and housing estates.

Very little thought was given to how the newly enlarged cake might be divided. Most subscribed to Lemass's comfortable dictum that a rising tide lifts all boats. Lemass himself, however, did not believe that this was the whole story. In a speech in May 1963 he said there was growing evidence that 'all have benefited in some degree [from economic success] . . . but that inequalities and distortions have emerged or widened is also true. It should be possible for a Christian nation . . . to develop methods of sharing the benefits of better living which economic progress makes realisable . . . This now in my view is the main issue of public policy arising in this country for settlement at this time . . . such a system would necessarily involve a willingness on the part of all sections to rely less on their own economic strength and bargaining power and more on the objective judgment of the institutions set up to help in carrying out this policy . . .'[14]

The advancing Catholic urban middle class saw such remarks as addressed not to them, but to the trade unions, which no doubt they were. However the audience to whom this speech was given (the National Convention of Junior Chambers of Commerce) suggests that Lemass may have had a wider target in mind. The middle class ignored this possibility and quietly got on with the business of amassing position, control and finally wealth. Distractions such as culture, religion or political philosophy were minimised.

They have achieved considerable success. As the Introduction to this book put it: 'nearly half of national income goes to the top-earning twenty per cent of the population; five per cent of the population own nearly two-thirds of the wealth . . . the middle classes have an unfair share of many state benefits, especially education and health care'.

There is still, thirty years after Lemass's speech, a question to be answered as to whether we have found the best, or even a satisfactory, method of dividing the product of the national labour.

Notes

Introduction (pp. 1–4)
1. B. Inglis, *West Briton*, (London 1962), 26—the list is based on one in T. de Vere White, *A Fretful Midge*, (London 1957), 11.
2. *Freeman's Journal*, 17 March 1907.
3. Democratic Programme of the First Dáil, quoted in Chubb, *Source Book of Irish Government*, revised ed, (Dublin 1983), 27–8; Fianna Fáil, *Coru agus Rialacha*, (1972), quoted in Chubb, *Source Book of Irish Government*, 133.
4. Michel Peillon, 'Stratification and Class' in P. Clancy *et al*, *Ireland—A Sociological Profile*, (Dublin 1986), 97–115.

Chapter 1 (pp. 7–18)
1. Tape-recorded reminiscences of Andrew Fayle of Orwell Park, by courtesy of Peter Costello.
2. See, for insance, the speech by John Redmond to the United Irish League National Assembly in Wicklow, reported in *Freeman's Journal*, 30 September 1907.
3. H. Robinson, *Memories: Wise and Otherwise*, (London 1924), 224.
4. H. Robinson, *Memories: Wise and Otherwise*, 148–9.
5. P.L. Dickinson, *The Dublin of Yesterday*, (London 1929), 14.
6. *Freeman's Journal*, 8 May 1907.
7. A generation before Matthew Arnold had noted, 'How often it happens in England that a cultivated person . . . talking to one of the lower classes . . . feels, and cannot but feel, that there is a wall of partition between himself and the other; that they seem to belong to different worlds. Thoughts, feelings, perceptions, susceptibilities, language, manners—everything is different.' M. Arnold, 'Equality' in Noel Annan ed, *Selected Essays*, (Oxford 1964), 198, 203.
8. N. Robertson, *Crowned Harp*, (Dublin 1960), 24.
9. *The Leader*, 2 March 1907.
10. N. Robertson, *Crowned Harp*, 74–5.
11. *The Leader*, 2 March 1907.
12. M.B. Pearse ed, *The Home Life of Padraig Pearse*, 2nd ed, (Cork 1979), 106.
13. C.S. Andrews, *Dublin Made Me*, (Cork 1979), 10–12.
14. Beatrice Lady Glenavy, *Today we will only gossip*, (London 1964), 13.
15. J.V. O'Brien, *Dear Dirty Dublin*, (California 1982), 40.
16. K. Kennedy *et al*, *The Economic Development of Ireland in the Twentieth Century*, (London 1988), 14.

17. *The Statist*, April 1907.
18. W. Bulfin, *Rambles in Eirinn*, 2nd ed, (Dublin 1912), 368.
19. J.V. O'Brien, *Dear Dirty Dublin*, 193.
20. P.L. Dickinson, *The Dublin of Yesterday*, 1.
21. H. Sutherland, *Ireland Yesterday and Today*, (Philadelphia 1909), 108.

Chapter 2 (pp. 19–33)
1. P.L. Dickinson, *The Dublin of Yesterday*, 76.
2. Sir C. Cameron, *Reminiscences*, (Dublin 1913), 166–72.
3. P.L. Dickinson, *The Dublin of Yesterday*, 76.
4. M. Daly, *Dublin—The Deposed Capital 1860–1914*, (Cork 1984), paperback ed 1985, chaps 1 & 2.
5. R. Barry O'Brien, *Dublin Castle and the Irish People*, (London 1909), 385–401.
6. *Royal Commission on Trinity College Dublin*, Appendix to First Report, (Dublin 1906), 11–18.
7. M. McCarthy, *Five Years in Ireland*, (London and Dublin 1901), 336; UCD Fellows, 282.
8. *A Century of Service*, A History of St Vincent's, (Dublin 1934), 84.
9. G. Birmingham, *The Search Party*, originally published 1909, 16th printing, (London 1918), 15.
10. R. Barry O'Brien, *Dublin Castle and the Irish People*, 387.
11. L. Cullen, *Eason & Son—A History*, (Dublin 1989), 286–93.
12. T. Farmar, *The Legendary, Lofty, Clattery Café*, (Dublin 1988), 29–30; *Irish Independent*, 2 December 1932.
13. M. Daly, *Dublin—The Deposed Capital*, 130.
14. C.S. Andrews, *Dublin Made Me*, (Cork 1979), 35.
15. C.S. Andrews, *Dublin Made Me*, 24.
16. P. Costello, *Dublin Churches*, (Dublin 1989), 124.
17. *Consumption and Cost of Food for Workingmen's Families in UK Urban Districts*, (1905), Cd 2337, lxxxiv, 25.
18. (Dublin 1905), 10. This little book was reprinted in 1906, 1908, 1910 and 1913.
19. C.S. Peel, *How to Keep House*, (London 1902), 57.
20. J.V. O'Brien, *Dear, Dirty Dublin*, (California 1982), 122–4.
21. A. Clarke, *Twice Round the Black Church*, (London 1962), 35.
22. C.S. Andrews, *Dublin Made Me*, 42.
23. E. Bowen, *Seven Winters*, (London 1943), 21.
24. Beatrice Lavery's grandmother did hers, at least while she was a girl. Beatrice Lady Glenavy, *Today We will only Gossip*, (London 1964), 20.
25. W. Bulfin, *Rambles in Eirinn*, (Dublin 1907), 63.
26. A. Clarke, *Twice Round the Black Church*, 114.
27. *Freeman's Journal*, 14 December 1907.
28. *ibid*, 5 January 1907.
29. Sir H. Robinson, *Memories, Wise and Otherwise*, (London 1924), 175.

Chapter 3 (pp. 34–46)

1. Rev. B. O'Reilly, *The Mirror of True Womanhood*, (New York 1877), reprinted from the 13th American edition, Dublin 1927, 55, 113. This book was published in Ireland by M.H. Gill in 1882 and six times between then and 1895.
2. Rev. B. O'Reilly, *The Mirror of True Womanhood*, 235, 266.
3. A.J. Humpheys, *New Dubliners*, (London 1966), 162–3, 217.
4. J. Meenan ed, *Centenary History of the Literary and Historical Society*, (Tralee 1955), 106–12.
5. M. Halliday, *Marriage on £200 a Year*, (London 1903), 79–80.
6. W.B. Stanford & R.B. McDowell, *Mahaffy*, (London 1971), paperback ed 1975, 67–103 *passim*.
7. Lecture to the Royal Dublin Society reported in the *Freeman's Journal*, 2 February 1907.
8. J.V. O'Brien, *Dear Dirty Dublin*, (California 1982), 188.
9. *Freeman's Journal*, 8 January 1907.
10. F. Bamford & V. Bankes, *Vicious Circle*, (London 1965), 10–11, 26, 94.
11. *Freeman's Journal*, 19 September 1907.
12. *ibid*, 24 October 1907.
13. C.S. Andrews, *Dublin Made Me*, (Cork 1979), 30–33.

Chapter 4 (pp. 47–58)

1. C.S. Andrews, *Dublin Made Me*, (Cork 1979), 34.
2. A. Briggs, *Victorian Things*, (London 1989), 56.
3. Unless otherwise mentioned the statements on the Exhibition are based on W. Dennehy, *Record: Irish International Exhibition 1907*, (Dublin 1909).
4. *Freeman's Journal*, 10 August 1907.
5. A. Clarke, *Twice Round the Black Church*, (London 1962), 10.
6. *Freeman's Journal*, 11 April 1907.
7. Lord and Lady Aberdeen, *More Cracks with 'We Twa'*, (London 1929), 140–41.
8. *Freeman's Journal*, 11 November 1907.
9. *ibid*, 29 August 1907.
10. W. Dennehy, *Record: Irish International Exhibition 1907*, (Dublin 1909), ccvi.
11. J.V. O'Brien, *Dear Dirty Dublin*, (California 1982), 102.
12. Lord and Lady Aberdeen, *More Cracks with 'We Twa'*, 160. Her Ladyship's figures are slightly adrift: J. Deeny, *Tuberculosis in Ireland*, (Dublin 1954), 21, gives rates of 2.10 for 1913 and 1.53 for 1924.

Chapter 5 (59–69)

1. L. Paul-Dubois, *Contemporary Ireland*, (Dublin 1908), 361–6.
2. 15 February 1902, quoted in R. Kee, *The Bold Fenian Men*, (London 1972), 1989 Penguin ed, 152.
3. *Freeman's Journal*, 2 January 1907.
4. W. Bulfin, *Rambles in Eirinn*, 2nd ed, (Dublin 1912), 99.

5. W. Bulfin, *Rambles in Eirinn*, 362.
6. W.A. Houston Collisson, *Dr Collisson in and on Ireland*, (London 1908), 43.
7. L. Paul-Dubois, *Contemporary Ireland*, 412.
8. P.L. Dickinson, *The Dublin of Yesterday*, (London 1929), 108–9.
9. L. Paul-Dubois, *Contemporary Ireland*, 399.
10. J. Carney, *The Playboy and the Yellow Lady*, (Dublin 1986), 207.
11. The reference was to an appalling case which had been widely reported in the 1890s, in which a group of villagers in County Tipperary had attempted over several days to burn the evil spirits out of the wife of one of them. The woman subsequently died of strangulation, burns and other ill treatment. A curious feature of the case is the ambivalent attitude of the local clergy. See M.J. McCarthy, *Five Years in Ireland*, (London and Dublin 1901), 142–74.
12. W. Starkie, *Scholars and Gypsies*, (London 1963), 37.
13. *The Leader*, 2 February 1907.
14. *Freeman's Journal*, 5 February 1907.
15. R. Kee, *The Bold Fenian Men*, (London 1972), Penguin ed 1989, 208.
16. Eugene Sheehy in J. Meenan ed, *Centenary History of the Literary and Historical Society*, (Tralee 1955), 79, 81.
17. J.V. O'Brien, *Dear Dirty Dublin*, (California 1982), 62.

Chapter 6 (pp. 73–86)
1. *Irish Independent*, 24 October 1932.
2. Dermot Keogh, *The Vatican, the Bishops and Irish Politics 1919–1939*, (Cambridge 1986), 182, 185.
3. T.P. Coogan, *Ireland since the Rising*, (London 1966), 70.
4. In his *Shape of things to Come*, (London 1933).
5. See E. Cahill, *The Framework of a Christian State*, (Dublin 1932).
6. L. Doyle, *The Spirit of Ireland*, (London 1935), 18.
7. L. Doyle, *The Spirit of Ireland*, 19–20.
8. *Irish Builder*, February 1932.
9. *Irish Ecclesiastical Record*, vol 42, 611.
10. *Bunreacht na hÉireann*, (Dublin 1937), Art 41.
11. Quoted in Lee, *Ireland 1912–1985*, (Cambridge 1990), 283.
12. Casual gardener from *Irish Builder*, January 1932; Westmeath labourers were paid 10s. to 15s., *Irish Independent*, 12 December 1932.
13. D. Murphy, *Wheels within Wheels*, (London 1979), paperback ed 1981, 4.
14. *Irish Independent*, 29 January 1932.
15. D. Murphy, *Wheels within Wheels*, 56.
16. O. Robertson, *Dublin Phoenix*, (London 1957), 91.
17. B. Inglis, *West Briton*, (London 1962), 15.
18. G. Seaver, *John Allen Fitzgerald Gregg Archbishop*, (Dublin and London 1963), 126.
19. M. Davie, *The Diaries of Evelyn Waugh*, (London 1976), paperback ed 1979, 783.

20. B. Inglis, *West Briton*, 19.
21. C.S. Andrews, *Man of No Property*, (Cork 1982), 13.
22. C.S. Andrews, *Man of No Property*, 30.
23. *The Outlook*, January 1932.
24. *Irish Independent*, 14 January 1932.
25. ibid, 9 May 1932. To put the Archbishop's comments in context, it should be noted that sheer fully fashioned silk stockings were only a few years current, and were directly related to the shorter skirts of the 1920s. See E. Ewing, *Dress and Undress*, (London 1978), paperback ed 1989, 140.
26. M. Holroyd, *Lytton Strachey*, (London 1967–8), paperback ed 1971, 1020–21.

Chapter 7 (pp. 87–98)
1. C. Arensberg, *The Irish Countryman*, (London 1937).
2. J. Lee, *Ireland: 1912–1985*, (Cambridge 1990), 197.
3. Figures from the *Irish Independent* as follows: Civil Service, Sweep on 6 June; breweries 14 November; railways 2 September.
4. *Statistical Abstract 1931*, (Dublin 1931), 111, 112.
5. C.S. Andrews, *Man of No Property*, (Cork 1982), 67.
6. R. Briscoe, *For the Life of Me*, (London 1958), 212.
7. *Irish Independent*, 20 December 1932.
8. *Irish Independent Careers Book*, (Dublin 1936), *passim*.
9. *Irish Independent*, 12 May 1932.
10. *Committee on the Cost of Living Figure*, P, no 992, (Dublin 1932). This Committee was part of a larger controversy on the size of civil service pay stimulated by the new Fianna Fáil Government, see R. Fanning, *The Irish Department of Finance 1922–58*, (Dublin 1978), 223–44.
11. 'Other People's Incomes', *The Bell*, August 1943–November 1943.
12. *The Irish Housewife—A Portrait*, (Dublin 1986), 26.
13. T. Farmar, *The Legendary Lofty Clattery Café*, (Dublin 1989), 37–8.
14. *Irish Nursing and Hospital World*, July 1932.
15. *Model Housekeeping*, 1931/2, 493.
16. *Irish Nursing and Hospital World*, 1932, 17.
17. Christian Brothers, *Christian Politeness*, (Dublin 1935), 43.
18. O. Wuerst, *Gastronomy*, (Dublin 1930).
19. *Committee on the Cost of Living Figure*, (Dublin 1932).
20. *Irish Independent*, 1 August 1932.
21. Advertisements in *Model Housekeeping*, 1931/2, 169, 275; *Irish Independent*, July 1932.

Chapter 8 (pp. 99–109)
1. *Irish Independent*, 5 August 1932.
2. Christian Brothers, *Christian Politeness*, (Dublin 1934), 40.
3. *Irish Ecclesiastical Record*, vol xxxix, 537.

4. G. Seaver, *John Allen Fitzgerald Gregg Archbishop*, (Dublin and London 1963), 204.
5. *Irish Independent*, 14 January 1932.
6. M. Butler, *The Ethics of Dress*, (Dublin 1927).
7. *Irish Independent*, 19 January 1932.
8. O. Robertson, *Dublin Phoenix*, (London 1957), 71.
9. *Talkie Topics*, (October 1932).
10. D. Keogh, *The Vatican, the Bishops and Irish Politics 1919–1939*, (Cambridge 1986), 137.
11. D. Keogh, *The Vatican, the Bishops and Irish Politics 1919–1939*, 201–2.
12. B. Inglis, *West Briton*, (London 1962), 29.
13. L. O'Broin, *No Man's Man*, (Dublin 1982), 145.
14. *Catholic Bulletin*, vol xxii, 5. This is about the current (audited) circulation of *Image* and twice that of *Business and Finance*.
15. ibid, vol xxii, 163.
16. ibid, vol xxii, 246.
17. T. de Vere White, 'Social Life in Ireland 1927–1937' in F. MacManus ed, *The Years of the Great Test 1926–39*, (Cork 1967), 25.
18. Christian Brothers, *Christian Politeness*, 49.
19. M. Holroyd, *Lytton Strachey*, (London 1967–8), paperback ed 1971, 1020–21.
20. N. Robertson, *Crowned Harp*, (Dublin 1960), 160–62.
21. O. Robertson, *Dublin Phoenix*, 27.
22. Quoted in T. de Vere White, 'Social Life in Ireland 1927–1937' in F. MacManus ed, *The Years of the Great Test 1926–39*, (Cork 1967).
23. The Hospitals Commission, *First General Report*, (Dublin 1936), 80.
24. *Irish Independent*, 23 May 1932.
25. *Woman's Mirror*, 4 June 1932.
26. *Model Housekeeping*, 1931/2, 295.
27. Christian Brothers, *Christian Politeness and Counsels for Youth*, (Dublin 1934). This is the twentieth edition (i.e. twentieth printing), which, so the preface says, has been 'carefully revised in order to meet the requirements of the present day'.
28. *Rerum Novarum*, (1891), 141, quoted in E. Cahill, *The Framework of a Christian State*, (Dublin 1932), 382.
29. H. Leonard, *Home before Night*, (London 1979), paperback ed 1981, 69.

Chapter 9 (pp. 110–123)
1. T.P. Coogan, *Ireland since the Rising*, (London 1966), 54–5.
2. L. Cullen, *Eason & Son: A History*, (Dublin 1989), 391.
3. T.P. Coogan, *The IRA*, (London 1970), paperback ed 1971, 71–3.
4 *Irish Independent*, 9 January 1932.
5 ibid, 3 February 1932.
6. L.O. Broin, *No Man's Man*, (Dublin 1982), 146.
7. K.A. Kennedy *et al*, *The Economic Development of Ireland in the Twentieth Century*, (London 1989), 41–2.

8. *Irish Independent*, 12 March 1932.
9. *ibid*, 9 February 1932.
10. *Catholic Bulletin*, 1932, 99.
11. T.P. Coogan, *Ireland Since the Rising*, 71.
12. L. O'Broin . . . *just like yesterday* . . ., (Dublin nd), 92.
13. J. Meenan, *Centenary History of the Literary and Historical Society 1855–1955*, (Tralee 1955), 228–49.
14. R. Briscoe, *For the Life of Me*, (London 1958), 60.
15. *Irish Independent*, 10 January 1932.
16. *ibid*, 15 February 1932.
17. *Derry Journal*, quoted in *Catholic Bulletin*, 1932, 258.
18. *Irish Independent*, 20 February 1932.
19. *ibid*, 22 February 1932.
20. N. Robertson, *Crowned Harp*, (Dublin 1960), 176.
21. Quoted in G. Seaver, *John Allen Allen Fitzgerald Gregg Archbishop*, (Dublin and London 1963), 125.
22. *Irish Independent*, 8 June 1932.
23. *Dáil Debates*, 15 July 1932.
24. *Irish Independent*, 19 September 1932.
25. L. O'Broin, *No Man's Man*, 147.
26. See, for instance, *Irish Independent*, 1 December 1932.
27. *ibid*, 24 September 1932.
28. *Dáil Debates*, 5 August 1932.
29. T.P. Coogan, *Ireland since the Rising*, 70.
30. *Irish Independent*, 5 September 1932.
31. *ibid*, 20 September 1932.
32. *ibid*, 31 December 1932.
33. T. Farmar, *A History of Craig Gardner*, (Dublin 1988), 144.
34. *Irish Independent*, 5 November 1932.

Chapter 10 (pp. 124–136)
1. Quoted in J. Bowman, *De Valera and the Ulster Question 1917–1973*, (Oxford 1982), paperback ed 1983, 107.
2. T.P. Coogan, *Ireland since the Rising*, (London 1966), 52.
3. A. Clarke, *Twice Round the Black Church*, (London 1962), 21.
4. G.K. Chesterton, *Christendom in Dublin*, (London 1932), 59.
5. This idea was reiterated by Leo XIII in 1884 who vividly described 'the two distinct and mutually hostile camps of the human race . . . two armies who have always been engaged in conflict throughout the ages'. Encyclical *Humanum Genus*, 1884.
6. *Irish Independent*, 1 November 1932.
7. The most elaborate working out of this concept was in the writings of E. Cahill, SJ, and Denis Fahey, a Holy Ghost Father who greatly influenced the thinking of John Charles McQuaid.
8. *Irish Independent*, 8 February 1932.

9. J.J. O'Riordan, *Irish Catholics*, (Dublin 1980), 68.
10. G. Seaver, *John Allen Fitzgerald Gregg Archbishop*, (London and Dublin 1963), 152–6.
11. P. Corish, *The Irish Catholic Experience*, (Dublin 1985), 167; O'Riordan, *Irish Spirituality*, (Dublin 1980), 74.
12. *The Irish Jesuit Directory and Year Book for 1932*, (Dublin 1932), 90–94.
13. P. Kavanagh, *The Green Fool*, (London 1938), 1975 paperback ed, 54.
14. *Irish Independent*, 19 May 1932.
15. *ibid*, 24 June 1932.
16. P. Boylan, *All Cultivated People*, (Gerrards Cross 1988), 185.
17. Unless otherwise stated, all quotations from newspapers describing the Congress are from the collection of press comments reprinted in *Eucharistic Congress 1932—Pictorial Record*, (Dublin nd), 149.
18. Organising Committee of the Eucharistic Congress, *Handbook of the Eucharistic Congress*, (Dublin 1932).
19. The feature writer JAP in *Irish Independent*, 22 June 1932.
20. J. Deeny, *To Cure and to Care*, (Dublin 1989), 38.
21. *Irish Independent*, 13 August 1932.

Chapter 11 (pp. 137–145)
1. *A Century of Service*—A record of One Hundred Years, published for the centenary of St Vincent's Hospital, (Dublin 1934), 118.
2. Hospitals Commission, *First General Report*, P no 1976, (Dublin 1936), 116–17.
3. The basic information about the origins of the Sweep are from A. Webb, *The Clean Sweep*, (London 1968), a source that needs to be treated with care. It contains, for instance, a vividly imagined scene of de Valera's Governor General, Donal Buckley, in June 1930 'coming back from his morning walk in the trimly-kept grounds of the Vice-Regal lodge in the Phoenix Park, Dublin. A small-time farmer from County Kildare, Buckley could never reconcile himself to his splendid isolation in that spacious, historic mansion . . .' before signing the enabling Act for the Sweep (see page 56).
4. Details of the income from individual Sweeps come from the accounts, as audited by Craig Gardner, which were distributed to every TD. Income was reported net of certain sales expenses, as directed by the Act. They are taken from the set in the Dáil Library, by courtesy of the Librarian.
5. *The Distributive Worker*, November 1932.
6. T.P. Coogan, *The IRA*, (London 1970), paperback ed 1971, 149.
7. Details from the published programmes of the Irish Hospitals Sweepstake.
8. *Irish Independent*, 3 June 1932.
9. Quoted in C. L'E. Ewen, *Lotteries and Sweepstakes*, (London 1932), 366.
10. *Catholic Bulletin*, 1932, 517.

11. J. Deeny, *To Cure and to Care*, (Dublin 1989), 142.
12. M. Adams, *Censorship—The Irish Experience*, (Dublin 1968), 122.

Chapter 12 (149–164)
1. B.F. Biever, *Religion Culture and Values*, (New York 1976), 240.
2. Alice Taylor, *To School through the Fields*, (Dingle 1988), 8.
3. D. Connery, *The Irish*, (London 1968), paperback ed 1972, 57.
4. M. Molloy, *The Book of Irish Courtesy*, (Cork 1968), 15.
5. *The Irish Times*, 3 May 1963.
6. L. O'Broin, *Frank Duff*, (Dublin 1982), 62–7.
7. J. Feeney, *John Charles McQuaid: the Man and the Mask*, (Cork 1974), 30–31, 44–7.
8. X. Rynne, *Letters from Vatican City*, (London 1963), 118.
9. Biever, who was an American Jesuit, did his research from 1963 to 1965, sending questionnaires to 1,500 Dubliners of whom 1,015 Catholics responded; Biever had supplementary interviews with 55 of these. His research compared attitudes to religion and other matters of native Irish and Irish American Catholics.
10. *The Irish Times*, 18 February 1963.
11. *ibid*, 13 February 1963.
12. D. Connery, *The Irish*, 29.
13. *The Irish Times*, 17 May 1963.
14. *Sunday Press*, 23 June 1963.
15. *Dáil Debates*, vol 204, no 8, 1311–12.
16. M. Nevin, 'A Study of the Social Background of Students in the Irish Universities', JSSISI, 1968.
17. J.J. Lee, *Ireland 1912–1985: Politics and Society*, (Cambridge 1989), paperback ed, 562–643, describes this problem in magisterial detail.
18. John McGahern interviewed by Fintan O'Toole, *The Irish Times*, 13 October 1990.
19. Brendan Behan, *Brendan Behan's Ireland*, (London 1962), paperback ed 1965, 19.
20. *The Irish Times*, 8 January 1963.
21. *ibid*, 19 February 1963.
22. Quoted in *Sunday Review*, 21 April 1963.
23. T. Stonier, *Nuclear Disaster*, (Harmondsworth 1964), 26.
24. *The Irish Times*, 23 October 1962.
25. *Dáil Debates*, 29 May 1963.
26. *The Irish Times*, 3 March 1963.
27. *Studies*, Winter 1964.

Chapter 13 (pp. 165–177)
1. G. FitzGerald, 'Economic Survey 1962' in *Irish Review and Annual*, *The Irish Times*, 1 January 1963.
2. *Sunday Press*, 1 September 1963.

3. F. Kennedy, *Family, Economy and Government in Ireland*, (Dublin 1989), 53.
4. D. Rottman and P. O'Connell, 'The Changing Social Structure', in F. Litton ed, *Unequal Achievement*, (Dublin 1982), 68–74.
5. Workers' Union of Ireland, *Report of General Executive Committee for 1963–64*, (Dublin 1964).
6. *Hibernia*, September 1963.
7. *The Irish Times*, 1 February 1963. The Limerick Rural Survey of 1962 noted that 'some kitchens have a screen down the centre to cut off the family from the workers'. Although the extreme inequalities of the 1930s were waning, the distinction was clear.
8. Quoted in D. Connery, *The Irish*, (London 1968), paperback ed 1972, 97.
9. Marion Fitzgerald in *Sunday Review*, 3 March 1963, see also John Broderick, *Don Juaneen*, (London 1963).
10. A. Humphreys, *New Dubliners*, (London 1966), 196.
11. P. Kelleher, 'Familism in Irish Capitalism in the 1950s' in *Economic and Social Review*, vol 18, no 2, January 1987, 75–94 at 90.
12. B. Haring, *The Sociology of the Family*, (Cork 1959), 56.
13. *Sunday Review*, 10 February 1963.
14. D. Purcell, 'Interview with Monica Barnes', *Sunday Tribune*, 3 June 1990.
15. R.C. Geary and F.S. O'Muircheartaigh, *Equalisation of Opportunity in Ireland: Statistical Aspects*, (Dublin 1968, 1974).
16. *The Irish Times*, 2 March 1963.
17. T. Farmar, *A History of Craig Gardner & Co.*, (Dublin 1988). The average industrial wage is calculated, as before, from *Statistical Abstract* as the cost of salaries and wages for all industries divided by the average number of persons employed. This figure includes administrative and clerical staff.
18. *Sunday Review*, 3 February 1963.
19. *ibid*, 13 January 1963.
20. *The Irish Times*, 15 February 1963.
21. *Report of Revenue Commissioners*, 1962/3.
22. J. McCarthy, *Ireland*, (New York 1964), 132.
23. *Statistical Abstract*, 1958 & 1963.
24. *The Irish Times*, 11 February 1963.
25. *Sunday Press*, 19 May 1963.
26. *The Irish Times*, 28 February 1963.
27. Public Record Office, Business Records, DUB 7.
28. 'An Irish Housewife', *I'm not afraid to die*, (Cork 1974), 119.
29. A. Clarke, *Twice Round the Black Church*, (London 1962), 116.
30. *The Irish Times*, 1 May 1963.
31. *Household Budget Inquiry 1965/6*, (Dublin 1969), Table 5.
32. *Facts about Ireland*, (Dublin 1963), 73.

Chapter 14 (pp. 178–189)
1. A. Humphreys, *New Dubliners*, (London 1966), 163.

2. 'An Irish Housewife', *I'm not afraid to die*, (Cork 1974), 73.
3. M. Molloy, *Book of Irish Courtesy*, (Cork 1968).
4. Christian Brothers, *Courtesy for Boys and Girls*, (Dublin 1962), vi.
5. F.X. Carty, *Why I said No to God*, (Dublin 1986), 24–5.
6. John McGahern interviewed by Fintan O'Toole, *The Irish Times*, 13 October 1990.
7. J. McCarthy, *Ireland*, (New York 1964), 135.
8. Mab Hickman in *Creation*, March 1963.
9. M. Sheridan, 'The Gastronomic Irishman' in O.D. Edwards ed, *Conor Cruise O'Brien introduces Ireland*, (London 1969), 229.
10. D. Connery, *The Irish*, (London 1968), paperback ed 1972, 90.
11. *The Irish Times*, 17 March 1990.
12. *ibid*, 16 February 1963.
13. *Sunday Press*, 7 April 1963.
14. *ibid*, 1 December 1963.
15. G. Howell, *In Vogue*, (London 1975), 280.
16. *Sunday Press*, 17 March 1963.
17. *The Irish Times*, 20 May 1963.
18. *ibid*, 20 May 1963.
19. J. Levine, *Sisters*, (Dublin 1982), 48.
20. *The Irish Times*, 29 May 1963.
21. *ibid*, 25 January 1963.
22. Most of the information in the next few paragraphs comes from Maxwell Sweeney's informative contemporary study, 'Irish Television: A compromise with commerce' in *Studies*, Winter 1963.
23. *Sunday Review*, 6 January 1963.
24. *The Irish Times*, 7 May 1963.
25. *Hibernia*, April 1963.
26. *The Irish Times*, 27 January 1963.
27. F.X. Carty, *Why I said No to God*, 104.
28. *The Irish Times*, 20 February 1963.
29. M. McLoone and J. MacMahon, *Television and Irish Society*, (Dublin 1984), 150. The *Household Budget Survey* of 1980 reported that 91 per cent of households had TV, 81 per cent running hot water and 83 per cent an internal lavatory.
30. *The Irish Times*, 20 January 1963.

Chapter 15 (190–201)
1. *The Irish Times*, 25 February 1963.
2. *Sunday Press*, 14 July 1963.
3. *The Irish Times*, 1, 25 May 1963.
4. *Sunday Press*, 18 September 1963.
5. D. Rohan, *Marriage Irish Style*, (Cork 1969), 69–70.
6. A. Humphries, *New Dubliners*, (London 1966), 139.
7. 'An Irish Housewife', *I'm not afraid to die*, (Cork 1974), 58.

8. Angela MacNamara in *Hibernia*, January 1963.
9. Quoted in B. MacMahon, 'Getting on the High Road Again' in J. O'Brien ed, *The Vanishing Irish*, (London 1954), 211.
10. John Canon McCarthy, *Problems in Theology*, (Dublin 1960), II: 195–6.
11. J. McCarthy, *Ireland*, (New York 1964), 79.
12. M. O'Beirne, *People people marry, people people don't*, (Dublin 1976), 29, 66.
13. *Sunday Press*, 8 September 1963.
14. Sean O Faolain, 'Love among the Irish' in J. O'Brien ed, *The Vanishing Irish*, (London 1954), 109.
15. A. Boylan, *Diaries* (unpublished), 25 November; 9, 10 December 1963.
16. *Hibernia*, January 1963.
17. F.X. Carty, *Why I said No to God*, (Dublin 1986), 94.
18. *Marriage*, December 1963—this was an Irish version of an American publication, edited and published in Dublin.
19. John Canon McCarthy, *Problems in Theology*, 214, 216.
20. See P. Brown, *The Body and Society*, (New York 1988), paperback ed 1990, chap 2.
21. B. Carr, *The Instant Tree*, (Cork 1975), 17.
22. *The Irish Times*, 5 March 1963.
23. B. Geldof, *Is that it?*, (London 1986), paperback ed, 43–7.
24. *The Irish Times*, 17 May 1963.
25. J. Levine, *Sisters*, (Dublin 1982), 30.
26. R. Sweetnam, *On Our Backs*, (London 1979), 139.
27. R. Cobb, *A Classical Education*, (London 1985), paperback ed 1986, 136–41.
28. A. Clarke, *Twice Round the Black Church*, (London 1962), 164.
29. L. Ott, *Fundamentals of Catholic Dogma*, sixth edition, (Cork 1963), 121–2, 480.

Chapter 16 (pp. 202–212)
1. Quoted in *Sunday Press*, 15 September 1963.
2. Quoted in G. Howell, *In Vogue*, (Harmondsworth 1975), paperback ed 1978, 254.
3. R. McNamara, *Blundering into Disaster*, (London 1987), 44, 45–60.
4. *The Irish Times*, 22 October 1962.
5. *Sunday Review*, 6 January 1963.
6. A. Boylan, *Diaries* (unpublished), 26 June 1963.
7. M.N. Hennessy, *I'll Come back in the Springtime*, (London 1967).
8. Quoted in D. Connery, *The Irish*, (London 1968), paperback ed 1972, 30–31.
9. Quoted in *Hibernia*, July 1963.
10. A. Boylan, *Diaries* (unpublished), 22–24 November 1963.
11. Garret FitzGerald's personal archive, quoted by permission.
12. A. Boylan, *Diaries* (unpublished), 26 November 1963.
13. H. Brody, *Inishkillane*, (London 1973), 71.
14. Speech in Tramore to National Convention of Junior Chambers of Commerce, quoted in the *Sunday Press*, 19 May 1963.

Index

abattoirs, in 1907, 28
Abbey Theatre, 99, 160, 172
   The Playboy of the Western World:
      showing in 1907, 59, 63–8
Aberdeen, Lady
   anti-tuberculosis campaign, 9, 56, 57–8
Aberdeen, Lord (Lord Lieutenant), 9, 11, 50, 54
Adelaide Hospital, 138
administration of government, in 1907, 9, 11–12
AE (George Russell), 106
agricultural exports
   Economic War, 120, 122–3
Aiken, Frank, 104, 120, 178, 204
Ailesbury Road, 54
air travel
   Amelia Earhart's solo flight across Atlantic, 131
   first flight from Ireland to Berlin, 1932, 73
Alexandra, Queen
   visit to 1907 Exhibition, 53–4
Allgood, Sara (actress), 65
Andrews, C.S. (Todd)
   Dublin Made Me, 13, 28, 45, 47, 59, 83, 85, 89, 90, 167
Anglesea Road
   house prices in 1932, 97
Anglo-Irish, 63, 81, 119
   military, in, 12
   symbols of the old order in 1910, 1
Annuities to British Government
   witholding of, in 1932, 113, 120–22
anti-tuberculosis campaign, 9, 28, 56–8, 79
appearance, importance of, 25
Aras an Uachtarain
   garden party for Kennedy visit (1963), 208
Army Comrades Association (Blueshirts), 73, 122, 123, 157
   membership in 1932, 123

Arnott's department store, 140
Arts Club, 20, 131
'at homes', in 1932, 106
Athlone radio transmitter, 85

baby boom, 202
Baggot Street, Upper
   shops in 1907, 30
Barnes, Monica, 169
Barrington's (Great Britain St), 45
   lemon soap, 57
barristers
   income, 22, 171
   training in 1907, 24
bathrooms, 56–7, 79, 151
Beatles, 193
   visit to Dublin (1963), 157
Beecham's Powders, 107
Behan, Brendan, 155, 159
Bell, The, 92
Berlin Wall, 160
Bewley, Charles (Irish ambassador to Rome), 102
Bewley, Ernest, 23
Bewley's cafes, 23, 77, 89, 93
Bewley's grocery stores, 20, 27–8
bicycles, 17, 32, 176
Biever, Fr B.F. (SJ), 153, 154, 170, 182, 190, 192, 198
Birmingham, George, 22
Birrell, Augustine (Chief Secretary), 9, 11, 12
births
   in 1907, 59
   in 1963, 178; illegitimate births, 191
   maternity hospitals, 138
Bishop Street, Jacob's factory, 45
Blackrock, 42
blind pig parties, 42
Bloody Sunday, 211
Blueshirts. *see* Army Comrades Association

225

Board of Works, 24
  officials' salaries in 1907, 20, 22
Boland, F.H., 155
Bolands Mills
  directors' salaries in 1907, 22
bona fide travellers, 42–3
books
  bestsellers in 1963, 186
  censorship, 86, 145, 159–60, 191
  Lady Chatterley trial (1960), 160
  paperbacks industry, 159–60
Bowen, Elizabeth, 28, 30
Boylan, Anna, 211
Boylan, Patricia, 167
Branigan, Garda 'Lugs', 157
breakfast dishes
  in 1932, 93, 95
Brennan, Joseph (Secretary of Dept of Finance), 68, 120
breweries
  numbers employed in 1932, 89
Briscoe, Robert (TD), 116
Britain
  administration of Ireland in 1907, 9, 11–12
  Economic War, 120, 122–3
  English 'paganism', 86, 190, 191
  Great Train Robbery (1963), 164
  Irish colony, 7–8
  Profumo scandal, 163
  sweep ticket sales, 140, 142, 144
British Empire, 24, 128
British influences
  in 1907, 59
  in 1932, 86
British national anthem, Anglo-Irish attachment to, 100
British publications
  circulation of, in 1907, 59
  comics, 59
bronchitis, 178
Bronco toilet paper, endorsed by clergymen, 108
Brookeborough, Lord, 3, 149
Brown Thomas's department store, 102
Browne, Cardinal Michael, 153, 155
Browne, Dr Noel (TD), 107, 204
building development
  in 1960s, 157
Bulfin, William, 17, 31, 62
Byrne, Frankie, 167

Byrne, Gay, 184, 187
  Late Late Show, 1, 187, 191
  taxable income in 1963, 171

Cadbury's Cocoa, 27
Cahill, Fr Edward (SJ), 75, 80, 152
Cameron, Sir Charles (Medical Officer of Health), 42
  Reminiscences, 19
cancer deaths
  in 1932, 106, 107
  in 1963, 178
Cantrell and Cochrane
  ginger ale, 27
Capitol Showband, 193
Carr, Bunny, 187, 198
Carrolls (P.J.) Ltd
  flotation in 1935, 123
Carty, F.X., 180, 187, 197
Casey's Circus, 59
Catholic Bulletin, The, 103, 115, 119, 124, 128, 143
Catholic Church, 75. *see also* Clergy; Eucharistic Congress (1932)
  charitable organisations, 127
  class distinctions, attitude to, 109
  clerical garb, reinforcement of rule, 99
  confraternities, meetings and sodalities, 126, 127
  control of education, 153
  'devotional revolution', 126–7, 128
  esteem for, in 1963, 153–4
  French Government's treatment of, 1907 protest against, 2
  Irish nationality bound up with, 128
  legal forms, obsession with, 127
  Mass attendances in 1932, 127
  moral concerns in 1963, 199–201
  Peter's Pence collections: in 1907, 25; in 1932, 96–7
  religious outlook in 1932, 124, 126–7
  Second Vatican Council, 145, 153
  sex, attitudes to, 192, 194, 197–8
  traditional devotional styles, disapproval of, 128
  women, attitudes to, 35, 80
Catholic middle class, 2–3
  class distinctions in 1907, 13–14
  Irish Independent as mouthpiece of, in 1932, 76
Catholic Welfare Bureau, 193

Index

censorship, 86, 145, 191
  books banned in 1963, 159
Censorship of Publications Board, 159–60
central heating, 176, 187
Chance, Sir Arthur, 82
Chanel, 31, 97
charitable donations, 176
charitable organisations, 127
chastity, 190–91, 192, 194
Cherry Blossom boot polish, 27
Chesterton, G.K., 124
child abuse, unknown frequency of, 198
children's upbringing
  difference in treatment between boys and girls, 35, 178–9
Chinese food, 182
Chips (comic), 59
Christ Church Cathedral School, 170
Christian Brothers
  etiquette books, 108–9, 179
Christmas shopping, in 1907, 30–31
Church of England Newspaper, 119
Church of Ireland, 127. see also Protestant community
  Synod in 1963, 155, 157, 198
cinema, 76, 126, 176;
  in 1932, 85–6
civil defence
  survival demonstration in 1962, 204
civil service
  employment prospects (1932), 87
  holiday entitlements (1932), 77
  household expenditure patterns (1932), 91–2
  numbers employed (1932), 89
  pay: in 1932, 80, 83, 90–91; in 1963, 172
Civil War, 157
Clancy, Basil, 155
Clann na Gael, 140
Clare, Anthony, 202
Clarke, Austin, 28, 32, 39, 45, 50, 124, 175, 199
class distinctions, 1–2
  in 1907, 12–14;
  in 1932, 80, 81, 83;
  in 1963, 167–70
  clergy's view of, 109
  dress, importance of, 99, 182
  food-buying and, 177
  snobbery, 168–9
cleanliness, Irishmen urged to, 56–7

clergy, 192
  clerical dress, rule reinforced, 99
  esteem for, in 1963, 153–4
  rise to importance, 34
  sexual jargon used by, 194
Clery's department store, 23, 102, 129, 137
  managing director's salary in 1932, 90
clothing. see also fashion
  in 1907, 31–2
  in 1932, 97, 98, 99–100
  in 1963, 182–3
  class distinctions, 99, 182
  department stores in 1932, 102
  dry cleaning, 32
  hats, 31–2, 98, 183
  personal tailoring, 32
  prices, 31–2, 98
  silk stockings, 86
  symbolism of, 99–100, 102, 104
  women's trousers, 183, 184
clubs
  religious divisions in 1932, 81, 83
cocktail parties, introduced to Dublin, 106
College Green, 45
Collins-O'Driscoll, Mrs (TD), 120
Collisson, Houston, 62
Colum, Padraic, 66
Comic Cuts (comic), 59
comics, in 1907, 59
communism, 73, 75, 124, 152, 178
  in IRA in 1930s, 73, 111
  Red scare in 1963, 160–61
company-keeping, 192, 197
condoms, 197–8
confessional, seal of, 200
confraternities, 126, 127
Congo, Irish army in, 160, 211
Connolly, Senator (Minister for Posts and Telegraphs), 85
Conroy, Bronwyn, 184
constipation, worries about, 107
Constitution of Ireland, 1937
  central position of family, 80, 165
consumption. see tuberculosis
contraception, 79–80, 194, 197–8
cookery
  in 1932, 93, 95–6
  in 1963, 180, 182
  Chinese food, 182
  cookbooks, 26, 95

cookery *continued*
   Economic Cookery Book (1905), 26
   necessary chore, seen as, 180
Cork
   population in 1901, 14
Cosgrave, William T., 76, 103, 110, 111, 155
   achievements in government, 110
   devout Catholic, 124
   dress sense, 102
   physical appearance, 115–16
   salary of, 114
Cosgrave Government (1922–32), 73, 110
cosmetics advertisements, in 1932, 107–8
cost of living
   in 1932, 91, 92
   in 1963, 172, 174
   civil servants' household budget (1932), 91–2
   equivalent values 1900–1990, 3–4
cost of living index (1932), 91
Costello, General M.J., 155, 171
Costello, J.A., 155
Craig Gardner (accountancy firm), 139
   entry system in 1963, 170–71
   partners' salaries: in 1907, 22; in 1932, 90; in 1963, 171
Craven A cigarettes, 107
Creation magazine, 164, 176, 182
crime
   in 1907, 15; Irish Crown Jewels, theft of, 43, 45
   in 1963, 190; Green Tureen murder, 164
   drink-related, 42
   prostitution, 15
Cuban missile crisis (1962), 203–4
Cullenswood parish (Beechwood Road)
   Peter's Pence collection: in 1907, 26
Cumann na nGaedheal, 49
   1932 election campaign, 76, 110–19
   Cosgrave Government (1922–32), 73, 110
   de Valera appeals for co-operation from, 122
   forms new party, Fine Gael, 123
   links with Blueshirts, 123
   rumoured coup in 1932, 73
customs duties
   1932 impositions, 119–20

dairies, private, 28, 79
Dame Street, 30
dance halls, 126, 192–3
dancing, condemnation of, 192, 194
Dargan, William, 47
de Beauvoir, Simone
   The Second Sex, 159
de Valera, Eamon, 68, 73, 104, 131, 138, 145, 192, 202, 208, 211. *see also* Fianna Fail Government (1932)
   1932 election campaign, 111–19
   audience with the Pope (1933), 102
   'Catholic first' assertion (1931 Ard Fheis), 124
   dress favoured by, 102
   economic objectives, 149, 151
   election appearances, 116
   land annuities issue, 113
   major policy aims, failure of, 149, 151
   performance at League of Nations, 122
   personal charm, 151
   personal qualities, 116
   popularity in 1963, 155
   rural idyll, 151
   welcome for John F. Kennedy, 207
deaths, causes of
   in 1932, 106–7
   in 1963, 178
   tuberculosis. *see* tuberculosis
Deeny, Dr James, 132, 145
Delany, Fr (President of UCD), 35
Dennehy, William (newspaper editor), 48
Department of Finance, Secretary's salary
   in 1907, 20
   in 1963, 171
devotional revolution, 126–7
diabolo (game), 40, 42
Dickinson, Page, 11, 18, 19, 20, 63
diet. *see also* food
   working class in 1907, of, 19–20
Dillon, John, 18
dinner menus, in 1932, 93, 95
dinner parties, 39–40, 104, 106
diseases. *see also* deaths; tuberculosis
   in 1932, 106–7
Distributive Worker, The, 161
divorce, 73, 79
doctors' income
   in 1907, 22
   in 1932, 90
Doctrine and Life, 154
D'Olier Street, 30
Dolphin Park F.C., 138

Index

domestic rates
  in 1963, 174
Donnybrook
  Peter's Pence collection in 1932, 97
Dorset Street, 28
Doyle, Lynn (writer), 76–7, 81
dress. *see also* clothing
  symbolism of, in 1932, 99–100
drinking. *see also* public houses
  in 1907, 39, 40, 42
  in 1932, 96
  in 1963, 168
  bona fide limits, extension of, 42–3
  crime related to, in 1907, 42
  drunkenness, 42, 79
driving licence examinations, 155
Drumcondra
  house prices in 1932, 97
dry cleaning, introduction of, 32
du Maurier, Daphne, 186
Dublin, 3
  building development in 1960s, 157
  Catholic middle class, 3
  Catholic population in 1907, 14
  characters in 1907, 45
  city and suburbs: social structure, differences in 1911, 20
  crime in 1907, 15
  lifestyle in 1932, 77
  Monto (brothel quarter), 15, 79, 199
  noise and smells in 1907, 45–6
  population: 1901, 14; 1911, 19
  prostitution, 15, 79
  slums, 14, 77; clearance and rehousing, 77
  suburbs: population in 1901, 14
  time difference in 1907, 7
Dublin Bay Sailing Club, 23
Dublin Castle, 11, 12
  levees, 11
  theft of Irish Crown Jewels from (1907), 43, 45
Dublin Chamber of Commerce, 110
Dublin Corporation, 14, 157
Dudley, Lord (Lord Lieutenant), 9, 11
Duff, Frank, 155, 187
Duggan, Richard (bookmaker, Sweep promoter), 139

Eason's, 89
  salaries and wages in 1907, 22, 23

Economic Development (1958), 155
Economic War, 120, 122–3, 149
economy
  in 1907, 19
  in 1932, 73, 75; value of Sweep funds to, 144–5
  in 1963, 149, 152, 155, 165
  crisis in 1930s, 73, 87
education
  Catholic Church controls, 153
  Intermediate Certificate exams, 1907, 32
  secondary and third level, in 1963, 170
  top schools in 1907, 32
  women, in 1963, 167, 168–9
Edward VII, 45
  visit to International Exhibition in 1907, 53–4
elections
  1932 campaign, 76, 77, 110–19; murder of Leitrim TD, 117
Elvery, Beatrice, 13–14
emigrants' remittances in 1907, 14
emigration, 14, 59, 75, 126, 149, 151, 207
Empire Theatre, 39, 59, 60
employment
  agricultural employment (1932), 87
  manufacturing industry (1907), 19
  marriage bar, 79, 165, 167
  married women (1963), 165, 167
  mobility, in, 24, 169–70
  opportunities: in 1907, 24; in 1932, 80–83, 87, 89; in 1963, 165
  personal contacts, importance of, 90
  professional premiums, 83, 87, 89
  recruitment methods (1907), 24
  religious divisions, 23–4, 170
  Sweep, numbers employed in 1932, 140
  university graduates (1932), 89
Endymion (Dublin character), 45
Eno's, 107
entertaining
  in 1907, 39–40
  in 1932, 104, 106
  in 1963, 182
  'at homes', 106
  cocktail parties, 106
  dinner parties, 104, 106, 182
  Lord Mayor's Easter Luncheon (1907), 39–40
  supper parties, 106

229

entertainment
  in 1907, 40–41, 42, 45–6, 59–60
  in 1932, 76, 85–6, 137
  in 1963, 176, 192–3
  blind pig parties, 42
  cinema, 76, 85–6, 176
  dancing, 126, 192–4
  diabolo, 40, 42
  Irish International Exhibition (1907), 53
  music halls, 45
  radio, 85
  sports (1932), 137
  street entertainment (1907), 45–6
  television (1963), 186–7
  theatre, 59–60, 172, 174, 176
  wrestling, 60
entertainment tax, 120
ESB, 89
  electrical output in 1963, 165
  Fitzwilliam St office controversy, 157
  Shannon scheme, 110, 113
etiquette
  books of, 99, 108–9, 179
  table manners, 108, 179, 180
Eucharistic Congress (1932), 76, 102, 104, 110
  arrival of Cardinal Lauri (Papal Legate), 131–2
  Blackrock College garden party, 132
  Children's Mass, 129
  daily activities, 131, 133
  final procession and Benediction, 134, 136
  floodlighting of buildings, 129
  foreign press reports, 133
  Girl Guides' offer of accommodation, 103
  government's meeting with Cardinal Lauri, 102
  Mass in Phoenix Park, 134
  Midnight Mass in city churches, 132
  preparations for, 128–9
  Protestant firms, reaction of, 131
  souvenir items, 129
  State reception, 132
  stoning of pilgrims in Northern Ireland, 133
  women's retreat, 131
evening eating
  dinner parties, 104, 106
  high tea, 104

exhibitions, 47–8. *see also* Irish International Exhibition (1907)
expenditure
  civil service households (1932), 91–2
  clothing: in 1907, 31–2; in 1932, 98
  daily patterns in 1963, 172–5
  drink, 96, 168
  education (1907), 32
  food: in 1932, 92
  health care (1932), 93, 95
  hire purchase, 174
  Household Budget Enquiry (1965/66), 177
  household budgets (1963), 172–7
  housing: in 1932, 97; in 1963, 174–5
  servants' wages (1907), 37
  transport (1907), 32–3

faction fighting, 15
Faith, Adam, 193
family, constitutional importance of, 80, 165
fascism, 75
fashion
  in 1907, 31
  in 1932, 97, 100, 102
  in 1963, 183, 184, 202
Feminine Mystique, The (Betty Friedan), 184, 186
feminism, 35, 184
Fianna Fail, 76, 157, 178, 211. *see also* Fianna Fail Government (1932)
  1932 election campaign, 76, 77, 110–19
  declared objectives, 2
  dress favoured by, 102
  self-sufficiency programme, 111, 114
Fianna Fail Government (1932), 73, 89
  annuities issue, 120–22
  Economic War, 120, 122–3
  Governor General, boycott of, 103–4
  Oath of Allegiance, abolition of, 129
  refusal (usually) to wear morning clothes, 102
  taxes and duties, 119–20
Findlater's stores, 20, 27
  women's magazine *The Lady of the House*, 28
Fine Gael
  formation of, 123
First Dail
  Democratic Programme, 2

Index

FitzGerald, Desmond (Minister for Defence), 116
FitzGerald, Garret, 164, 210, 211
Fitzwilliam St
   ESB office controversy, 157
Flanagan, Oliver J. (TD), 157, 163, 191
food
   cheese, dislike of, 20, 96
   Chinese food, 182
   cookbooks, 26, 95
   cookery, 93, 95–6, 180, 182
   cookery in 1932, 93, 95–6
   dinner parties, 39–40, 104, 106, 182
   enjoyment of, seen as unbecoming, 180
   family menus (1932), 93, 95
   family spending on: in 1907, 26–7; in 1932, 92; in 1963, 176
   hygiene (1932), 79
   milk supply, 28, 79
   new dishes in 1963, 182
   packaged products, 27
   private dairies, 28, 79
   private slaughterhouses, 28
   pub dinners (1907), 20
   Shelbourne dinner menu (1932), 96, 97
   steak fondue, 182
   supper parties, 106
   supply (1907), 27
   table manners, advice on, 108–9, 179–80
   working-class diet in 1907, 19–20
food-buying
   in 1907, 26–7
   in 1932, 92–3
   in 1963, 175–6
   bulk purchasing, 176
   fridge, effects of, 1, 176
   grocery shops, 27–8, 175–6
   popular products in 1907, 27
   social status and, 177
   supermarkets, 176
Foxrock, 175
   house prices in 1963, 174
franchise, 34, 35, 80, 186
Freeman, Spencer (Sweep promotor), 139, 142
Freeman's Journal, 9, 11, 14, 17, 18, 23, 25, 28, 32, 34, 37, 39, 43, 55, 60, 76
   Exhibition of 1907, 49, 53, 54
   Playboy at Abbey (1907), 64, 65, 66, 67, 68
Freemasons, 115, 124, 152, 178

French, Percy, 62
fridge, 1, 176

GAA, 49
Gaelic games, 68, 120
Gaelic League, 13, 60, 62, 63, 64, 68, 104, 190
   number of branches in 1907, 18
   opposition to International Exhibition of 1907, 49
Gaiety Theatre, 59
Gallaher's, 24
Gate Theatre, 174
Geary, Roy, 169
Geldof, Bob, 198
Gem (comic), 59
Georgian buildings
   replacement by high office blocks, 157
German nationals, land purchasing by, 163
Germany
   economic depression in 1932, 75
   in 1930s, 75
   scandals at court (1907), 45
Gerry and the Pacemakers, 193
Gill, M.H., 103
Girl Guide movement
   oath controversy (1932), 103
gloves, 25
government administration
   1907, 9, 11–12
government ministers, 3
   salaries in 1932, 114
Governor General
   boycott by Fianna Fail Government, 103–4, 132
Grafton Street (Dublin), 17
Grand Canal
   Corporation's plans to fill in, 157
Great Exhibition (1851), 47
Great Train Robbery (1963), 164
Green Tureen restaurant (Harcourt St), 164
Gregg, John (Archbishop of Dublin), 82, 99–100, 119
   opposition to Sweep, 143
grocery trade
   in 1907, 27–8
   in 1963, 175–6
   supermarkets, 176
gross national income
   distribution of, 2

Ordinary Lives

Grosvenor Hotel (Westland Row), 55
Guinness's brewery, 24, 45, 89, 134
Gye biscuit (Jacob's), 167

Hackenschmidt, George (wrestler), 60
Haddington Road Church
    Peter's Pence collections, 25, 96
hair tonics, 108
hats, 31, 32, 97, 183
Haughey, Charles, 182, 202
Haughey, Maureen, 182, 187
Hawkins House, 157
Hayes, Canon (Muintir na Tire), 75
health. *see also* deaths; tuberculosis
    Dublin slums (1932), 77
    popular medicines (1932), 107
health care
    in 1932, 93, 95
    in 1963, 174
heart disease, 106, 178
Hennessy, Dr Thomas (TD), 100
Henry Street Warehouse, 31
herbal ointments, 107
Herbert Park
    creation of, 55–6
    discovery of bodies in (1907), 48–9
    Irish International Exhibition of 1907, 47, 48
Hibernia, 152, 160, 167, 174, 190, 205
Irish Honours list, 1963, 155
high tea, political status of, 104
hire-purchase, 174
Hogan, Patrick (Minister for Agriculture), 116, 122
Holmes millinery shop, 31–2
Holy Ghost Seminary, 180, 197
holy wells, Church's dislike of, 128
Home Rule, 7, 9, 18, 60, 63, 69
homosexuality, 43, 45, 198–9
horse-drawn traffic, 17
horse-racing. *see* Sweep
Horse Show Week, 1, 39, 100
    in 1907, 55
    in 1932, 77, 138
hospitals
    development programme 1945–65, 145
    financial difficulties in 1932, 138
    health care in 1932, 93, 95
    lottery to raise funds for. *see* Sweep
Hospitals Commission, 107
Hospitals Trust, 90, 139. *see also* Sweep

Hotel and Tourist Association, 55
household allowance, 175
Household Budget Enquiry (1965/66), 177
household budgets
    in 1963, 172–7
housework
    boys and girls treated differently in relation to, 35, 178
    servants, 37–9
housing
    in 1907: fashionable areas, 25–6
    in 1932, 96–7
    in 1963, 174
    indoor lavatory facilities, 56–7, 79, 151
    prices: in 1932, 97; in 1963, 174
Howth, 42–3
huckster's shops, 46
humour, 40, 191
Hyde, Douglas, 31, 63, 64
hygiene
    anti-tuberculosis campaign, 56–7
    bathrooms, 56–7, 79, 151
    food hygiene in 1932, 79
    personal hygiene in 1932, 79
    Turkish baths, 57

illegitimate births
    in 1963, 191
Imperial Economic Conference (Ottawa, 1932), 100, 102, 120
income
    average industrial wage: in 1932, 90; in 1963, 171, 172
    distribution of: in 1907, 14
    government ministers: in 1932, 114
    levels: in 1907, 14, 19, 20, 25; in 1932, 80–81, 90; in 1963, 171, 172
income tax, 92, 96, 119, 165, 171
indoor lavatories, lack of, 56–7, 79, 151
Intermediate Certificate exams (1907), 32
international exhibitions. *see* Irish International Exhibition (1907)
IRA, 89, 122
    arms importations in 1930s, 122
    militant communism in, 73, 111
Irish
    linked with 'Catholic', 128
Irish Army
    cadets at Kennedy funeral, 210–11
    Congo, in, 160, 211

Index

Irish Association of Sweet Manufacturers, 163
Irish Commercial Travellers' Association, 39
Irish Crown Jewels, theft of, 20, 43, 45, 55
Irish Ecclesiastical Record, 79–80, 127, 194, 200
Irish flag, 99, 103
Irish Free State, 75
   attitude of Church of Ireland to, 82
   population in 1926, 87
Irish Hospitals Sweepstakes. *see* Sweep
Irish Housewife, 175, 176
Irish Housewives Association, 186
Irish Independent, 73, 75, 81, 86, 90, 99, 108, 114, 120, 122, 137, 142, 205
   daily sales, 1932, 76
   Eucharistic Congress (1932), 129, 131, 132
   Guide to Careers (1956), 171, 172
   mouthpiece of Catholic middle class in 1932, 76
   readership in 1907, 45
Irish Industrial Association, 49
Irish International Exhibition (1907), 43, 47–58
   anti-tuberculosis campaign, stimulation given to, 56–7, 58
   bad weather during, 55
   catering, 50
   closing hymn offensive to Catholics, 50
   entertainments, 53
   exhibitions, 49
   financial failure of, 55
   Irish firms represented, 49
   official opening, 50, 53
   opposition and hostility to, 49–50, 55
   Royal visit, 53–5
   siting in Herbert Park, 48–9
   Somali village, 53, 54
   Trinity students' prank, 54
Irish-Ireland movement, 60, 62–9
Irish language movement, 63, 151
Irish Motor Show, 1907, 17
Irish Parliamentary Party, 7
   denunciation of International Exhibition of 1907, 49
Irish Press, 126, 134
   in 1932, 76
Irish Rosary, The, 50
Irish Rugby Union
   refusal to fly Irish flag over Lansdowne Road ground, 103
Irish Tatler and Sketch, 106
Irish Times, 114, 119, 159, 160, 161, 177, 184, 186, 189, 202, 203, 204, 208
   in 1932, 76
Irish Tourist Authority, 90
Island Golf Club, 82

Jacob's biscuits, 27, 45, 89
   Gye biscuit (1963), 167
Jammets restaurant, 22, 96, 177, 182
Jews, attitudes to, 53, 57, 115, 124, 127, 152, 153, 178, 201
   reputation for cleanliness, 57
John XXIII, Pope, 153, 211
Joyce, James, 198
judges' salaries (1907), 20
Junior Army and Navy store (D'Olier St), 30
Jury's Hotel, 129

Kavanagh, Patrick, 83, 128, 191, 198
Kennedy, John F. (US President), 160
   assassination and funeral of, 210–11
   attraction of, 202–3
   Cuban missile crisis (1962), 203–4
   Irish visit (1963), 177, 189, 205–8;
   garden party in Aras an Uachtarain, 208
Kettle, Tom (MP), 54
Kilmahunna, 152
Kingstown, 42, 54
   Peter's Pence collection (1907), 25

Labour Party, 103, 119, 123
Labourers Question (1907), 9
labourers' wages
   in 1907, 19
   in 1932, 80–81
   in 1963, 172
Lady Chatterley trial (1960), 160
Lady of the House (Findlater's magazine), 28
Land Act, 1903, 9
land annuities
   witholding of, 113, 120–22
land purchase by Germans, 163
Land Question, 9
Land War, 7
landlord power
   dismantling of, 9, 12

language revival movement, 63, 151
Lansdowne Road football ground
   Irish flag over, 103
Late Late Show, 1, 187, 191
Lauri, Cardinal (Papal Legate), 102, 131
Le Marin, Constant (wrestler), 60
Leader (journal), 67, 69, 103
League of Nations, 75, 122
Leddy, Joseph, 117
Legion of Mary, 79, 127, 153
Leinster Alley, 20
Leinster (mailboat), 139
Lemass, Sean (Taoiseach), 102, 111, 145, 155, 157, 165, 202, 212
   income in 1963, 171
Lenihan, Brian (TD), 157, 202
Leo XIII, Pope, 109
Leonard, Hugh, 109
letter boxes, change of colour, 103
Leverett and Frye, 20, 27
Lever's Sunlight Soap, 27
Levine, June, 186, 198
liberals, 75, 152
Liberty Hall, 157
librarians' pay (1907), 25
Licensing Act, 1907, 42
life expectation, in 1963, 178
Lipton's Tea, 27
Lisdoonvarna (Co. Clare), 194
Local Government Board, 24
Locke's Distillery case (1948), 157
Lord Chancellor
   salary in 1907, 20
Lord Lieutenant, 9, 11, 50, 54
Lord Mayor's Luncheon (Easter Sunday 1907), 39–40
Lucey, Rev. Dr (Bishop of Cork), 153, 155

McArdle, J. (Surgeon), 22
McBirneys department store, 31, 42
MacBride, Sean, 160
McCarthy, Canon, 194, 201
   Problems in Theology, 199
McCourt, Kevin, 171
MacDonnell, Sir Anthony (Under-Secretary), 11, 20, 24
McDowell, Richard, 39
MacEntee, Sean (Minister for Finance), 80, 115, 119, 120
McEoin, Sean, 155
McGahern, John, 159, 180, 198

McGrath, Joe (Sweep promoter), 139, 140
McKenna, Rev. Dr (Bishop of Clogher)
   Lenten letter 1932, 126
McKenna, Siobhan, 155
MacLiammoir, Micheal, 155
   The Importance of being Oscar, 186
MacNamara, Angela, 165, 189, 191, 195
MacNeill, James (Governor General), 104, 132
McQuaid, John Charles (Archbishop of Dublin), 132, 152, 153, 155
McVeagh, Jeremiah (MP), 9
Magnet (comic), 59
Maguire, Ben, 115
Mahaffy, J.P. (Provost of TCD), 22, 40, 63
Mahon, Brid, 189, 193–4
Manchester Martyrs
   monuments to, 60, 62
manners
   books of etiquette, 108–9, 179
manufacturing industry
   employment in 1907, 19
   output in 1963, 165
marriage
   countryman's approach to, in 1963, 194–5
   introduction bureau, discouragement of (1963), 193
   minimum age in 1963, 155–6
   mixed marriages, 201
   purpose of, Church's view on, 192, 197
   rates: in 1907, 35, 37, 59; in 1963, 178, 191
   sex in, 192, 197
marriage bar, 79, 165, 170, 178
Martin, Mother Mary, 155
maternity hospitals
   financial difficulties in 1932, 138
May, Juno (female wrestler), 60
Mazawattee tea, 1, 27
McVitie's biscuits, 27
meat supply
   private slaughterhouses (1907), 28
medicines, in 1932, 107
menus, in 1932, 93, 95
Merchant's Quay Franciscan Church
   blessing of throats in 1963, 155
Metropole Hotel (Dublin), 39, 55
Miami Showband, 193
military establishment in 1907, 12

Index

milk supply
  private dairies, 28, 79
  tuberculosis linked to, 28, 79
Milltown
  house prices in 1932, 97
  Peter's Pence collection in 1907, 26
Mini cars, 163
miniskirt, 1
Mitchell, Caroline, 164
mixed marriages, 82
Model Housekeeping, 79, 96, 106, 182
modelling agencies, 183
Mohangi, Shan, 164
Montgomery, James (film censor), 102
Monto (brothel quarter), 15
  closing down of, 79, 199
Moore, Seamus (TD), 90
Moore, Sean (Lord Mayor), 157
Moore Street, 28
moral law, 199–200
morality, 190
  chastity, 190–91
  moral concerns in 1963, 199–201
  scrupulosity, 200
  sexual attitudes and experiences, 190–99
Moran, D.P., 12, 13, 17
  The Leader journal, 67
Morrisroe, Rev. Dr (Bishop of Achonry), 126
motor cars, 32–3
  driving licence examinations, 155
  expenditure on: in 1907, 32–3; in 1963, 174
  Irish Motor Show, 1907, 17
  numbers on road, 99, 165
  prices (1907), 32–3
  traffic accidents (1907), 17
Moynihan, Sean, 127
Muintir na Tire, 75
Mulkerns, Val, 184
Murphy, William Martin, 48, 54, 55
Murphy's grocery (Mary's Abbey), 28
music halls, 45
Mutesco Hair Tonic, 108
Myles na Gopaleen, 159

Nannetti, J.P. (Lord Mayor), 55
national anthem, 100
National Concert Hall, 48
national flag, 99, 103

National Gallery, 157
national schoolteacher's salary
  in 1907, 22
  in 1932, 90
nationalism, 60, 62. *see also* Gaelic League; Home Rule; Irish-Ireland movement
  in 1907, 18
  denationalisation process, 59
Nelson's Pillar, 30
neutrality, 149
newspapers
  in 1907, 45
  in 1932, 76
noise of streets
  in 1907, 45
Norris, David, 198–9
North Circular Road (Dublin), 17
  rents in 1907, 26
Northern Ireland, 149
  Catholic middle class, 3
  civil rights movement, 3
  stoning of pilgrims to Eucharistic Congress, 133
nuclear war, fears of, 161
  anti-fall-out sweet, 163
nurses' pay (1932), 90

Oath of Allegiance controversy, 102–3, 111–12, 117
  abolition legislation, 119, 129
Oath of allegiance controversy, 111–12
O'Brien, Judge Barra, 168
O'Brien, Cruise, 67
O'Brien, Edna, 159
Observer, 207
O'Buchalla, Donal (Governor General), 104
O'Casey, Sean, 155
O'Connell Bridge House, 157
O'Connor, Ulick, 168
O'Dalaigh, Cearbhall (Chief Justice), 186
O'Donnell, Peadar, 75
O'Duffy, General Eoin, 134, 143
O'Faolain, Sean, 92, 194, 197, 198
  Vive Moi, 197
office development, in 1960s, 157
official salaries
  in 1907, 14, 19, 20
  in 1932, 80, 90
  in 1963, 171, 172

O'Higgins, Kevin
    assassination of, 111, 122
O'hUiginn, Brian
    Fun O' the Forge, 115
O'Kane, Rev. Dr (Bishop of Derry), 126
O'Kelly, Sean T., 102, 103–4, 155
Olympic Games (Los Angeles, 1932),
    137, 138
O'Malley, Donogh, 202
O'Neill, Captain Terence (Prime
    Minister, NI), 3
Ottawa
    Imperial Economic Conference (1932),
    100, 102, 113, 120

package tax, 120
paperback publishing, impact on
    censorship, 159–60
Park St
    collapse of wall in 1907, 15
Parnell statue (O'Connell St), 60
Parnellism, 7
Patterson, 'Banker' (loan shark), 23
Paul VI, Pope, 189
PAYE tax system, 165
Peak Freen biscuits, 27
Pearse, Patrick, 32
Pearson's Weekly, 59
Pembroke, Lord, 48, 55
Pembroke District Council, 48
personal appearance
    cosmetics in 1932, 107–8
personal hygiene
    in 1907, 56–7
    in 1932, 79
personal identity
    four determinants of, 1
personal tailoring, 32
Peter's Pence collections
    in 1907, 25–6
    in 1963, 96–7
Philbin, Rev. Dr, 155
Phoenix Park
    Eucharistic Congress (1932), 134
    playing fields, 68
Pius XI, Pope, 129
    Castii Connubii encyclical (1930), 80
Playboy of the Western World (Synge)
    Abbey showing in 1907, 59, 63–8
Plaza dance hall (Middle Abbey St)
    Sweep draw, 142

plumbing in houses, 107
pneumonia, 178
pocket money, 177
pop art, 163
pop songs, in 1963, 193
population
    1901, 14
    1911, 19
    1926, 87
    Protestant percentage in 1932, 81
post-war baby boom, 202
post-war economic boom, 149
poteen making, 15, 126
poverty, 14–15, 19, 59, 76
Powerscourt, Viscountess, 103
premarital sex, 198
Prescott's laundry, 32
Prevention of Corruption Act
    servants' perks, 37
prices
    clothing, 31, 98
    housing, 19, 26, 97, 174
    motor cars (1907), 32–3
    refrigerators (1963), 176
    theatre tickets, 172, 174
private dairies, 28, 79
private slaughterhouses, 28
professions
    entry premiums (1932), 83, 87, 89
    income levels, 22, 90, 171
    Protestant representation in 1907, 14
Professor, The (Dublin character), 45
Profumo affair (1963), 163
prostitution, 15
protectionism, 149
Protestant community, 12, 14, 81, 152, 153
    attitude to Irish Free State, 82
    discrimination in favour of, in 1907,
        23–4
    financial institutions, dominance of, 81
    proportion of population in 1932, 81
    reaction to Eucharistic Congress
        (1932), 131
    representation in professions in 1907,
        14
    stance in 1932 elections, 119
prudishness, 100
prurience, 191
public houses
    in 1907, 42, 59
    bona fide limit, extension of, 42–3

cooked meals: barmen's protest
     against, 174
  dinner menu in 1907, 20
  early closing in 1907, 42
public transport, in 1907, 17
Punchestown races, 1, 202
puritanism, 59, 83
Purser, Sarah, 106

racism, 53, 65. *see also* Jews, attitudes to
radio, 85, 87
  2RN, 85
railways
  numbers employed in 1932, 89
Ranelagh
  rents in 1907, 26
Rathfarnham, 42
Rathgar, 175
  house prices: in 1932, 97; in 1963, 174
Rathmines and Rathgar
  Peter's Pence collection: in 1907, 26; in 1932, 97
recession in 1930s, 73
Recorder of Dublin
  salary in 1907, 20
Red scare (1963), 160–61
Redmond, John (MP), 9
refrigerators, 1, 176
religion, 1, 2. *see also* Catholic Church; Jews; Protestant Community
  boycotting of non-Catholic traders, 201
  employment and, 23–4, 170
  social divisions in 1932, 80–83
religious broadcasting, 189
religious expenditure, 176
religious outlook, importance of, in 1932, 124, 126
rents
  in 1907, 19, 26
republicans, 83. *see also* nationalism
  dress favoured by, 102
  employment prospects (1932), 89
  puritanical outlook, 83, 85
respectability, maintenance of, 25
restaurants, 180, 182
  Jammets, 22, 96, 177, 182
retail trade. *see also* grocery trade
  pay in 1907, 22–3
Reynolds, Pat (TD), 115
  murder of, 117
Ring, Christy, 155

Ringsend parish
  Peter's Pence collection (1907), 26
road accidents, in 1907, 17
Robinson, Lennox, 106
Robinson, Sir Henry, 33
Ross, J.N. (Senator), 170
Rotunda
  Living Pictures (1907), 60
Rotunda Hospital
  Master's salary in 1907, 22
Royal Dublin Society, 47
  Irish Motor Show (1907), 17
Royal Showband, 193
rural areas
  employment in 1932, 87
  German land-buying, 163
  support for Fianna Fail, 114–15
rural society, 12, 81, 151
Russia
  communist revolution, 73
  Cuban missile crisis (1962), 203–4
  Stalin, 75
Russian occupation, fears of, 161

'Sackcloth and Ashes' (Dublin character), 45
St Andrew's Church (Westland Row)
  Eucharistic Congress Midnight Mass, 132
  Peter's Pence collection (1907), 25
St Patrick's teacher training college, 180
St Vincent de Paul Society, 127, 175, 176
St Vincent's Hospital, 57
Sandymount
  typical rents in 1907, 26
schools
  top schools in 1907, 32
science graduates
  employment prospects in 1932, 89
Second Vatican Council, 145, 153
secondary education, 170, 174
self-sufficiency, national, 86, 111, 114
servants, 37–9, 176–7
  daily routine, 38
  division of functions, 37
sex
  child abuse, 198
  Church's attitude to, 192, 194, 197–8, 199
  company-keeping and dancing, dangers of, 192, 193, 194, 197
  contraception in 1963, 197–8

sex *continued*
   dangers to chastity (1963), 192, 194
   differences in aspirations between sexes in 1963, 193
   differences in upbringing of boys and girls, 35, 178–9
   experiences of, in 1963, 191–2, 198
   feelings of 'badness', 191
   homosexuality, 43, 45, 198–9
   ignorance about, 195, 197
   kissing, 191, 194, 195
   lack of enjoyment in, 191
   marriage, in, 191, 192, 197
   Monto brothels, 15, 199
   premarital relations, 198
   reticence about, 68, 191
   scandals, 43, 45, 163
   student dating in 1963, 195
   taking pleasure in: seen as abuse of order of nature, 192
sex education, 195, 197
sexual repression, 191
Shackleton, Francis (Dublin Herald), 38, 43, 45
Shamrock Rovers, 138
Shannon Lawn Tennis Club, drunkenness in, 79
Shannon scheme, 110, 113
Shelbourne Hotel, 1, 205
   dinner menus, 96
shops
   Andrews grocery, Terenure, 30
   Barry's sweetshop, 28
   in 1907, 27–31; cash collecting system, 30
   wages and conditions, 22–3
   chain stores, 27–8
   Christmas shopping in 1907, 30–31
   department stores in 1932, 102
   grocery stores, 27–8, 175–6
   religious divisions, 81
showbands, 193
silk stockings, 86
sin, 200
Sinn Fein, 65, 69, 111
   Irish Year Book, 62
   United Irishman, 62
slacks, 184
slang, 109
slaughterhouses, 28
slums, 14, 19, 77
   clearances, 77

small farmers
   support for de Valera in 1932, 114–15
small-town snobbery, 169
smells, on streets in 1907, 45–6
Smithson, Annie M.P. (novelist), 95
smoking, 174
   Craven A as cure for sore throats, 107
snobbery, in 1963, 168–9
social divisions, 81–3. *see also* class distinctions
social education
   anti-tuberculosis campaign, 56–8
social pressures
   in 1932, 93, 99
social status
   expenditure on food and, 177
sodalities, 126, 127
spending. *see* expenditure
spirituality
   in 1932, 124
sporting activities, in 1932, 137–8
Starkey, Walter, 65, 106
stations, 128, 151
Stephen's Green (Dublin), 15
Stillorgan
   house prices in 1963, 174
stock exchange index
   in 1963, 165
Strachey, Lytton, 86, 106
Straffan House, 56–7
Straw Boys, 109
street entertainment, 45
street noises, in 1907, 45
street smells, in 1907, 45–6
strokes, deaths from, 178
suburban population
   social structure in 1911, 20
suffragettes, 34, 35
Sunday Press, 161, 183, 184, 189, 191, 202, 207, 208
Sunday Review, 168
supermarkets, 176
supper parties, 106
surtax, 90, 119, 171
Sweep (Irish Hospitals Sweepstakes), 90, 138–45
   distribution of receipts in 1932, 144
   numbers employed in 1932, 89, 140
   opposition to, 143
   organisation and excitement of draw, 142–3

Index

smuggling of tickets, 140, 142
  value to Irish economy, 144–5
Switzer's department store, 102, 176
symbolism, in 1932, 99–109
Synge, John Millington
  The Riders to the Sea, 65
  The Playboy of the Western World:
    showing at Abbey in 1907, 59, 63–8

table manners, advice on
  in 1932, 108–9
  in 1963, 179–80
Tailteann Games (1932), 76, 136, 137
tampons
  use of, regarded as morally suspect, 194
Tara (Co. Meath), 62
tax inspectors
  income in 1932, 90
taxation
  in 1932, 92, 96, 119–20
  in 1963, 165, 171
  PAYE system, 165
  surtax, 90, 119
  turnover tax, 157
teachers' salaries, 22, 90
Telefis Eireann, 186–7. *see also* television
  Director-General's salary in 1963, 171
telephones, 174
television, 176, 186–9, 211–12
  favourite programmes in 1963, 187
  Late Late Show, 187, 191
  licence evasion in 1963, 189
  'Monica's Kitchen', 180
  public affairs programmes, audiences for, 187
  religious broadcasting, 189
tenements, 14, 19, 77
That Was the Week That Was (BBC), 163, 189
theatre, 59–60, 126, 176
  seat prices in 1963, 172, 174
Theatre Royal, 60
Thom's Directory, 24
Titbits, 59
Tivoli Theatre, 60
Tobin, Surgeon, 57
tonic wine, 108
Tourist Board, 83
Townsend Street, 28
transport. *see also* motor cars
  in 1907, 17, 32–3
  in 1963, 176
  bicycles, 17, 32, 176
  personal transport revolution, 17
  public transport in 1907, 17
Trevaskis, Brian, 211
Trinity College Dublin
  fees in 1963, 170
  modelling and beauty class (1963), 183
  Provost's salary in 1907, 22
  students' prank at 1907 Exhibition, 54
Trinity Week, 1
tuberculosis, 9, 11, 178
  anti-tuberculosis campaign, 9, 28, 56–8, 79
  death rates: 1907, 9, 56, 59; 1932, 106–7; 1913–32, 57–8
  milk supply and, 28, 79
Tulloch, Hill, 131
Turkish Baths (Leinster St), 57
turnover tax, 157
twist (dance), 163
2RN radio, 85

Ulster amateur boxers
  non-participation in Tailteann Games (1932), 137
Ulysses, 57
  Leopold Bloom, 46, 57, 59
Under-Secretary
  salary in 1907, 20
unemployment, 75
  in 1932, 113–14
Union Jack (comic), 59
United Irish League, 7, 9, 69
United Irishman (Sinn Fein paper), 60
United States, 160
  civil rights movement, 3, 207
  Cuban missile crisis, 203–4
  depression of 1929, 73
  Sweep ticket sales, 140
universal franchise, 80
University College Dublin
  fees in 1963, 170
  Fellows' salaries in 1907, 22
  Literary and Historical Society, 68, 116, 202; admission
  of women to debates, 35
  religious observance among students in 1963, 153
  student dating in 1963, 195
  trousers ban, 183

university education. *see also* Trinity College; University College Dublin
  in 1963, 170
  fees in 1963, 170
  graduates' employment prospects in 1932, 89
  students' attitudes in 1963, 19
  teachers' salaries in 1907, 22

values
  influence of cinema on, 85–6
Vatican Council, 145, 153
Veet hair-remover, 108
Vicars, Sir Arthur (Ulster King of Arms), 38
  salary in 1907, 20
  and theft of Irish Crown Jewels in 1907, 43
votes for women, 34, 35, 80, 186

wages. *see* income
Wallace, Edgar, 142
Walsh, Caroline, 183
Walsh, J.J. (Minister for Posts and Telegraphs), 90
Warren, K.
  The Tailteann Cookery Book, 95, 96
water consumption
  in 1932, 79
wealth, distribution of, 2–3
wealth, ownership of, 2
weather
  summer of 1907, 55
Westland Row, 25, 28, 132
Westminster parliament
  questions to Chief Secretary, 1907, 9
Williams and Woods
  jams, 27
Wincarnis, 108

wit
  in 1907, 40
  in 1932, 106
Wogan, Terry, 184, 187
Woman's Mirror, 107, 131, 133
women
  The Mirror of True Womanhood (1907), 35
  dependency of, in 1963, 175
  education of, in 1963, 167, 168–9
  employment prospects: in 1932, 140; in 1963, 165, 167
  Eucharistic Congress Mass for, 133–4
  fashions: in 1907, 31; in 1932, 79, 97, 100, 102; in 1963, 183, 184
  household allowances, 175
  marriage bar, 165
  position and status of: in 1907, 34–5; Church's views on, 35, 80, 186
  trousers worn by, 183, 184
  votes for, 34, 35, 80, 186
women undergraduates
  modelling and beauty classes in 1963, 183
women's magazines, 28, 79
Women's National Health Association of Ireland
  anti-tuberculosis campaign, 56–8
Word, The, 178
working-class
  diet in 1907, 19–20
  expenditure patterns (1932), 91
  food expenditure (1907), 26
  Peter's Pence collections (1907), 26
Workmen's Compensation Act, 37
wrestling, 60

Yeats, Jack, 67
Yeats, William Butler, 66, 67

Zam-buk (herbal ointment), 107